S0-AFA-299

acclaim for
BREAKTHROUGH

"Highly convincing evidence of a government cover-up regarding UFO's."
—*Kirkus Reviews*

"Raises important questions about humankind's place in the universe."
—*San Francisco Chronicle*

"[An] intriguing scenario about the interplay of mind, matter, and belief systems."
—*Pittsburgh Post-Gazette*

"Compelling proof of the existence of extraterrestrials here on earth."
—*Telegraph* (Dixon, IL)

Books by Whitley Strieber

Communion
Transformation
Majestic
The Wolfen
The Hunger
Warday
Nature's End
*Breakthrough**

*Published by HarperPaperbacks

HarperSpotlight

BREAKTHROUGH
The Next Step

Whitley Strieber

HarperPaperbacks
A Division of HarperCollinsPublishers

HarperPaperbacks   *A Division of* HarperCollins*Publishers*
10 East 53rd Street, New York, N.Y. 10022

A hardcover edition of this book was published in 1995 by HarperCollins*Publishers*.

Cover photograph by FPG International/Jack Zehrt

First HarperPaperbacks printing: June 1996

Printed in the United States of America

HarperPaperbacks, HarperSpotlight, and colophon are trademarks of HarperCollins*Publishers*

❖ 10 9 8 7 6 5 4 3 2

CONTENTS

SECTION THREE:
The Official Story
219

Appendices
301

SECTION ONE

The Communication

The sky is waiting
to be touched by a hand
Of fabulous childhood
—*Edmond Vandercammen*

I

something very new

Steadily rising over the past fifty years, a chorus of voices has been claiming that unidentified flying objects are real and that mankind is coming into contact with extraterrestrials. Other voices, as loud or louder, have claimed that this is all nonsense. As the evidence has built, official denial has become more strident. At the same time, the number of people who do not believe the government, science, and the press has grown until it is now a substantial majority.

One of the reasons is that the denials are not convincing. Another is that more and more people are having the contact experience. Thirty years ago, practically nobody knew of a person who thought they might have encountered visitors. Now, most of us know, or have heard of, such a person. And we also know that this person, in the vast majority of cases, is as normal as we are.

In December 1985, I found myself swept up in the tide of contact. I had a series of encounters that seemed to me to be almost undeniably real, with strange, fierce, and quite amazing creatures who did not appear to bear any reference to earthly life. When I wrote about these experiences in my 1987 book, *Communion*, I was astonished as much at the public response as I was at the stridency of the rejection and denial that the book met with in the media.

To me, the book was an adventure—a series of speculations about a fascinating and bizarre experience. At the time, I left the question open. When I withdrew from public life in 1989, I left saying that I would not return until I had something truly new to say.

Also in that year, I got strikingly convincing proof that the visitors were real. Frankly, I was astonished, not only at its emergence, but also at the subtle and highly ethical manner in which it was presented. It provides reasonable assurance that the visitors are real to those who need this to go forward. But it doesn't simply flatten the case of the skeptics. Instead it gently suggests to them that they might consider reassessing their position. The visitors do not, it appears, intend to shatter any minds by their coming.

I said little about the proof when it appeared, because it suggested so many unpredictable consequences. My own expectation had been that this was an essentially human experience. But suddenly, I could no longer deny that somebody was out there, and they did not appear to be human at all.

I was thrown into a state of confusion and deep concern. Would publication bring the visitors closer to us? That had happened after *Communion* appeared in the bookstores. I had thousands of letters attesting to it. The visitors seemed almost to view the book as a signal. Publication of the proof might be an even stronger one.

This presented me with some difficult issues. Based on a stunning experience I'd had a couple of years before, I knew something about the very secret things that they were doing to people, and there was undoubtedly something sublime there. But I also had many letters that told a less appealing story, so I was torn.

I had many more questions that had to be answered before I went on with this. I had to absolutely assure myself that they were not an evil force, and to do this I had to gain deep understanding of their aims and methods. Why were they sometimes so good, other times not? I also had to know how long-term contact would change us. And what about all the scary stories, my own included? If the almost universal fear was inappropriate, then I had to unlock its mystery so that we could truly get past it. I'd already discovered that no amount of familiarity with the phenomenon would do it. The fear was too deep.

I finally decided to move ahead, but cautiously.

It has been six years, but the questions I posed have been adequately addressed under the rigorous conditions that I demanded: nothing counted unless there were multiple witnesses. And by that I did not simply mean two people in a room seeing the same thing. Encounters had to develop as real experiences. The structure of each encounter that led to an answer had to be provably nonhallucinatory, and to involve numbers of people, and no hypnotically derived memories counted.

Given what I have learned under these conditions, I feel that I can say that contact with the visitors is safe, though extremely challenging. I feel that their coming is a call to change. My most accurate speculation about them during my years of public life was probably that they might be what the force of evolution looks like when it applies itself to a conscious mind.

In a series of stunning experiences—all witnessed by others—I saw from the visitors' viewpoint how they propose to enter our lives and what they regard as important. I found a probable reason for why they are here, and how we can sensibly respond. I observed them going to the home of friends and watched as they conducted an encounter with them, and was able to see over a period of years the changes that this brought to my friends' lives. Some people at my cabin in upstate New York came face-to-face with one of them, touched hands, and got detailed physical descriptions. From these and other incidents, I learned extraordinary things about the visitors' true aims.

In this era when so many of us, especially among the young, are beginning to fear that we do not have a future, I discovered that the absolute opposite is probably true: not only do we have a future, it is full of potential more wondrous by far than we have even dared speculate.

Contact, coming in the middle of our era, with all its upheavals, its exploding knowledge base, and growing population pressure, appears to be intended to direct us toward a power that lies undiscovered within us. If we change in the way that I think the visitors are saying that we can, what happens will make our most imaginative hopes seem ridiculously small.

As knowledge grows, we are losing the superstitions that have surrounded and obscured the presence of the visitors, perhaps from time immemorial. We are beginning to see that something real lies behind the old myths and gods—a strange otherness that is beginning to respond. It must never be forgotten that contact was not initiated by the visitors. It was initiated by the growing richness of the human mind.

My readers have provided me with an amazingly varied view of this phenomenon, revealing its vastness and complexity, and completely shattering most of my early assumptions. For example, the "abduction scenario" that has become a media cliché, where the witness is taken into a UFO and examined on a table by apparent aliens, is not often mentioned. There is also no compelling evidence that the visitors are evil, or that people are being hurt, kidnapped, or killed. With regard to religion, I found my own faith and understanding immeasurably enhanced; indeed, contact with the visitors will inevitably lead us to rediscover the richness of all our religions. It will lead to a new foundation, and I cannot imagine that they would challenge or deny any expression of faith. Far from it.

But that does not mean that encounter is easy. It is hard and demanding. What is happening is far more involving, subtle, and strange than would result if we were dealing with a scientific expedition from another planet. This is more—much more.

A few months after my first experiences, I discovered that elements of the government have apparently taken a secret interest in the visitors, and that they guard their secret fiercely.

I also saw, as the letters kept coming, that the visitors have responded to this by simply bypassing our official institutions. They are making direct contact. What the government or any other authority does or does not do at this point is not important.

The reason that the government has been removed from the picture appears to lie in its early response to the visitors. It seems likely that our modern encounter with them began in 1947, with the well-reported sightings of "flying disks" over Mt. Rainier and the Air Force's announcement in July of that year that it had captured a crashed disk. Although it denied that statement shortly after making it, and in 1994 further claimed that the debris recovered was a balloon, I can demonstrate with assurance that both of these claims are false. This is based on what I learned by getting caught up in a secret, although informal, congressional inquiry that is unrelated to the present Government Accounting Office investigation of UFO issues, and is referred to publicly for the first time in this book.

The originators of the policy of secrecy and denial have apparently bypassed the elective government, ignoring legal mandates to congressional oversight and executive supervision.

From the first, the visitors were seeking a response from us. Their initial effort was directed at official America, and emerged into public view in July of 1952, precisely five years after the initial sightings. On the night of July 19–20, 1952, there was a spectacular display of unidentified flying objects over Washington, D.C. They were sighted visually from the ground and by pilots in the air, and tracked by radar at Washington National Airport and at Andrews and Bolling Air Force bases. They soon became a cause célèbre in the press worldwide. On July 29, Drew Pearson reported in his column that the Air Force was getting "less skeptical" about flying saucers, and headlines saying "Saucers Swarm Over Capital" blanketed the country.

I feel, based on my experience of the way that they communicate, that the visitors responded to this public declaration of interest when they returned to the capital that same night. As many as twelve UFOs at a time were tracked by radar, but no visual sightings were made. On that night, there was an opportunity for a coherent response that would have been confined to the official world, because of the lack of public sightings. But the only official reaction was to explain the display away as radar ghosting due to a temperature inversion. However, on other nights there had been dozens of radar contacts that were combined with sightings by the public, and by both airline and military pilots.

The problem was that nobody had any idea of how to effect contact and that the relationship between the way we were reacting in our own press and what was happening in the skies was not recognized. The dialogue was simply not noticed.

Instead, it was assumed that the visitors, if present, must be like we would be in a similar situation: only dimly aware of how the culture being contacted was operating. But the visitors are not dimly aware. It has become quite obvious that they understand us better than we do and, as will be amply demonstrated in these pages, can enter the details of our lives in startlingly insightful ways. This is due to the fact that they possess the very sort of hyperconsciousness that they are pressuring us to activate in ourselves.

Publicly, the official world has taken a stance of denial from the beginning and has sought and obtained the unwavering support of the scientific community and the press. This is not because particular individuals within the bureaucracy have been foolish or evil or blind, but because bureaucracy is at its worst responding to the unknown and the unexpected. The authorities were hoping that a day would come when they could control the contact process. That day never came and it never will, but the secrecy gradually became institutionalized as the basis of a broad culture of denial.

Because the official response was inadequate, the visitors took their case to ordinary people. As a result of the massive and more-or-less concealed effort that they had been making over the years, there was an electrifying response to the publication of *Communion* in 1987. It turned out that vastly more people than anybody had ever dreamed had encountered the visitors in the dead of night and the privacy of their lives. Nearly 140,000 letters have revealed a situation radically different from every previously accepted belief about the visitors. We are in contact with something that is not only bizarre beyond our most fanciful notions, but also at least as complicated and full of contradictions as we ourselves are, and probably more so.

On the one hand, science has always maintained that actual contact with aliens would be unimaginably weird—but then, when such strangeness is reported, it is rejected as too bizarre to be real. Actually, what is happening is so far beyond even the wildest imagination that it is too bizarre not to be real. As a result of a very natural desire on the part of UFO researchers to convince, there has been a tendency over the years to filter media reports in the direction of easier believability. Much of the material reported here—so familiar to witnesses—is going to be very surprising to those who have had to rely on public reports for their information. I do not propose to edit for believability, but only for accuracy.

The proof I am about to present is quite sufficient to pass the "reasonable man" test. It would satisfy a jury. With it, anybody who is not committed to denial for emotional or official reasons can safely and assuredly entertain the prospect that our visitors are very real.

They do not demand faith, and they present an ethical structure of such compelling power that nobody entering into deep communication with them can fail to look to his own soul, and seek renewal in his own way. In fact, I do not think that it is possible to relate usefully to them without addressing the existence of the soul in some manner. Thus the currently fashionable intellectual conceit that the physical world as we know it is the whole world, and that the visible body of man is the whole of man, is probably the one consistent barrier to contact that exists. It is why almost our entire intellectual community has been left behind.

However, the recognition that the soul is actually as

much a part of the physical world as the body—a conclusion that is, to me, almost inescapable at this point—
will inevitably lead to the discovery of previously
undetected extensions of reality. The world is not
divided into the physical and the supernatural at all; it is
simply that the physical is much larger, more various,
and richer in content than we have dared to dream.

As it turns out, this is accurately reflected in most
religious texts, including the Christian. Relegating the
soul to some other realm was the beginning of the long
process of becoming blind to it.

The soul is measurable and observable, and when we
become able to feel and taste and touch it within ourselves—to literally extend our nervous systems into this
forgotten level of sensation—we will burst into the same
hyperconsciousness that the visitors possess.

When we learn how to touch it with the instruments
of knowledge, we will also see into the vast, timeless,
and wondrous beyond where it dwells, and will find at
that portal a new way of living that will at once connect
us with worlds undreamed and enable us to gain
unprecedented control over the very nature and appearance of physical reality. We will then reconceive ourselves as creatures beyond time, founded in the
beginning of the world and destined for eternity.

I hope that we will make a new start with the visitors,
based on a clear awareness of their importance and—
above all—their availability. It is hard, but far from
impossible, to become involved with them. No authorities, leaders, or bureaucracies stand between the individual and contact and all of its benefits. If people want
groups, they can form them among their own relatives,
friends, and neighbors. The visitors place a premium on
the individual and the family, and that is where the
foundation of our relationship with them will begin.

The sheer pressure of encounter, as the mind battles

to understand, can cause stunning personal expansion. The hyperconscious state in which the visitors live is available to us now, in embryonic form. Later, as the number of people who can enter it grows, it will become more powerful. We must work as individuals, as families, and as a species all at once, because personal gains and general gains occur together. Unless we advance hand in hand, we do not advance. This is not for leaders or followers. It is for the free.

Obviously, as this process comes to include most or all of humanity, our world is going to be dramatically altered.

But will that be good or bad? Maybe we don't want the visitors' brand of change.

These are issues that must be explored in the light of reason and calm reflection. All of the emotional responses—the hysterical denial of the official world and the media, the dire assumptions of a vocal group of UFO researchers, the fear of us witnesses—must also be acknowledged with tenderness and compassion if we are to make useful progress. The failures within the government must be accepted as inevitable under the circumstances, and the wrongs, as they are revealed, righted gently and with attention to the value of our republic and its future potential as a medium of exchange with worlds beyond.

What the visitors possess is superior knowledge, which is why so much of what they do seems like magic of the sort that is repudiated by science as "psychism" and "the supernatural." It is not magic, it is a whole new combination of mind and science, and if we could not learn its secrets equally well, they would not be here.

These next few years are going to be an incredible time. Something new has happened, something truly amazing. The visitors are here, they are available, and they are ready. And so are we.

2

public proof

Like everything the visitors do, the proof unfolded in precise increments. Although I didn't know it at the time, it had actually begun to emerge as early as the summer of 1986. *Communion* was finished and at the publisher's, and I really expected that the experience would stop. But it did not stop. Incredibly and appallingly, the visitors hadn't just visited me, they seemed to have come to stay.

My whole understanding collapsed. At first, I saw them as an almost robotic, emotionless, and very tough presence. But later I began to see personality. I discovered morality and ethics there, behind all the fear and confusion. I found—and this was the main thing that kept me interested—that they were bypassing every single trace of official authority there was and going right to the individual.

This was the first thing about them that seemed to form a real common ground between them and me, and it drew me, along with my overwhelming curiosity, to

start walking in the woods at night, returning again and
again to the place where I had originally been taken, trying to see what I could do to make my half of this wild
new relationship work.

By then, I'd already started to hear the terror-tales
spread by the UFO community, of gene robbers and
soul thieves. I'd read the documents floating around the
fringes about underground alien bases and human body
parts boiling in vats. But I went on anyway, because I
didn't see that I had any other moral choice. By writing
Communion, I had committed myself to this search, and
also I suspected that the stories were all false. When we
face the unknown, I had said in *Communion*, "the enig-
matic presence of the human mind winks back from the
dark."

On the night of August 27, 1986, I had one whale of a
mind-bending experience. I was sitting in the living
room at my upstate New York cabin reading one of Dr.
John Gliedman's essays on physics, when I was struck
by the words, "the mind is not the playwright of reality." I thought: my God, what if he's wrong, and the
more esoteric interpretations of reality are true? What if
reality is to a degree created by our perception of it?

At that precise moment, there came nine knocks on
the side of the house. There were three groups of three,
with an expectant hush between each group. I was petri-
fied. The absolute precision, the bizarre loudness—the
whole feeling of the moment—told me that I was facing
the unknown. I wanted to get up and go outside, but
instead just sat there, frightened and thinking, I'm not
ready for this. At the end, when I did not go outside to
investigate, there was a little double-knock that eloquently communicated failure.

I did not go outside, at least not while in a normal,
conscious state of mind, and the knocks were not
repeated.

I was just absolutely stunned. The visitors were real. Damned real.

I reported this experience in *Transformation*, which was given to the publisher in late 1987 and published in March 1988. These dates are important to my proof, and—as will be seen—reveal that the visitors have far more insight into our activities than we have ever thought possible.

For me, the nine knocks were personal confirmation. They were obviously physical. They came from a spot near the ceiling where nobody could have been standing. Their ultra-precision was completely singular. I was hearing something perfect, and the effect was startling.

The next day I attempted to duplicate the knocks but wasn't able to achieve anything similar. I also had the reaction of my cats, who had responded with obvious fear, to confirm what I had heard. To me, their reactions were the best test of whether or not these phenomena were imaginary. They had stared right at the spot where the knocks were coming from and both had hissed.

But personal proof is a long way from public proof. Before that came, there would be many other personal incidents of overwhelming power. There would be one, especially, that would reveal a great deal about why the visitors have themselves chosen secrecy.

I had asked for contact, but when it was offered I held back. Clearly, I should have gone outside, but the fear had really been amazing. And look at the animals: when I experimented with knocking on the wall, they weren't afraid. That night, though, they had been in deathly terror.

I could not see the reason for the fear, but I certainly saw that it was the main problem. It had just ruined a prime chance, maybe my only chance. My response was to continue to try, in the hope that I would have more chances. My method would be to demonstrate by my actions that I was still challenging my fear.

I went out into the woods at night, night after night, deeper and deeper. I soon began to discover that the psychology of my response was much more complicated than I had thought, and my fear far more extreme. My battle against the power of the night became a way of life.

During this time, also, my experience began to change. There were many new types of communication, ranging from sentences heard in my mind to vivid images.

In late December of 1987, I began seeing flashes of pictures in my head that seemed related to the visitors. These were not like the images I had seen before, of such things as the anatomy of a visitor's body and an astonishingly complicated map of the earth's atmosphere. They were different—less vivid, of shorter duration, but of much greater emotional impact.

They were like briefly glimpsed photographs, and they showed me coming out of the house, standing on the little hill that led down to the spot in the woods where I'd originally experienced encounter, then sitting on a stone bench I had had built a short distance away. At that point, an image would flash past of a visitor sitting next to me.

This visitor seemed to be somebody who knew me and had feelings for me.

Then came Thursday, January 7, 1988: I awakened suddenly before dawn, sitting upright in bed. It was a silent, gray morning, just at the edge between dark and light, the moment when day replaces night.

I thought I'd heard a sound, maybe a trumpet. I grew furtive, concerned by the suddenness of my awakening, immediately wondering if the visitors were somehow involved.

Something made me want to go outside, and not only that, to act at once. There was a sense of urgency—go quick, quick!

I grabbed my robe, thrust my feet into my slippers, and went racing downstairs, out the side door, up the hill past our pool, and into the woods beyond.

At once everything changed. Dawn had not reached the lower woods. Before me was a path thick with shadows. But it was also clear that somebody was there, down beyond the woods. I could not see in detail, but I could certainly see through the trees enough to perceive a large, gray object there.

I heard a voice whisper, "He's naked." It was insinuating, sinister . . . and sounded as if it found my "nakedness" interesting in a quite nasty way. There was also, however, something oddly childish about it, as if a little boy was spying on another in a private moment.

I remember how vulnerable it made me feel, how the goosebumps rose. It is interesting to reflect that, if I had literally thrown off my clothes and gone striding down into that meadow, I would have been unclothed, but no longer naked—vulnerable—in the way that was meant. In that sense, my nakedness had to do not with physical nudity, but with the fear.

I stopped at the near end of the small bridge that led to the deeper woods, made to hesitate by the tone. Then I heard another, similar voice say, "Come on, come on." This voice was furtive and impatient. The words did not sound as if I was meant to overhear them. They were like the whispered mutterings of over-eager hunters waiting for a deer to come down the fatal path.

All of these words were inside my head, but not like thoughts. It was more like I had on earphones that created the familiar illusion that the sound was in the center of the brain.

Coming from the meadow I could also hear a certain

sound that I identified with the machines of the visitors. This sound had been mentioned, now and again, by my early correspondents, but it had—and has—not been described in any publication of which I am aware. When people hear it, they cannot fail to notice its unique nature. It is not the sort of science-fictional humming or whirring described in the popular literature. For this reason, I am not going to describe it here, because whenever I see it mentioned, I can be assured that there was something authentic about the experience being related.

So here I was facing sinister voices and that same noise, all alone, with my family asleep in the cabin behind me and the dark woods ahead.

A new, deeper, even more visceral fear was my basic response. Growing out of it was a strong concern that, if I went down there, I might not come back.

Beyond that, though, there was something that I wasn't ready to do, something that I did not understand. The visitors knew, though, which was why they were warning me away even as they called me. This wasn't a meeting, it was a lesson about why a meeting was not yet possible.

The voices had been effective: I couldn't do it. I turned and went back to the cabin, which was just now being touched by the dawn's light. My emotional state made me acutely aware of everything around me, of the sharp scent of the frosty air, of the sound of my feet crunching against the frozen grass, of the cold leaking in around my body.

Then something happened that remains with me to this day, as vividly real as it was at that moment. The instant that my hand touched the doorknob there came three sharp, clear cries from the direction of the meadow beyond the woods. I stopped, turned, looked back.

Those remain the most emotionally alive, most heart-rending sounds I have ever heard. They were so vibrant with love, with longing, with hurt that I can hardly express their impact. I have since realized that they were also incredibly rich, far richer than music, richer than the most emotional of our voices.

It felt as if some deep, enormous, and lost part of being was calling me from the other side of the woods. This was absolutely real, absolutely physical. If anybody else had been with me, I have no doubt that they would have heard exactly what I did.

Beyond the tremendous emotional complexity and power of the tones, there was also a remarkable precision of delivery, which instantly reminded me of the knocks. Had they been recorded, I would not be surprised to find that they were each exactly the same length and spaced apart exactly the same amount of time, down to the millionth of a second, or the billionth . . . or to infinity.

This absolute precision, with its sense of something mechanical combined with gigantic emotionality, created an effect that was at once confusing and shocking. Because we do not have this combination in our world, the feeling of the different was very strong. Nothing alive is that precise, and no machine possesses emotion.

Even in our machines, I haven't heard precision that great, and combined with emotional richness it is alien.

Thus the lesson ended—with a stirring call to the deepest possible communion between us and these incredibly exact, vibrantly alive others.

The lesson was multilayered and offered the first clear look at exactly what was preventing real contact. When I had been standing in those woods, I sensed that this other consciousness was in some nameless way challenging my own. I felt as if I was under attack, somehow. There had been a threat, not so much of physical harm as of disappearance—as if I were going to be absorbed in something and simply cease to exist. This

emerged in me as the fear that I was about to be kidnapped.

It made me wonder what happened when two minds
as different as ours and the visitors' try to perceive the
same part of physical reality.

It has become clear to me, from my observation of
them, that they possess an additional perceptual dimension that causes them to perceive the world in a very different way from us, and maybe matter can shape itself
into only one reality at a time. There are theories of
physics that suggest that perception may affect reality,
and that we live inside a kind of envelope of meaning
that confers structure on an indeterminate universe. It is
as if everything is a sort of field before we perceive it,
and that perception itself resolves it into the world we
see and understand.

If so, there would be a deep conflict between us and
the visitors that could only be resolved by taking the
greatest care. In physics, when a particle and an anti-
particle collide, there is complete conversion of matter to
energy—annihilation. Is what happens when minds as
different as ours attempt to form the same physical material into different realities also a sort of annihilation?

If so, that would explain why they are so careful
about going too far too fast—and also how willing they
are to keep trying. Perhaps the challenge is to create
together a new and greater reality that includes both our
meaning and theirs.

Maybe, but not on the morning of January 7, 1988. At
the time, I thought of my fear as an entirely emotional
condition. They were meeting me more than halfway. A
couple of months before, they'd even showed me what
they were doing. So I should never have been that
scared. I blamed myself for it. I had no idea that there
would emerge this fundamental physical component
that could only be approached if millions of people,

each individually, made their own unique contact. I did not understand the patience that would be needed or the gigantic scale of effort that would be called for.

Our sense of reality belongs not just to us, but to all living things on the earth. We all share it, but the visitors do not share it. Until this extension takes place, we will remain isolated from one another.

On that morning, all I knew was that the situation was too big for me to handle. I went back upstairs, threw off my robe and slippers, and returned to bed. Almost at once, something more happened. It seemed as if an enormous presence had entered the room. My wife, Anne, moaned, tossed away from me.

It felt exactly like somebody was standing beside the bed. The only thing missing was a physical body.

Whereupon the following extraordinary thing happened.

I was plunged in an instant back into my earliest childhood—my babyhood, in fact. It was not a dream or a memory. It was as if my adult consciousness had entered my baby body. Whitley, the bedroom, the moment—all were gone. In an instant present reality became less to me than a dream.

At first I did not know where I was. There were tall, thin sticks all around me. I was moving among them, gliding, floating. Sunlight was pouring in the window and it seemed alive, as if the light was an old friend, somebody I knew well.

Then things began to focus. I saw my mother's desk looming up above me. I saw her bed with the clothes all rumpled. I saw the shade half-drawn on the window. At last, I realized what I was doing. This wonderful, miraculous gliding motion was me walking, and I knew that it was the first time. I did not know I had legs and was taking steps. It felt as if I had risen up and was floating. The sensation was exquisite.

Somehow, the triumphant moment of my first step had been dragged out of the depths of childhood amnesia and given back to me.

Right now my heart is aching for just another few seconds of that experience. I was so completely open, so awake, so free of wants, desires, needs. I was just there, in a bedroom flooded with living light.

The sheets unkempt upon the morning bed of childhood, the dust-motes drifting in a shaft of that light, the whisper of leaves beyond the window: glory was piled on glory, I was a king in the palace of an ordinary moment.

But we know how babies suffer. We see it, their impotent rage, their wailing, their eager gobbling of their food. We know that they are animals, feeding, screaming, and evacuating their bowels. But they know more: they are also the confidential friends of the sunlight.

My time in that precious world lasted only a few moments. Then I was back in my bedroom at our cabin. I woke Anne and told her the whole story.

Later I went down to the meadow. There was no trace, no evidence of the complex and wonderful mystery that had come and gone.

But I had taken my first step and I knew it, and I was at once filled with anguish that it had not been a bigger one and joy that it had happened at all.

The purpose of the encounter is clear: it was to throw me into conflict, to upend my understanding, to cause me to doubt myself. For these reasons, it created such an intensity of desire to understand that deeper energies than I even knew I possessed were mobilized.

As the days passed and the woods remained silent, a sense of failure began to eat at me. But what could I do? I had to wait.

I returned to my night walks, kept trying to present

myself as available. Despite all that happened, I was still full of questions, even basic ones about the degree of reality involved.

On my first night with the visitors in late 1985, I had attempted to fix the event in reality by asking if I could smell them. On another occasion, I would take one of my cats. No matter how real an experience seemed at first, though, the strangeness always wore it down. It just would not fix itself in reality, and I knew that this had to happen if things were going to develop.

It was now February of 1988 and *Transformation* was being bound and shipped. Thus, nothing in the book could now be changed, and only I, my editors, and some friends knew its contents. Reviewers were just beginning to get copies. In the second week of March, the first few books would appear in stores in the larger cities.

It was at this precise moment in the life of *Transformation*—after it had been finished and could no longer be altered, but before the public knew about it— that the second part of the proof came.

On February 27, 1988, eighteen months to the day after the incident of the nine knocks at my cabin, but before they could have been publicly known, a large number of people in Glenrock, Wyoming, were awakened at 2:45 A.M. by a series of nine knocks in three groups of three on their cars, on the sides or roofs of their houses, or on their doors. The *Glenrock Independent* reported on Thursday, March 3, that "strange, unexplained noises interrupted the slumber of many Glenrock residents early Sunday morning. The three part series of three dull thuds at 2:45 A.M. was reported by many residents who believed it was made by direct physical contact on the outside of their dwellings."

In other words, despite the near-simultaneity of the sounds, numerous people thought that their individual homes were being affected. That they all heard the sounds at virtually the same time is supported by the sudden surge in police calls. All this only adds to the strength of the proof, because it requires that any hoax be extremely elaborate and that it involve many people, all knocking on houses at the same time. Residents hearing the knocks, "discounted the possibility of a hoax being performed on a seemingly random number of houses. The residents quickly either looked outside or physically inspected their property." A UFO was also observed in the area.

In the end, the *Independent* said, "The UFO, like the knocking, remains a mystery."

Although this happened in early 1988, it was not until nearly a year later that I became aware of the incident through a clipping service. I can well remember how stunned I was when *San Antonio Express-News* reporter Ed Conroy called it to my attention. It could not have been an accident, not something so distinctive and precisely timed.

Somebody was out there.

Conroy spoke to some of the residents about events of that night. "I went downstairs, thinking somebody was at the door," one recalled. "On my way down, I heard three more knocks." The lower floor of her house was "bathed in a bright orange-golden glow." Another resident was awakened by "very loud knocking" and went to the door and looked up into the sky. "I saw the stars," she reported, "but there was a very bright haze. Then I saw shadows running against the garage." Her dogs would not chase these shadows. One resident saw a light in the sky. "I went outside and it was kind of foggy . . . up in the sky the light was, it was red and green." The light remained in the same position for about an hour. She pointed it out to a passing police patrolman, who speculated that it might be a satellite. Residents varied in their recollection of the exact number of knocks they had heard. None of them, even when interviewed, were aware of *Transformation* and the significance of the sequence, but the fact remains that the original newspaper report is clear.

A town official, who refused to be identified, said that an alternative explanation was that Glenrock is on a honeycomb of old mine shafts, and the sounds may have been caused by a collapse.

However, residents located outside the area of the mine shafts also heard the sounds, and the National Earthquake Information Center in Golden, Colorado, told Conroy that "no activity was registered in this area during the time of the Glenrock incidents." A collapsing mine shaft that made that much noise would have easily generated enough seismic activity to be recorded on their instruments.

After agonizing about whether or not it was time for another book, I finally decided to document the incident in the *Communion Letter*, which I was then publishing as a more rational antidote to all the cultic material that was floating around in those days. I felt that I had to make sense of the fear, understand what the visitors were doing, and what they wanted us to do in response—at least those three things—before I proceeded.

The remarkable story of the Glenrock incident, as it turned out, did not end in 1989. Rather, it ended at the exact moment that I was finishing this chapter.

On November 15, 1994, my wife opened a letter postmarked earlier in the month from Casper, Wyoming. As I was still writing this book at that time, it was not possible that this witness, Darin Young, could have been aware of its contents. Certainly he could not have been aware of the specific relevance to it of the Glenrock incident, because nobody knew about that but me.

He wrote, "I live in a small town in Wyoming called Glenrock." He continued that he had been reading

Transformation for the fourth or fifth time when the section on the nine knocks suddenly drew his attention. "I don't know why I'm writing you about this now, years after I first read your book and made the connection, but I thought you might like to hear about it."

His letter was the first I had received about the incident, and it had come despite the fact that my public mail had ceased to be delivered beginning in October, for reasons that the post office has been unable to correct. It was one of twenty-one letters that got through, compared to a volume of nearly three hundred the previous month.

In 1987, Darin was living in Arizona. He had gotten a call from his mother in Glenrock. Subsequently, he had asked friends about the incident, and now described it. "The entire town was covered with a dense fog that hovered approximately ten feet off the ground. In the space of fifteen minutes the Glenrock police department got almost fifty prowler and disturbance calls. All through the town, seemingly on the sides of houses, roofs, gates, etc., came the mechanical rapping, knocking sound: three sets of three knocks.

"I know people who said they saw something hovering above their trailer park on the north end of town and rumor has it that our town paper photographer got pictures of this (I haven't seen them, though). My mom said that the sound was like a big truck downshifting combined with a nut with a sledgehammer hitting the side of the house.

"I heard that the police vehicles wouldn't start and I talked to one lady who said she thought she saw small children in aluminum suits running through her back yard on that night. This all happened at about three or three thirty in the morning."

When I obtained permission to quote from his letter and use his name, I found Mr. Young to be a sincere and straightforward man. Since the claims he made in the letter are already supported by published news reports, they cannot be disputed. And nobody could possibly have controlled the timing of his letter, which is the only anomalous thing about it.

The way that it was delivered on the precise day that it was most needed, so long after the event, is very typical of the visitor experience. That eerie precision again.

Of course, the whole incident will be dismissed by science and any elements of the press that continue to support uncritical denial. Various officials—perhaps the local mayor and police chief—will be brought forward to say that the sounds were easily explainable, that they didn't occur in three groups of three, and so forth. Citizens will be quoted who heard nothing, or who heard sounds but with no pattern. In the end, it will be put down to coincidence in the hope that the whole thing will simply be forgotten.

This time, however, that is less likely to happen than ever before.

It would seem to me that there are serious moral issues involved at this point in upholding denial, especially if the act itself is an impediment to contact. Every human being alive has a right to meet the visitors that is as fundamental as the right to breathe, and those who knowingly contrive to spread denial, confusion, and fear must be violating a moral law of singular importance.

Over the course of this book, I will show that the visitors can influence minds and read what is happening inside our lives with extraordinary accuracy. When Young said, "I don't know why I'm writing you," my belief, based on experiences that I will examine in later chapters, is that he was unknowingly referring to the influence of the visitors.

Since the book was written, I have had it read by all of the named witnesses and by a number of other people.

To a quite unprecedented degree, the visitors appear to be aware of these readings, and I expect that they will enter the lives of other readers as well. Linda G. Jordan, a witness mentioned later and one of my early readers, wrote on January 5, 1995, that she was getting ready for work when she "heard KNOCK KNOCK KNOCK KNOCK KNOCK KNOCK KNOCK KNOCK KNOCK," on the side of her house. "I stood there frozen in time. I replayed what I had just heard and counted. Whitley, it was nine knocks." Her dog reacted like my cats. "She immediately came racing through the house barking her head off and would not stop."

There is communication taking place. The proverbial opportunity has come knocking, and we have every reason to take notice, and seriously consider how to answer.

3

the secret of the knocks

Shortly after *Communion* was published, I received a telephone call from Ed Conroy, then a reporter from the *San Antonio Express-News.* When he explained that he had also edited a book entitled *Combating Cult Mind Control* (by Steven Hassan), I realized that he brought more depth of knowledge than most reporters. To help allay the suspicion that I was a cult leader, I decided to open my life to this expert on cults. Over the next six months, he questioned me closely, following up every detail of *Communion,* even finding childhood friends I had mentioned to see if their recollections supported mine.

Ed's interview became so extensive that it turned into a book, which he published in 1989 as *Report on Communion.* He was not involved in the UFO movement and seemed exceptionally objective, so I began hiring him freelance for the *Communion Letter.*

On October 23, 1994, I interviewed the interviewer over the telephone from my cabin. My first question to him concerned the time he became aware of the Glenrock incident.

"After reading a clipping about it from the *Rocky Mountain News*."

I remembered his call.

"Whitley," he said, "I think I've found something that's going to surprise you." He then read me the clipping, and I shouted to my wife, "They've just proved it!" From that moment to this, I have been struggling to make something that would be worthy of what they did.

I asked Ed, "What did you do in response to the story?"

"I phoned a number of people in Glenrock who were mentioned in the story. I spoke with one witness, Linda Martin, at length. I got a long interview. She gave me further details about the phenomenon regarding the strange mist that surrounded her trailer, which was quite unlike anything she'd ever seen, and about the quality of the light that shone down from the object that hovered above her neighborhood."

There have been a number of descriptions of this light, and I wonder, if we could learn more about it, if we might gain some insight into the visitors' technology, if that is the right word for it. "How did she describe the quality of the light?"

"It was an eerie glow that seemed bright, but didn't cast a lot of actual light. I'd heard the description before in regard to similar phenomena."

"How did she react, in general, to your interest?"

"She was quite candid and seemed interested that some reporter from Texas would want to talk to her about it."

"Did she have any idea about the existence of

Transformation? At the point you did the interview, it had already been published."

"I recall not. She was not in any way connected with the UFO phenomenon through reading about it or in any other way."

I hadn't known that she was this divorced from the phenomenon. In a way, though, the fact that Glenrock was in general unsuspecting and unaware was even stronger confirmation. "Was there anyone you interviewed in Glenrock who was aware of *Transformation*?"

"No. Not at all."

"Were any of them involved in the UFO community?"

"None. Later I met a woman at a UFO conference in Laramie who knew some people from Glenrock socially, but that was as close as it got."

I wanted Ed to confirm the crucial piece of information about the timing of my publication of my book and the newspaper's report of the incident. "And you were aware that I had written my version of the nine knocks before the Glenrock incident and given it to my publisher?"

"Yes, I can confirm that."

"And that *Transformation* had not been published when the incident took place?"

"Yes."

Another area that had to be addressed was alternate explanations. What if the Glenrock incident could be explained as a natural phenomenon? Despite the careful pattern of the knocks, I wanted Ed to recall where his investigation had taken him in this regard. "Did you make any effort to find out if there was an alternative explanation for the Glenrock incident?"

"Naturally, I phoned the authorities and attempted to get their version of what had gone on. The sheriff was convinced that there was nothing odd about it whatsoever. If there were any strange noises, he thought that

they might have been sounds that had come from the
shifting of earth under Glenrock, which had a lot of
mineshafts underneath it."

"Did you follow this aspect up?"

"I called the National Earthquake Center in Golden,
Colorado, and attempted to determine if there had been
any indication of seismic activity in Glenrock at that
time, and I got a negative response. I was able to dis-
count that as a factor. I must also say that there was ner-
vousness in the voice of the sheriff when he was telling
me his theory. He seemed to be wondering whether or
not I'd buy his explanation. It seemed very unlikely to
me that there would be such a rhythmic pattern to the
collapse of an old mineshaft, and one witness I interviewed pointed out that her trailer was located in a
neighborhood some distance from the mineshafts. The
knocks were heard all over town, not just in the area of
the shafts."

That seemed quite a thorough approach. "Tell me a
little bit about your awareness of the rhythmic pattern.
How did you become aware of this, outside of the newspaper accounts?"

"From Linda Martin. She was quite specific about
that."

"What was the pattern?"

"She said that she heard three series of three knocks.
She wasn't quite sure if the first series was two or three.
Then it was three, pause, and three more. She was flab-
bergasted by it. Then she went outside and saw the light.
I might note that in certain Masonic initiations that the
pattern of three knocks is important. The rhythm also
appears in Mozart's Masonic opera, *The Magic Flute*. It's
an indication of a move from a lower level to a higher."

An initiation to a new level, then. Maybe the visitors
had also revealed, in tendering their proof, the primary
aim of contact.

But was that the whole meaning of the nine knocks? I had offered my own interpretation of them in *Transformation*, but it has always seemed to me to lack the depth and dimension I associate with the visitors. In January 1995, I was introduced to a gentleman called Swale Fenley, a personal fitness trainer from Houston who has had a deep effect on many people and who was known to me by reputation from his years of work in Los Angeles. Swale had an immediate reaction to the idea of the nine knocks. He told me that the concept of three groups of three is present in the Tibetan Buddhist tradition, where it refers to progress in past, present, and future time. I related this to the widespread ancient notion of the three-in-one—positive, negative, and balancing forces—being the basis of the universe.

In this sense, then, the nine knocks are literally a call to ascension: to rise above the plain of life upon which we have been created and where we have always dwelled. They are not only a call to contact, but a statement of its aim. The new level that the visitors challenge us to attain is above time, it would seem, and looks down upon the past, the present, and the future as the eagle looks down upon the naked world.

4

night work

Along with all the other things that happened in the fall of 1987, there had been an incident of such overwhelming importance and incredible strangeness that it took years to evaluate and understand.

What I had wanted to know the most at that time, even before the proof galvanized all my questions, was what the encounter stories and abduction reports were really *about*. *Should* I be scared? It haunted me that I was still so unsure about this. Should *Transformation* have contained a message of warning?

I had finally decided that what I needed was to see behind the scenes. I needed to watch the visitors at their work. Why all the secrecy, for example? Maybe it was because they were doing things we wouldn't want done, if we understood. Obviously, the official secrecy I was just then discovering had to be supported by the visitors themselves or it wouldn't survive, if only because they could obviously make themselves known in an instant and didn't.

When people hide, it is often for a sinister reason. What if I was opening a door to hell or something? I am not interested in helping demons. They seem to do fine on their own.

But if an answer was there, I had a responsibility to try and get it, so I went to the cabin once again, waited until about ten on a drippy night, then went down and sat in the stone circle I had built on the site of my first encounter. I pleaded my case: take me with you. If you're doing something good, show me. I hoped to God that they were, because we were so helpless otherwise.

The stone was dank beneath me, the bare forest that surrounded my circle stood naked against a rushing, clouded sky. The wind blew softly, cold mist sifted down, the darkness caressed and—as always—unsettled me. I sat with my legs folded under me, attempting to reach out with my mind. Would it work? This had led to lots of things, but never to what I was now looking for. Maybe the sheer intensity of the effort would help.

Because they seemed to be able to read thoughts, I had taken to simply sitting quietly and thinking my requests. I would do it in two ways: first in words, then in mental images.

I did this now, forming my question carefully, then trying to imagine it in pictures. I told them, I want to see what you do to people. I want to see some of these encounters everybody is writing me about, but from your viewpoint. Please take me with you. I found that there were no pictures for this. I had no idea how it would look.

When my experience had a subtext that it might be imaginary, I could never have made such a request. But the original nine knocks had turned my personal under-standing upside down: I knew for certain that it was all physical and the visitors were entirely real. I sat out there for a long, long time that night struggling to repeat my question, hoping I'd be listened to.

But it did seem like a completely impossible request. Nobody had ever told me that they'd understood what had happened to them.

I tried to wash my mind of the stories of weird medical tests and incubators full of human-alien hybrids that the UFO community whispered about because I just hadn't gotten enough letters about this sort of thing to justify concern. But out there in the dark, it wasn't easy.

Eventually the mist turned to slow, dripping rain, the wind rose, and I began to shiver. The rain got harder, and my knees started hurting. My resolve wore away with the night, and after about two hours I dragged myself to my feet and stumbled off on legs that were tingling so much from lack of circulation that I could hardly walk.

I went up through the woods, crossed the deck, and returned to the house. As far as I was concerned, it was just another failed attempt. The visitors did what they wanted, not what I wanted.

I went upstairs and took off my wet clothes. My warm pajamas were a relief, and it felt good to crawl into bed. Beside me, Anne slept softly. As I settled down, my old black cat, Sadie, came and curled up on the foot of the bed.

I had trouble sleeping. I was caught in a double-bind. I wanted to understand the visitors. But I didn't want to face them. Now that I'd stated my case, I was afraid that they'd actually take me up on it. I eventually slept, I don't know how long. It was about three o'clock in the morning when I awoke.

I was immediately aware that I was in a very different state from the ordinary. There appeared to be a deep internal vibration taking place, accompanied by a sensation as if static electricity coated my skin. The feeling wasn't unpleasant at all; on the contrary, there was a much richer sense of my body, as if I was far more than ordinarily alive. I thought, Oh, I'm like this again.

I went downstairs, moving so quickly that it was hard to tell if my feet were even on the floor. Sadie watched me rise from the bed, watched me cross the room. I sailed down the stairs. Our other cat, Coe, hissed at me from the entrance to the kitchen.

I was sailing, almost flying, and I feel now that I was experiencing yet another physical capability that we do not believe that we possess; and indeed, this has been a matter central to my whole experience: to discover that the mind, or some unknown component of being, may mediate our relationship to physical laws in many remarkable ways that we have always assumed were impossible.

I wasn't surprised or confused by my state. I'd been like this before, and many of my correspondents had reported similar experiences. I wasn't asleep, but I also wasn't awake in the normal sense.

As if being drawn by some magnetic force, I went outside. The night was still cloudy, but the rain had stopped. The air was clear and cold and very still. At the corner of the deck, I was confused to see something solid that was about the size of a car. Given the strength of the deck's structure, a car would certainly have crashed through.

I approached it, trying to understand what it was doing there. As I got closer, I saw that it was dark and silent.

Later, Edward Conroy would see a similar object in exactly the same place on this deck, also thinking at first that it was a car, and recount his experience of entering it in *Report on Communion*. At that time, he was not aware of what had happened to me. He would never remember the details of his own encounter.

The next thing I knew, the "car" seemed to be something else. I cannot remember a specific shape, except that I had the impression that it was not only a conveyance, that it was a kind of supermachine: a device, but alive.

At that moment, someone might have spoken to me, and I was aware that there were people on the deck around me—a group of young women, in fact, who appeared extraordinarily indifferent to me, and communicated a powerful impression that their interest extended to the job they were doing and not an inch farther.

They shoved at me—strange little pushing gestures—and I found myself inside the vehicle. It was cramped, with two seats in front, two immediately behind, and a bay in the back stacked with what I thought were thick black logs.

Between the two front seats was a large object that looked like iron that had been beaten into the shape of a globe.

I was seated in the left front seat. Beside me was a very fair-skinned man wearing a white, short-sleeved shirt and white pants. Before us were two windows that faced down and looked like narrow, angrily slanted eyes.

At this point, my psycho-physical state was still very distorted. I tingled and felt a sense of dislocation, but there was no longer any feeling that I might be dreaming. At the time, I did not understand why this altered state was necessary. Now that I do, I'm glad for it. Without it, I might well have been reduced to a screaming jelly, just as I had been during my first recalled encounter.

When I tried to look at the man beside me, craning to see his face, he turned away. The more I twisted, the more he avoided me. He began working his hand across the iron globe. There was no sense that we were moving. But a low voice behind me began to speak, giving instructions in an oddly stilted, archaic English.

We were going to see a child, and she and her mother would be greatly distressed, so much so that the mother would not be able to help the little girl after we were finished. This would be done instead by another woman, with whom the child had a special relationship. I was told that I was not under any circumstances to allow this woman to see my face or to look at hers, and that I was in every respect to do exactly as I was told when we arrived at our destination.

Immediately, I wondered about the man beside me. Why wouldn't he let me see his face? Was he another ordinary human being who had been told the same thing? This was a very new idea for me, the notion that people might be somehow in complicity with the visitors.

There was as yet no sense of motion at all, and I was confused when lights began flying past us. Until then, it had appeared to me that we were in a room with only the small slits as windows. Because of the total lack of movement, my assumption was that we were still on the deck. "What is this?" I asked. The flowing lights looked unlike anything I'd ever seen before, as if we were passing through a vast swarm of enormous fireflies.

The reply, almost disdainful, was, "It's a city."

I do not think that I was seeing the lights of streets and buildings, though. These strange, rich luminosities were, I now feel, the living souls of the inhabitants.

A moment later a change came, sudden and silent. As in a dream, the surroundings arbitrarily transformed to address the needs of the moment.

I got out—and received a tremendous shock. We were in an ordinary neighborhood, clearly in the United States, but nowhere near upstate New York. The Rocky

Mountains loomed just a few miles away, glowing in moonlight.

How had this happened? Could it possibly be real? No, of course not. This was a dream, it had to be.

I walked across the dark street, feeling the pavement under my feet, being made uncomfortable by gravel digging into my bare soles. At this point I felt physically more normal, but the sense of psychological dissociation became really profound.

I was deep in the strange, indeterminate reality of the visitors. Was this all completely true in the simplest and most straightforward sense or was my imagination being used as a sort of tool of communication . . . or were both things in part true?

On balance, I think that I was actually there. I think that this happened in the real, physical world. I suppose the thing that makes me want to impute it to my imagination is that it was just so completely incredible. But the possibility is certainly there.

I remember looking up toward those beautiful old Rockies in the moonlight and realizing that I was in Boulder, a town that I'm very familiar with. I inhaled real air, touched a bush in front of the house we were approaching. The best way I can describe this is that it was like being inside a living picture.

I bent down and touched the driveway. I remember that I put some little stones in my mouth, a gesture that seemed entirely natural at the time, and which I suppose was an instinctive attempt to gain some sort of coherent sense of place.

How long had it taken to get there? Not more than a few seconds. Certainly under a minute. The whole situation, although clearly impossible, appeared now to be indisputably physical. I vividly recall the empty streets, the small detail that all the streetlights I could see were out, and the absolute, uncanny silence. There was a timelessness to the moment, as if we were not simply intruding into a place, but almost as if we had somehow slipped between the moments of time itself. The sense of the furtive was thrilling. I felt as if I had become part of something very secret and extraordinary.

Then I was rocked back on my heels by the realization that the neighborhood was familiar to me. I had been in the house I was approaching half a dozen times. It was the home of an old friend, Dora Ruffner, and her daughter, people whom I loved as if they were family.

I had met Dora when she was exploring the ideas of the Gurdjieff Foundation in the early eighties. Despite the fact that she was then only twenty-two, she had struck me immediately with her accurate grasp of the material and her intelligent, skeptical approach. She had brought that same skepticism to my tales of the visitors; she was no UFO believer, but she had never wavered in her loyalty to me as a friend. Her insights had always been uncannily accurate, and I owed her a great deal for her willingness to listen to me when almost everybody except Anne and my son thought I was going completely mad.

In fact, two of the key insights in this book are Dora's: the one I have already touched on about the possibility that an actual, physical transformation of the body could be involved, and another about the key to resolving the fear.

I had wanted them to let me see what they did, but I surely hadn't bargained that they'd demonstrate on one of my closest friends.

I was then aware that the man who had brought us here had come up beside me. I was also aware of a presence in back of me, and it was oppressive, as if it had hungry eyes. When I started to turn around, a gentle hand restrained me from behind and, mixed with the sense of the predator, came a sort of stern compassion. I knew that presence, as I had known the incredibly low voice that had spoken while inside the machine. In *Communion* and *Transformation* I had identified what seemed to me to be a woman of extraordinary power. It is her face that is on the cover of *Communion*. She was, I think, the visitor whom I had seen most clearly on the night of December 26, 1985, whose presence seems to me to be bound up in the whole unfolding divinity of the feminine—the open, giving, fertile essence of birth itself.

The man grasped my arm to move me ahead, and I could feel his touch through my thin pajamas, fingers hard, more like plastic than skin. The thought that he might also be some sort of machine crossed my mind, and I had to force back a burst of raw fear. But then there was another feeling, that he wasn't like that at all—that he was, in fact, entirely human.

As we crossed the driveway, the objects that had seemed like logs came gliding around us. They were small, indistinct figures, all moving in exact sequence, as if they were attached on rails. The effect was really incredibly strange. They appeared alive, they seemed to have a sort of character—almost droll—but they moved in such an oddly linked way that it was hard to believe that they were any more than a weird toy, or even a bizarre weapon. Readers who have also seen them have described them variously as "trolls in uniform" and "wrinkled robots," who are "toadlike" in appearance.

One witness, pregnant, was reading in bed one night in 1957 when such figures entered her room. When she grew terrified, the leader said, as if to reassure her, "We aren't interested in you, but in the girl child you're carrying." She cried out that they were hideously ugly, to which he responded, "Just wait, my dear, one day you will look exactly like us." I mention this exchange at this particular point to illustrate that the incredible intimacy and strangeness of the whole contact experience is as likely to mean that we do not know what *we* are as it is to suggest that the visitors are extraterrestrials.

We entered the house, the two lines of linked creatures probing ahead with the slick caution of snakes.

As I walked into the living room, I felt strangely oversized. The place seemed diminished, like one's grade-school classroom reentered as an adult. Seeing this familiar place—the couch with the little girl's books still scattered on it, the big TV against the wall—was all so deeply moving, I almost wanted to weep. I ran my hand along the cool top of the TV, then turned toward the kitchen, where a light had gone on. There had also been a sound, the creak of the kitchen door. I heard another noise, a faint scrape. Somebody was moving about in the kitchen. I went closer, trying to see who it was.

There was a woman sitting at the small kitchen table. If I was careful, I could observe her from the relative darkness of the living room. She was in her twenties or thirties, I thought, with blond coloring and a pleasant profile. Her hands were primly folded before her and she was staring at the wall. She wore an open white windbreaker with a sweater underneath, but I couldn't see more details without coming into her field of view.

As I look back, there emerges into memory a disjointed image of this woman seen from above as she walked down the middle of an empty, silent street, her arms folded as if she was a little cold. I do not recall the specific moment that I witnessed this part of her approach.

Suddenly hands came onto my shoulders from behind, and I was drawn backward, guided toward the small bedroom where Dora slept. Her little girl was in a bedroom in the basement.

Dora has played a large role in my personal search

toward higher consciousness, sometimes as a student of my ideas, but more often as a guide when I have gotten myself lost down some blind alley. There is about her a quality of assurance—sometimes fierce, always compassionate—that has impressed me from the day I met her. It is because of this quality that I modeled the character of Amanda, the determined searcher in my novel *Catmagic*, on her.

But she had always taken the visitor business with a fairly large grain of salt. She was open about it, but not convinced that anybody, let alone me, had ever explained it correctly. So why were we here, at the home of this gentle skeptic?

Maybe that's why.

When I looked down on her in her bed, my heart almost burst with the intensity of the emotion I felt. She was so small and helpless looking, but so incredibly, surpassingly beautiful. She lay with her hand out, as if in blessing.

Then a scream came—a horrible shriek. It went through me like a burning arrow. Dora's eyes flew open, she lurched up, staring right at me, but her eyes were strange and dark and I knew immediately that they were seeing only into the world of nightmare.

She struggled, but something prevented her from rising. She would lunge forward, then stop as if she was slamming into a glass wall. It looked like she was doing this to herself, in an odd way holding herself back. But I also felt somehow responsible. Very responsible. I was holding her down somehow.

There were shapes against the ceiling that made me think of enormous insects. These were the things that had been stacked behind us in the vehicle like cordwood, that had entered the house as if on rails. Now they seemed insectoid, but also as if they exuded some sort of strange emotion. I heard a low sound coming from them, like the drone of a bagpipe, and I found it a little numbing, as if it was slightly anesthetic.

Another scream came, and another, and they were terrible to hear, terrible. I knew who was screaming; it was Dora's daughter. Even writing this brings back the agony that I felt then, and tears spring to my eyes again.

Dora was flopping and struggling, her eyes open but unseeing. The droning sound got louder and Dora finally fell back, her whole body communicating defeat. I could see her nostrils dilating, could see every muscle in her body straining, and in her open eyes an awareness of some very different kind, as if she also knew . . . as if we all know.

I was getting more numb, but I could still move. I had to get to the little girl, I had to help her. I ran into the kitchen, right past the woman at the table, who remained motionless. I took the stairs three at a time, slamming my shoulder painfully against the wall as I made the turn.

The bedroom was blazing with light. A strange stick-figure with a bobbing head and great, liquid eyes had the child by the leg and was striking the base of her spine with a small object.

The girl was trying to crawl away, shrieking terribly. She saw me and there seemed to be some recognition in her eyes, but it was distant. She was lost in desperation. The most awful thing was that her spine was glowing through her skin, as if the bone was burning like a coal. Each blow that was struck made it glow more brightly. The child struggled and clawed and howled. The absolute reality of every detail—the clothes tossed on the floor, the familiar toys, the books strewn around—made the scene all the more appalling.

Then the goblin that had her in its grasp suddenly stopped and came buzzing toward me. I was powerfully reminded of what I had gone through in 1985, and I batted at it as if it were a gigantic fly.

Of all things, I felt an emotion coming from it, and it was not malevolence. Rather, it seemed as if something close to embarrassment was involved. In that moment, I understood that the girl's spine was being stiffened, as if it was being adjusted to provide her with a strength and determination she would need all her life.

The embarrassment seemed to stem from a feeling that the screaming and the pain were inappropriate, that the whole interaction could have been much different, more conscious, more gentle, more truly reflective of the beauty of the inner work that was being done.

Then the woman in the windbreaker came trotting downstairs and scooped the little one up in her arms, cooing to her and loving her, smoothing her hair back, wiping the sweat from her brow. The cries subsided to barks of pain and then—abruptly—the girl was asleep.

I watched that woman take the girl in her arms, I looked at her face even though I'd been told not to . . . or perhaps because I had. She was so completely directed toward the child that I could not make her hear me even though I tried to talk to her.

We band of intruders returned to the night.

I got in the vehicle, and once again the same man was beside me who'd been there before, and he now seemed very much like an ordinary person. I asked him who he was, but got no reply. When I once again tried to look at him, he turned far away from me.

From behind me, I heard a low chuckle—and the creature that had previously seemed so alien and insectoid now acquired a very human quality as well.

I could see that the man beside me was moving his fingers across the black iron ball, working them along as if he was tracing a route. He was very still, and there was a sense of deep concentration.

Now I bent forward and looked out the down-facing, slit-like windows. At first I could see nothing. Then I saw trees sweeping about below me. It was the same effect that one gets from viewing film taken out the window of a diving airplane: the world seems to move while the immediate surroundings remain still. I could see that we were flying. So why didn't it feel like we were? Later, a physicist to whom I described this experience came up with the notion that the outside world might appear as it did if the conveyance I'd been in possessed its own independent gravity.

I saw that we were back at my cabin. I knew that my time in this wonderful machine was about to end, and I wanted to try to fly it. As a matter of fact, I wanted to steal it. But when I tried to put my hand on the iron ball, the person in the back slapped at it as if I was a little boy. The low voice said, "Of course not," even though I hadn't actually asked. I had the feeling that my desire to steal the thing was perfectly obvious to her, and that she was sardonically amused.

The next thing I knew, I was standing on my deck. I don't remember leaving the little conveyance, and I don't remember seeing it fly off into the night.

Had it ever even been there? In the dank silence, I wondered. Immediately, the high level of strangeness made the experience take on the quality of a dream. It was just so fabulously impossible, it seemed that it couldn't have been real.

In retrospect, my feeling is that I was participating consciously in a kind of event that is probably fairly common, but which we do not allow ourselves to remember, because if we did we would then see the design behind our lives and the impact of life's surprises would be diminished, perhaps disastrously. For the living lesson that is earthly experience to have its full effect on us, it must be—or, at least, seem—completely spontaneous.

Early in my relationship with them, the visitors called our world "a school," one of the few things they have ever said to me aloud. If that is true, then it must be that it is a school for souls, a sort of masterpiece of illusion in which we take the lessons that carve our beings.

However, based on what I witnessed that night, I do not think that the workings of it need be as hidden as they are. It could also be that the design of one's life, if participated in consciously at every level, could be elevated to a craft, and finally a literal art of being, that would have immeasurable potency of a completely new kind. In short, if we participated in the construction of our own lives in the way that this experience suggests might be possible, we would ourselves take control over the lesson plan that is now being managed by the visitors. We would gain, at last, control over our own destinies, as individuals, as peoples and nations, as a species.

I stood out on the deck for a long time, watching the clouds, listening to the misty silence, just inhaling the sweet air of home. I walked along touching the rail, feeling the wetness and the cold penetrating my fingers, feeling it under my feet. I wanted the sensations, I wanted to feel solid and physical.

A very pleasant idea came to mind: I could go inside and have some tea. I went to the door, and when I was suddenly back in my own living room with the stove crinkling and a half-finished *New Yorker* on the coffee table, I broke down completely. For a long time, I wept. It was as if I had finally gone through a door where I'd been hesitating for years and years.

At length, I put a few more logs in the stove and then went to the kitchen and boiled water. While I was waiting, I remember that I held the teabag in my cupped hands and inhaled, enjoying the scent.

As I sat drinking the tea, tasting it, inhaling the

aroma, my surroundings seemed charged with a beauty and mystery I had never noticed before.

I considered calling Dora right then and there. But it was three-thirty in New York, which meant that it was one-thirty mountain time. Also, I had no idea what it might mean to wake her up at this point.

I had been given a gift by the visitors, I saw that, a fabulous gift, and I would have to handle matters very carefully if I was going to take full advantage of it. This was much more than just a chance to see what they were doing during their contacts. I could watch how this unfolded in Dora and her daughter's lives.

Best to wait and see if she mentioned it on her own.

But then I thought—what if they aren't all right? What if they're hurt? I have no idea what might have happened in Boulder and I'm being incredibly selfish not to check on them.

But also, what if nothing whatsoever had happened in Boulder? I couldn't very well call Dora in the middle of the night just to say hello.

Finally I decided that, if it had really happened, the tremendous compassion and love that had overlaid the entire experience would never have hurt them.

After a time I took a shower, concerned that maybe I wasn't too clean. The seat I'd been in had been kind of dirty, actually. The little compartment had a stink to it, and the worn surfaces were slick, as if greasy from ceaseless use or as if they were a living skin.

Before I bathed, I checked to see if there was any gravel on my feet or any mark on my pajamas that would support a physical explanation for my experience, but there was nothing. The gravel I'd taken in my mouth had gone.

In bed again, I couldn't even begin to sleep.

I had asked for this experience, begged for it, worked toward it for months. Now I lay there sweating and listening to the rain patter on the roof . . . and realizing that my shoulder hurt. I got up and went into the bathroom to look at it. There was redness, the beginning of a bruise. I remembered falling against the wall as I ran downstairs at Dora's house. Or had something else happened? Was the bruise proof of something or simply a coincidence?

I stared at myself in the mirror, my hand on my shoulder, trying to see beyond those haggard eyes into the real man. What in God's name was I, that these things were happening to me? And what if I'd caused some awful doom to visit Dora and her little one? How dare I, in my arrogance, bring this unknown thing down on them?

I stared at the phone on the bedside table. I really wanted to call, really wanted to tell Dora to go downstairs and check on her girl.

I went to a chair, but when I closed my eyes, I saw shadowy, insectlike figures, I heard the strange, numbing buzz and the child's shrieking.

Toward dawn I slept a little, still in the chair. When I woke up I was cramped. It was nearly eight and I got dressed and went to mass. By the time I returned home, my wife and son were awake and I made our usual Sunday breakfast of pancakes.

At twelve the phone rang. My heart almost stopped when I heard Dora's voice. She said that she'd had a dream about me the night before and had waked up wanting to call me. I was shocked, but I determined not to say anything about what I remembered. We talked for a time, but the dream wasn't referred to again.

Later that day, she called again. We talked for quite some time about the nature of consciousness and methods of leading a more conscious life, but nothing was referred to that would suggest the least thing out of the ordinary. Then she put her daughter on, who proceeded to tell me that a fairy had come to see her in the night. Dora got back on and said that it had been an unsettled night. She had vague memories of loud noises.

There matters stood for about ten days. I had the feeling that they had been trying to tell me something that they'd been unable to articulate. Or maybe the calls were simply a coincidence, and maybe I was reading things into what had been said that weren't really there.

One night during that week another call came from Dora. She said that her daughter's kindergarten teacher wanted to meet me. Dora had mentioned to her that she knew me. The woman had said, "I think I'm involved in that." Dora went on to mention that her daughter and the teacher had "a very special relationship."

I didn't call the teacher, but rather asked if we could meet the next time I was in Boulder. I fought the desire to jump on the next plane. As Dora already knew, I planned to attend the World Affairs Conference there the next spring, so I said that I would do it then. But I did ask Dora to find out the nature of the woman's interest.

She called back with the teacher's story. To my disappointment, it had nothing to do with what I remembered. She had been driving in the mountains with friends some years before when they came upon a small egg-shaped object standing beside the road on three legs. They'd seen an opening in the side and gone up to it. Her friends had been afraid and stayed in the car. The thing had appeared to be about six feet high—not large—and the opening had been filled with machinery. As she walked closer, the door closed and it shot into the air with a loud buzzing sound.

With the wide information net that had been cast as a result of my books and travels, I could often get an interesting perspective on stories like that. For example, this woman's encounter was similar to one described to me by a book publicist in Ireland, who'd had the story related to him by a friend. The shape and size of the object, the small door revealing interior machinery, the buzzing departure—these descriptions were exactly the same.

In April I went to Boulder and met the teacher.

Dora's house was quite a strange place for me to be. I found it exactly the same as it had been on that night six months before—with one quite striking exception. The house seemed to be physically oriented in exactly the opposite direction that it had been on that night. I have never been able to explain this to myself.

Then I saw Dora's girl. She came running up to me wanting to sit on my knee and play "this is how the farmer rides," which we'd been doing since she was tiny. Already a beautiful child, she was glowingly alive, almost charismatic in her impact. Dora said that her mind was burgeoning, that she'd learned to read very suddenly and very well although she was barely past five, that she seemed to be bursting out in every possible intellectual direction. There was a deeply spiritual side to her as well.

She has remained one of the loveliest and most wonderful of people, with her remarkable soul shining with determination. For a child, her ideas and opinions are very complex and well developed. For example, she is strongly oriented toward concerns about the earth. She's a vegetarian and completely determined to maintain her belief in this in spite of all the obstacles and temptations that naturally fall in the way of a child.

She also has a remarkable ability to concentrate and is perfectly capable of reading at an adult level if she wishes, and has been doing so for some years.

I do not know the degree to which the "stiffening" of her spine that I saw (or dreamed up) relates to what she is like, but I do wish to say that she is an unusual and quite marvelous young person.

The kindergarten teacher could easily have been the woman I remembered from that night. When I met her, she was wearing a white windbreaker. She related the encounter with the strange object personally to me, then told me of another, more recent experience, which had involved walking down a street in the middle of the night. It was too vague, though. It proved nothing.

Over the next few months, Dora began to make changes. She started examining a good life carefully, as if to seek within it even greater richness.

At a convention in San Francisco I suddenly found myself introducing her to Ed Conroy. At the time, I felt like I was following a sort of choreography, that the visitors were the real engineers of their meeting. I sensed again there was a concealed script involved here and maybe in much more of life than we have realized, and I wondered who the real author of these scripts was.

Within a matter of months, Dora and Ed were in love, and not long after that they married. A new family embarked, and Dora soon bore a child of this marriage, another little girl.

During that time, the visitors took on a completely new dimension for me. How far what I actually saw was from the idea that they are here "stealing genetic material" to renew their faded species, how far from the notion of preying on the human soul.

I wonder if I did not observe—if not physically, then certainly in a sort of controlled journey using the imagination—the weavers of life at their work that night. Despite the abundant indirect evidence, I must qualify my assertion that this was a physical experience, because Dora never had a clear and direct memory of seeing me at her house.

In the years that followed the encounter, I found

myself watching the growth of the family. When I hold Ed and Dora's little one in my arms, I feel a sense of the presence of all children, and I see in the girl's eyes a flicker of mystery, as if the great secret that is humanity is finally about to open itself to its own understanding, and I feel that when we discover our truth at last, it will disclose itself first through our children.

5

behind the hidden drama: a dialogue between whitley and dora

In April 1994, I gave Dora the previous chapter, which had just been written. Afterward, we discussed her memories of the original occurrence as well as her experience upon reading the piece. Although she did not remember anything directly, there were certainly signs that something very unusual had taken place.

"It was a time," Dora told me, "when I was waking up a lot at night. I would wake up feeling either frightened or anxious and feeling that my heart was racing. A number of things were going on then. There was a lot of tension, a lot of fear."

I wanted to draw her out, but even now I didn't want to put ideas in her head. Carefully, I continued my questioning. "Do you remember anything specific about the event?"

"No, but when I read it to Ed I got into a similar feeling. A highly charged feeling. Like I would wake up with then. A panic state."

I watched her carefully as we talked. She showed no evidence of panic now. She was simply remembering. "What happened to the state back then?"

"It faded after a while."

I could recall her telling me about it, and aching at the time to tell her why I thought she had been feeling it. But I had forced myself not to, not for a year. "What do you remember my telling you? I believe that I told you something about this about a year after."

"What you told me was that you traveled here in the middle of the night, and you came into my bedroom, and your job was to keep me there, because something was being done to my girl."

The resonance of Dora's voice, the slight change of intonation that sounded a protective note caused me to suddenly recall something that I had suppressed. "I've blocked out the part about holding you down. It makes me very uneasy to hear it."

"You said you put some sort of a slab on me."

I recalled, not a slab, but a feeling that I had been holding her down in some way. "It's very difficult to face the fact that I remember your struggles to get out of that bed. The idea that I might have been responsible . . . it's terribly upsetting to me."

Dora gazed at me in a way that seemed to say, why are you doing this? I tried to find in myself the reason that I might have wanted to take our years-long search in this direction. "You know, I never would have written this down at all, except for the things that happened afterward that corroborated it. Like the fact that you phoned me so much the day after it happened. It was so odd that I would wake up with the memory of this happening, and then you would start calling me, with strangely related things. Other things. Do you remember those calls?"

She did not, and that forced me to bring back to mind something that I sometimes want to bury, because it is so much easier to simply assume that everything is exactly as it appears—with this experience, obviously a great mistake. I can never forget that what I may be seeing is, in essence, a context without ready access to language. I may have described my trip to Dora's house not because it actually happened that way in the physical world, but because I have no other way to express the meaning of the experience except as a physical journey.

Then again, it is also true that I don't relish becoming identified with trips in flying saucers. Obviously, this is going to make me yet another kind of a fool when it is published. Maybe the best thing is to just face the truth: I don't know what happened, but something certainly did. "They told me that there'd be someone special there for your girl. Do you remember me asking you about that?"

"Yes." She glanced away, as if recalling that moment, which had been so apocalyptic for me. "I told you that there was a special person in her life. I told you that that was her preschool teacher."

"Let's talk about her. It was the fact that she had a special relationship with your daughter, and—when I met her—she looked exactly like the person I'd seen in your house that night—that made me think that something about this was real."

I still remember vividly how the teacher had been dressed when I saw her, and how much she seemed, from her face, from the way she moved, from so many small cues, to be the woman who had been at Dora's kitchen table. She obviously had not the faintest idea of what she had done. If I was correct about the identification, she was totally amnesiac about the event.

I'd been fascinated when she'd told me about the fact that she'd seen one of the little machines up close. So many people who have sightings also turn out to be involved in the experience in other ways, and often they are like her, with only minimal memories.

It is quite awesome to contemplate that we may literally be leading double lives, some of us, going out in the secret night to work in support of the visitors, returning home with no memory of it.

"Would you say that there were any changes you noticed in your daughter after this?"

"She was always very intuitive and open, and at that age she was particularly expressive and very in touch with her intuition."

"I recall that she talked about Jesus."

Dora glanced at me, blinked. "She was very interested in baby Jesus and whether or not baby Jesus was alive. At one point, she wanted to know where baby Jesus was if he was alive. Then she said, 'I know, He's in my heart.' About that time she started saying that baby Jesus came to her at night and woke her up and talked with her. There was certainly a feeling that things were going on at night for her."

"Anything else?"

"In relation to the visitors in particular, when *Communion* came out, she looked at the face on the cover and said right away, 'Oh, there's one of Whitley's friends.'"

Dora had been quite amazed by that, because her daughter was barely four when the book was published, and had been told nothing whatsoever about the visitors. Sitting here now, so many years after the experience, it impacted me yet again. It was just so unimaginable that I could have ended up in a place so strange as that little craft—or crossed half a continent in seconds. "How did I end up in your house in the middle of the night like that? God, how could it have happened?"

"Your descriptions of the house were really accurate. The details."

On normal visits, I usually stayed in the kitchen and living room. While I'd seen the kids' bedroom in the basement, I had never been in Dora's bedroom, not until that night.

"You described things you couldn't have seen, I think."

Of course, it was almost as large an issue as my apparent prior knowledge of the teacher. Still, I was loathe to draw conclusions. "I was in the house other times. But that night—the memory is just so very vivid. After I wrote the piece, I remembered more about what it was like when we went there. There was a musical note sounding over the whole area. Like a trumpet note that you could hear deep down inside—vibrating in your teeth. I remember a lot going on in the neighborhood. I got the feeling that your house wasn't the only place involved. All kinds of movement, and this strange quality that everything was happening automatically. Strange movement, moving on rails. It was all on such a high level of strangeness, that I don't think even my imagination could have dreamed it up. It's fantastic to me that there could be the least suggestion that this actually happened. Yet I do see hints of it, vibrations of it in our lives. The teacher exists, for example. And I saw her sitting right there in your kitchen. Saw her profile. And then later, when we were introduced . . . the same woman. Good Lord."

Dora smiled. "And my daughter's turned out to be very unusual."

"She was always unusual." I recalled that stiffening

of the spine, and thought to myself that this had helped her, somehow, to focus and clarify herself as a human being. She'd become, as I recalled, quite determined about certain things, and it had been very unusual for a preschooler.

"She's a vegetarian, and she's completely unswayed by peer pressure. It's part of a whole belief system that she seems to have about the sacredness of the earth and life on earth. She doesn't like wooden houses because they kill too many trees. Also afraid of fire. She complained about whales being used in makeup. It'd be hard to say that I didn't influence her, but it goes way beyond me. She's far more aware and committed than me."

"I wonder what she really is, where she came from and what she's going to do?"

"She has a strong sense of right and wrong and does not like religious dogma."

"Her relationship with Christ is the most natural one I've ever known anybody to have. Incredible." But not conventionally religious. She'd struggled with the idea of Christ and I remembered how distressed she'd been when she'd seen some of the more cruel excesses that have attached themselves to certain of our religions.

"For a long time she didn't like Jesus. She didn't like the Old Testament God or his son. She didn't care for all the punishment. She got interested in Greek mythology. She liked the play of personality and character, and the sense of choice. Then she read *The Mists of Avalon*—"

I think that I gave her that book. I know that I enjoyed it enormously. But I was quite surprised that the girl had read it herself. "That's a thousand-page book. How old was she?"

"Ten. What she got from that was that there was a certain prudish and life-suppressing nature to the church that was coming into play. So she was starting to discriminate and form her own ideas about religion. She was very taken by Avalon, and the idea of matrilineal society."

I have been privileged to meet a number of very brilliant children in connection with this experience, and I cannot help but wonder if the visitors might not be enhancing them. I understood the stiffening of the spine as being a sort of physical metaphor. But what if it had meant even more than that?

If the visitors increased the intelligence of even a few thousand children, they would potentially change our world. But they operate on such a large scale that if it is happening, it must be far more than that. Also, they are so totally indifferent to the concept of an elite, I can't imagine them singling a few out over the many. In this regard, they once told me that I was the "chosen one," which at the time really impressed me. Later, I began to get letters from lots of other people who had been told the same thing, and I saw that it meant all of us.

"I noticed after the encounter that you changed. I didn't tell you for a year. I didn't, because if the whole thing was just in my own dumb imagination, it wasn't fair for me to drag you into it. But I noticed that you became very different. How do you react to that statement?"

Dora grew reflective. "I'm thinking about how when I read the chapter to Ed, it really seemed to be something important to me, and that surprised me. And it did seem to be attached to some real memory of something." Her voice gained tension, she leaned forward. "But I can't get to that memory. I think that there was a struggle—and maybe what that was about was that it somehow focused my ability to struggle effectively in life."

"The struggle on the bed?"

"Had a larger meaning. It was a hidden drama of my life struggle, trying to reach and protect my child. Afterward, I saw the issues more clearly, and began to focus more."

Suddenly I saw it: the physical struggle had literally been a model on which her subsequent life effort had been based. "So the act of struggling to get up and help her on that night translated into a struggle in life?"

Dora was silent for a moment. "That might be why it seems so deeply real."

"You became much more focused and directed. You rebuilt your whole life. A year later, you were in a different world."

Dora gave me a quizzical look. "There's also the matter of how Ed and I met."

There had been strong feelings about this in me. I'd brought Ed and Dora together, because it seemed to me that, in some nonverbal way, the visitors had asked me to do this. "Ed—he just went—totally in love immediately."

"You know about the voice?"

I had no idea what she was talking about.

"You've forgotten about the voice?"

I still couldn't remember.

Dora helped me. "The morning before Ed met me, he woke up and heard an audible voice—not an inner voice, but an audible voice—that said, 'Today you'll meet a woman who you'll take back home with you.'"

Now I recalled Ed telling me about that. It had amazed him quite a bit at the time.

"The two of you had breakfast and you were talking about your book *Catmagic* and he was saying how he'd fallen in love with the character Amanda, and the second you told him that I was Amanda, I walked up and sat down at the table. That was the moment we met."

"Tell me more about this voice. I only have a vague recollection."

"When he heard that voice, it was so real to him, that he decided to wear something sloppy because he didn't want to start a new relationship. Later we wrote each other, and he told me about the voice, and I told him that I had no intention of moving."

"Tell me about what happened when you read the chapter to Ed the other night?"

"We suddenly got very tired and tried to go to sleep. But there was a high sexual charge. All this energy. There was this real feeling of there being something else present."

I wondered what, exactly, she might mean. "Present in what sense?"

"In the sense that there was something asking me to surrender. That lovemaking could mean another person being made. A soul was there, and it wanted to be born. The sense of presence was tangible, like someone physical was also there, doing some kind of mind communication."

This was a remarkable statement, suddenly emerging like this. Surely she was referring to some internal state, an effect of their reading the chapter and recalling the early days of their marriage. "Were there any physical signs in the house?"

"Well, there were. But first let me tell you that Ed confirmed that he felt this presence. I asked him if he felt anything unusual. And he said, 'I really feel like I got asked to make a baby.' Of course, it could just be that I was at my fertile moment. But I never experienced anything like this before. It really put the issue of another child on the table for us."

"Anything else?"

"I couldn't go to sleep again that night. I got up and sat in the living room, and I said, 'If you're here, let me know—but don't let me know too much!' I was feeling fear."

This interested me. I feel strongly that fear is the key thing that prevents us from living the richer, more vital life that is implied by this whole experience. "How did that fear feel?"

"It took me back to that time. That, if it were really to approach me while I was awake, it would just be over-whelming. So, the fear isn't like I want to run away or that there's something malevolent. It was more a fear of something being so contradictory to my reality, that if it's there, I can't be anymore."

Suddenly I understood the basic cause of all our fear. "As if its manifestation would push you out of exis-tence?"

"And that's unacceptable. For somebody to take away my reality."

Exactly. It's a fear of annihilation. That's why it won't go away even when one gets used to the visitors. To be with them feels as if our very reality is being swept away—not because their perceptions are better than ours, but because they are simply so different.

The instant I heard Dora's words, I understood that it was the first entirely clear description of the core fear that is holding us back, and I saw what we could do to change things.

A clear understanding of what this is will be a strong foundation for deeper contact. We must find a way to convince our deepest selves that our small world is not going to be crushed out of existence if we allow our-selves to enter their larger one. It is not going to be a matter of simply brushing something aside. This fear is in the blood of man, in every drop of blood on this planet.

What we are afraid of is sharing what the visitors have, which is unlimited vision of what is real. We cling to our narrow perspective because it seems to protect our souls from knowing more than is good for them.

But my suspicion is that living on a larger scale doesn't actually lessen the spontaneity of existence and may even increase it. If so, then this increase in scale will enable us to truly join the universe at last, as active participants in its evolution as well as our own.

6

fire from heaven

No matter the cosmic implications, I was bothered by the fact that I had, in all that experience, hardly glimpsed the visitor who had been behind me. Not since my first remembered encounter in December 1985 had I really looked into the visitors' eyes, and I now began to wonder what they might be hiding. In the back of my mind was the thought that demons might not be able to conceal their evil, and maybe that was the reason for all the secrecy and concealment.

Going to Dora's with them had revealed a startling new dimension. Watching her life unfold afterward was giving me a positive message. But what about the other side? I knew there was one, I had been exposed to it myself.

In 1988 we were making the *Communion* movie and I was worried that it might cause the spreading incidence of contact to become an avalanche. But I had no time to go to the woods during that summer because I was in Los Angeles writing *Majestic* and watching the progress of the film. Despite my titles as coproducer and screenwriter, I was not much involved in the creative process, but it was interesting to be there.

In the fall of 1988, I was contacted by filmmaker Drew Cummings, who wanted to make a television documentary for release in connection with the film. I got the idea that maybe I could finally see the visitors up close and get them on tape besides.

In 1987 we'd had a remarkable group experience at my cabin. It hadn't been exactly clear what had happened, but the visitors had certainly shown up when a group was there.

Cummings was eager to come to the cabin and try to get footage of the visitors, but he was also very specific in saying that he was not committed to my ideas, a position that I understood completely. With this as a basic condition, we made plans.

The question was, what would I do with him when he got here? I felt that I had to work hard to get the visitors to respond more, especially as the relationship was so difficult in so many ways. After some thought, I came up with a new idea about how to get their attention.

Under hypnosis by Dr. Donald Klein, I had described getting lost on an old road not far from the cabin and seeing a black entrance into the ground. Many times, I'd hiked out looking for that spot, but had not found it. However, there is a cave back in the woods that has lots of local legends connected with it. Judging from a ritual axe-head found there, it was probably also a medicine site during or before the woodland Indian period. I decided that I would try going to the cave, if only to demonstrate my eagerness.

A week before Cummings and his crew were due, I

went out at about ten at night, trying to find out if anything would happen at the cave.

Half a mile from my house I stopped on a small hill. The cave was another half mile farther on, and this was scary.

I remembered that road, that entrance.

Did the cave go to the same weird place? Was that why some local people had once seen the stream that flowed past the cave running backward and the full moon doubled in the sky?

Forcing myself, I walked on. The woods were seething with activity, the frantic rustling of creatures in the last warm nights. Overhead, the stars shone down in their multitudes. Wary coons hanging back in the shadows growled at me from time to time.

The closer I got to the cave, the taller the trees became. Soon I was moving in absolute blackness. I turned on a spelunker's light I'd bought for the purpose. Eventually I found the crooked path that led to the cave. I went carefully down the cliff, until I could hear the stream sounding just below me. There had been recent rain, and the water was bellowing along the stones with a throaty roar.

I clambered into the narrow entrance and across the damp rocks, struggling to squeeze through. Night seemed to intensify the sense of confinement, and I felt at one point as if the breath was almost being crushed out of me. Finally, I reached the floor of the cave. When I turned out my light, the darkness was absolute.

The sense of vulnerability was total, as if my body had ceased to be a barrier. I felt as if I was going to literally be consumed by the dark. Nobody would hear a sound I made in here. Anything could happen to me and there would be no help at all. I had given myself to the night.

I had been there about ten minutes, alternately turning

the light off, then feeling trapped and turning it on again. Finally, I took out the battery so that I would not be able to turn it on quickly, no matter how much I wanted to. To do this, I had to accept the fear and act against it. After all, I was trying to tempt the visitors nearer, not stave them off.

I emptied my mind and sat with my eyes closed. For a time, I did overtone chanting, a vocal discipline I had taught myself years before after listening to a record of Tibetan monks. It requires an interesting balance of surrender and effort to chant two separate tones at the same time, and I don't think that I can reach such a deep meditational level any other way.

After I chanted, I waited. And waited. The stream roared, the cave began to seem dank and cold. In the end I had to admit defeat. Others might have found wonderful things in this cave, but all I'd gotten out of coming here was mosquito bites on my bald spot.

I went home and went to bed. I considered my own motives. Why did I think going out to the cave would help? A hypnotic memory, with all its associated problems, probably wasn't a valid foundation on which to base any assumptions. Maybe the night sky would be a better place to look.

But then, the next night, I thought: it's not the cave, it's the effort to overcome my fear that matters. Without regard to where the visitors were or weren't, going to the cave was a tremendous battle for me. Engaging in this sort of struggle had brought them closer before. Maybe it would get them to come and show themselves in clear light when the filmmakers were here.

Considering what they'd just done for me, it didn't seem like such an outrageous request.

So I went out once again. But the weather had deteriorated; there were low clouds scudding, and a wind was moaning in from the west.

As I was walking along the ridge, my mind began to attack me with a ghastly sense of vulnerability. I decided that my emotional state was due to the phantom-choked appearance of the sky, and the blackness that resulted from the thick clouds and the fact that the moon had not yet risen.

I had been sitting in the cave for about five minutes when I began to feel my skin crawl. It was pitch black, and it was all I could do not to turn on my light. But I waited. Closing my eyes, I heard low voices, coming, it seemed, from inside the stones around me. I couldn't make out any words, and I wondered if what I might be hearing was an echo of the voices of campers somewhere in the area.

I began to feel a distinct tingling, not unpleasant. When I opened my eyes, I beheld great change: my whole body was glowing with a blue light. It was bright enough to reflect off the stone walls around me. I thought: static effect, St. Elmo's fire. But there was no flicker, no wavering. I held up my hand and just stared at it, amazed by what I was seeing.

I touched my skin. The light seemed to be coming from inside me, and there was a sensation as if of a warm breeze blowing through my bones. It was among the oddest, most unusual feelings that I'd ever had, and it was accompanied by an emotion a little bit akin to elation.

Could it have something to do with magnetism or electromagnetic energy? The area has an iron-laden subsurface, and the stone in the region is among the oldest in the world.

In 1803 rocks in the town of Stone Ridge, not thirty miles away, had allegedly levitated, an incident that is still talked about locally and that has been reported in various places as an exceptionally odd event of the last century. The incident is mentioned in a compendium of unusual legends called *Weird America*.

Gradually, the glow around me faded and with it the delicious sensation. I almost felt as if I'd taken on new physical properties, as if I was starting to become . . . something else. For a moment it had seemed as if the earth itself was conscious and had in some way been talking to me, and that I had been changing, my body altering cell by cell.

For a time I simply sat there, feeling a mixture of elation and fear, but mostly fear. As soon as I started to leave, the fear overcame me and I ended up scrabbling out in a panic. I hit my head and almost tumbled down the cliff.

I went through the next day reading and meditating. As I recall, I read in the *Tao te Ching* of Lao Tzu, and thought about life on the pathless path, and how close that concept seemed to my own experiences. I remember one line that particularly struck me at the time: "The best leader is no more than a shadow to his people."

The leadership of the visitors in my life was so soft and indirect that it seemed as if I was doing it myself, and it was good to be reminded that this was very far from true.

Then the sun set, and it came time to return to the cave. I couldn't do it. Just could not manage it. The day's sage contemplations became the fears of the night, and this time they were really powerful. There had been no question about that light: it had been physical, and I sensed that it signaled a transformation . . . but into what? I have gotten numerous letters from people who have had brief experiences where they have appeared to change form.

There is an author called Satprem, an Indian who has led one of those extraordinary searcher's lives, wandering the world after a horrific encounter with the Gestapo in 1943, trying to put his broken self back together. Satprem studied for many years with Sri Aurobindo, who believed that mankind was a transitional species, destined to literally be re-created physically in a new form. This concept is embedded deeply in secret Tantric traditions and has emerged in the twentieth century as the notion that our bodies contain the potential for just the sort of reformation that seemed on the edge of happening to me in that cave.

Satprem chronicled the lifelong effort of Mother, a woman who also worked closely with Sri Aurobindo, to enter what they called the "overlife," which is the milieu of the next species.

At the time, I did not know about Satprem's work, but I certainly felt that some kind of physical change had been underway in my body. I did not go out to the cave that night. I did not want to face this new possibility.

The next day my friends would start arriving. Among the people I had invited were Lorie Barnes, Raven Dana, and Colleen Langley, all of whom I'd met through their letters. Edward Conroy came, in connection with his book. Dora came also. I invited Fred Max, a hypnotist who had experience with close-encounter witnesses, because Cummings wanted to show this process in his film.

Late that night, Conroy telephoned me for last-minute directions. In the course of the conversation, he mentioned seeing an odd black helicopter come down to the window of his apartment, which was extremely strange because he lived in a crowded downtown area and the craft had been in blatant and outrageous violation of the law. As he talked, the clatter of a helicopter on our television seemed to leap out of the set and fill the entire room. I was so startled that I dropped the phone. We rushed out onto the deck and saw directly over the house a gigantic helicopter, by far the largest I have ever seen. It was thundering. The fuselage was long and thin and dark; the blade was tremendous. As we watched, this bizarre machine went slowly off over the woods and was lost to sight.

Bemused by the odd coincidence, I concluded the call. We finished watching the film and went to bed. In the middle of the night, I was awakened by a persistent beeping sound. At first I thought it was the clock radio, then perhaps the oven or a smoke alarm with a low battery. But everything was in order. As I was returning to bed, I distinctly heard somebody tell me to go to the window. The voice startled me; I assumed that somebody was in the house. I ran around turning on lights, but couldn't find anybody. I should have thought of my letters: hundreds of people reported being stirred from their sleep by beeping or ringing sounds.

Witnesses also often report being directed to look up or go outside or go to a window during the course of their experiences.

It was typical of me, however, to focus on the wrong thing. After my search through the house, I went back to bed. It never even crossed my mind to so much as glance out the window.

When the instruction was repeated—by a voice that sounded very much like a young soldier on a radio—I finally responded. This time I leaped up out of bed, rushed to the window, and fumbled the screen open. Against the clouds, I saw a helicopter. It was hanging dead still, the blade rotating so fast that it was a blur.

"Look at us," a brisk female voice whispered. "We've got to shine a light on your forehead." I stared at the helicopter, which had begun maneuvering in a bizarre manner. The fuselage was turning here and there beneath the speeding blade, as if being aimed. The machine was so steady that it looked as if it was standing on a tabletop. Today's helicopters don't perform like that. But a discussion some months later with an engineer who specialized in helicopters revealed to me that a machine with a really high-speed blade might present such an appearance. Perhaps this is how helicopters might look in the future.

An instant later my eyes were dazzled and I heard what sounded like somebody reading a list very quickly. Simultaneously, I saw a series of images of the cave. They weren't strange images, simply mental snapshots of what I'd seen while I was in it and had my light on.

Then I found myself leaning out the bedroom window into a silent night, my face pressed against the screen. There was no helicopter and no more activity of any kind. So I returned to bed and went to sleep.

The next day Cummings arrived with his crew: a producer and two camera operators. One by one, my friends appeared, until by late afternoon the house was teeming with people.

Cummings had brought a low-light camera that could be left on for eight hours without running out of tape. He also brought with him a lot of skepticism that I regarded, as always, as healthy. Why does anybody ever believe anything that they haven't seen with their own eyes? I am not a believer by nature, and I am much more comfortable with people who demand that their understanding be based on proof.

The first night, a Friday, passed uneventfully. The low-light camera didn't pick anything up. The next day we took turns giving interviews. After supper, Colleen, who is a professional entertainer, did some of her routines, and we had a lot of fun.

At about eight, I suddenly began to hear that list being read again—not really hear it, but more to remember it as one might remember hearing a lecture. I still couldn't make out the words, though, but soon discovered that if I just relaxed I would start interacting with the rest of the group in a most curious, automatic manner, as if I was an external observer to my own words and actions.

I found myself saying that I wanted to take one group of people out to the cave, and for others to stay behind. Cummings said that he couldn't take his low-light equipment anyway, because it was too bulky.

I was surprised to hear myself say that we were going to a place where the visitors stayed when they were in the area, and that we would try to get them to come down to the house and go before the camera.

I felt no sense of inner compulsion. It was more as if I agreed to play out the program because I thought it was a good one. Had I considered it wrong, I don't think I would have been forced to comply. I want to stress that I did not have the impression, at any time, that I had lost control of my own will.

So I took a gang out into a dripping night. I wasn't looking forward to guiding them down the slippery cliff face. Somebody could even get killed. I stopped them before we began to negotiate the rocky path and warned them all of the dangers.

Nobody wanted to stay back, nobody wanted to return to the cabin, not even when I said that I'd gladly accompany them.

Down we went, and it was hell. I had to guide them one by one, and there was more than one panic attack as we slid along the ledges. Even though I went up and down the cliff face five times, normally a hard climb even once, I didn't get tired.

We got into the cave. We all waited. Nothing. Might as well have been in a movie theater during a power outage.

After half an hour, and feeling like a complete idiot, I guided them all back up to the surface, and we straggled home wet and muddy, with more than one article of clothing ripped to shreds and not a few head bumps from overhanging stones.

The filmmakers had heard various sounds in the house while we were gone, and they were rather spooked. They'd set up their low-light camera and were ready to go to bed.

Because the house was so crowded, my son and I were going to camp out at the stone circle that marked the site of my first encounter, and Ed and Dora decided to join us.

So we went down and pitched some tents and settled down to a perfectly normal night. This was the time when Ed and Dora came so much closer together, and their growing love spread a glow over the whole weekend for all of us.

It was nice listening to the soft whisper of rain on the tent, and I slept deeply—until six A.M., when I was suddenly wide awake.

I sat up, listened, heard nothing unusual. I looked outside the tent. All seemed well. The dawn chorus was just starting and the clouds had blown off, so the morning was beginning to get bright.

I roused my son and we went back to the house. As we were climbing up a low hill that overlooks the property, we distinctly saw a silver shadow move swiftly along the deck, across the back yard, and then go flitting off into the woods. It looked like a small, hooded figure made of silver mist.

It clearly wasn't a bird or a trick of light or anything like that. My son shouted with surprise; we stopped in our tracks.

Its color reminded me of the light that had come off me in the cave. Disembodied, I would have looked much like this. I noted, also, that the figure darted from side to side to avoid trees. Translucent it might be, but it obviously had to obey physical laws.

A moment later, the figure was gone. We went inside—to find Cummings and his companions in a state of some alarm. They'd had an unsettled night, and just moments before, a startling experience.

In the hour before dawn, they told us, a couple of blows on a convertible couch had awakened its occupant. Against the gray light coming in a nearby window, he had seen a small figure, which had at first seemed to be a child. Then it had looked at the observer with big, black eyes and this, plus the very narrow face, had confirmed that something extremely unusual was present. Another moment, and it had transformed into an apparition with the head of an eagle or falcon.

Then it had disappeared. He'd been wondering what had been there when there was a sudden burst of heat so intense that the bed had seemed to be on fire and he'd leaped up in fright.

It was the next moment that we'd mounted the hill and seen the figure hurrying into the woods.

The structure of this series of perceptions is, very simply, the structure of real experience. It had both simultaneous and sequential elements, and had unfolded in a perfectly normal way. The only part of it that made it in any way questionable was what we'd seen.

The sharp blows of awakening were typical of my own experience. The combination of the eagle vision and the feeling of great heat felt by the filmmaker seemed to me to fit with much of the visitor experience as it has been described to me by my readers and has emerged in the testimony of such witnesses as Betty Andreasson Luca. This material suggests that there are dimensions to the experience beyond what would be present if it represented only a relationship with extraterrestrials of recent arrival.

In human mythology, the eagle is a symbol not only

of strength and power, but of heat, purifying change, and the intelligence associated in many cultures with the light of the sun. Among the ancient Greeks, Zeus, the chief god in their pantheon, was believed to take the shape of an eagle to receive men's souls when they were initiated into the Mysteries of the Sun. The eagle was connected with rites involving drawing fire out of heaven. Sacrificial victims who were burned were thought to ascend into heaven in the form of eagles. The firebird, or Phoenix, took the form of an eagle. Betty Luca, at the height of her visitor experience faced a Phoenix in the context of terrible heat. Among American Indians, the thunderbird was associated with the body of the sun, as was the Garuda of eastern mythology, who, like the Greek Prometheus who was also associated with the eagle, stole the secrets of the gods.

I viewed this event as I had others, as a message spoken in the ancient language of myth: burn away your ignorance and your sins, then you can ascend.

Cummings was hopeful that he'd gotten something on film. We reviewed the footage but could find nothing on it except a few unexplained sounds.

He was amazed to have to admit that he'd been so close to encounter. He was awed. But, as this could not be called absolute proof, he remained a skeptic, although perhaps a shaken one.

Then Raven Dana came staggering out of her bedroom. Her face was flushed, her eyes were swollen closed and streaming, and her lungs hissed and rattled like those of somebody with a cold or severe hay fever. "I've seen the visitors," she said quietly.

7

a dark, reflective eye

Raven had just become the first person I'd ever heard of to touch a visitor while in normal consciousness. She'd had face-to-face physical contact which, incredibly, was corroborated by Lorie Barnes.

Over the morning, I had interviewed each member of the group and determined who had and who had not had encounters. Raven and Lorie had both had incredible experiences. Colleen Langley, who had been in the room with Lorie, had not awakened. The filmmaker's experience was already known to me. And my son and I had seen the silver figure.

I realized that a communication had just taken place. I'd been given detailed information not only concerning the visitors' exact appearance, but what they could do with their bodies. There had even been a remarkable show of symbolism that had communicated its meaning eloquently.

After that first morning, I intended to refrain from questioning any of these witnesses about their experiences for some substantial time, to see if their memories changed or deteriorated. In reality, it was six years before I felt ready to call them again. I was primarily interested in Lorie and Raven, because their experiences had been the most extensive. In the fall of 1994 we met at my new cabin.

I spoke to each of them separately. As they did not know each other well and had never discussed the incident together, I also thought that it would also be instructive to see how their recollections compared.

Raven and I sat down together after breakfast and took ourselves back to those days. She remembered how bad her allergies had been. I commented that close physical encounter is often accompanied by such a reaction. After my first few experiences with them, the visitors had warned me off sweets of all kinds. I had experienced a life-threatening increase in my allergic response, with sugar being a special area of sensitivity. I must take four allergy shots a month at this point to be comfortable.

I asked Raven to remember back. "Could you describe what happened that night?"

"Well, the first thing I remember is waking up because the automatic lights had come on outside. I looked out the window and then opened it, because I was feeling hot, even though it was kind of cold out. Then I fell asleep for a while. Then I woke up again, because something I thought was a raccoon or a skunk or a cat had come through the window, as if something had stepped in onto the window ledge and was coming down onto the bed, like an animal or small child. I felt it pressing against my leg."

"Did it bother you that the window had a locked screen in it?"

"The thought never even occurred to me. My first thought was, oh, great, if I move I'm going to get skunked."

The mind seeks the normal, always. The stranger the event, the harder it tries to wend its way back to what it knows. "How heavy did you feel that this object was?"

"Small dog, large cat, small child."

We'd left our cats in our city apartment because there were going to be so many people in the house that weekend. "What weight, would you estimate?"

"Maybe about twenty to forty pounds, hard to tell. But a definite sense of weight, and I could feel it stop moving suddenly when I woke up. Like it had sensed it and stopped moving. I had the feeling that if I was very still I could see it before it jumped back out the window."

"And what happened then?"

"I very slowly turned my head, until I could see the outline against the window."

She had known that something was there, but unlike me had not been plunged at once into terror. I have always envied Raven Dana her poise in the face of this experience. But I must also add that she has reported her share of fear, as have we all. "What kind of an outline?"

"Like a small child."

"How tall?"

"It was crouched. In that position, two and a half feet. It had a knee bent and a foot on the bed."

Her memories remained detailed, even after all this time. It was fascinating to talk to her, to look into her eyes. She'd been so close to them, so very close. "An aggressive crouch?"

"It wasn't an aggressive crouch. More frozen, like it hadn't expected me to wake up. That kind of a crouch. I wanted my eyes to adjust to the light."

I reminded her that it had been a cloudy night, but that there had been a fair amount of ambient light.

"Well, I could see, but not a lot of detail. I was very acutely aware of its presence in a way that I can't physically describe. Except, where it was touching my leg, I could sense a sort of electric charge. Not unpleasant. I could feel it through the sheet. It was the kind of sensation you might feel if your hair was standing on end, or if somebody was holding a tuning fork against your leg."

"Any other sensation?"

"Light pressure. Like a small child or animal. I remember thinking how normal this seemed. How much like an animal this was. There was an incredible awakening of my own animal nature. At that point, I thought, should I get up, get out of the bed, or what? I didn't want to frighten it, but I was a little frightened myself. As I was thinking, What do I do, it raised its hand. I could see the outline against the window."

An animal—just what she'd said back in 1989. She had not forgotten that detail, and it's a telling one. At the least, it means that there were absolutely no common points of cultural reference, no clues at all that would have enabled her to identify it as possessing any element of humanity. I don't think that anybody inventing this story could ever have dreamed up such an unlikely detail. With hindsight, it makes sense, but I doubt very much that it is something somebody who was not having real contact could have imagined.

"At this point, what exactly had you seen?"

"The outline, and when it turned its head, I could see the cheekbone—a high cheekbone—and one of its eyes. A long, black eye."

I have thought a great deal about those eyes. Why are they like that and—above all—why do they have that effect on us? Those eyes take you to your conscience, those brilliant eyes. "What sort of face did you see?"

"A little bit longer than usual, mostly human-looking face with a bald head. The eye had no pupil. Just a dark, reflective eye."

But human—subtly human. She was seeing something so strange, then, that it struck her as possessing the affect of an animal, but having a face that suggested the human. What was she really seeing? What was there? I decided to change my approach a little, trying to come at it from another direction. "Any impression of age?"

"As far as age is concerned, I had the feeling that it was very old and very young at the same time."

Were those just words, or could she get more exact? "How do you reconcile that?"

"It communicated the sense of curiosity and wonder to me that you get from a small child that still hasn't made judgments about the world, and sees everything as fresh and new. I had the feeling that it was looking at the world that way. There was a certain sense of innocence that you don't find in adults, yet at the same time the wisdom and serenity you see in somebody very old, who has reconciled to life."

So far, nothing had been said between her and the creature, so where was all this communication coming from? There is what I would call an ambiance about the visitors, as if they are surrounded by a field of self that is larger than their bodies.

"Did you hear anything?"

"No."

"Smell anything?"

"Kind of a musty odor, like the wet fur of an animal. Not unpleasant, but very woodsy."

I have been very interested in their odors, because I think of smell and touch as confirming senses, much more so than sight and sound. Over the years, I've tried to smell them and touch them as much as I could, and have noticed many different odors, the most notable of which was the human smell of some of them. "Let's go back to the hand. What was it like?"

"The forearm was extraordinarily long and thin. Very long compared to the body. Very delicate, in the sense of very finely chiseled."

I returned to the issue of the degree of humanity she was perceiving. "You said at first that there seemed to be an animal presence, then that there was a human quality. What did you mean by human?"

"My sense was the same as it would have been if a person had poked their head into the room and felt caught. I had the feeling that it was conscious, that this was a self-aware individual, and it was aware that I was awake."

I was struck, at this point, by how carefully preserved these perceptions were, even after all these years. This had been no dream. "Describe the raised hand."

"The hand wasn't raised in a threatening way, but more as if asking a question. What do you want to do next? That sort of thing."

I could picture the scene, Raven and the visitor frozen in this incredible moment, and I thought: when we come together as species, it will seem like this to us all. "How did the hand look?"

"I couldn't see much, but I could see three long, thin fingers silhouetted against the window. Although I was frightened, I was very drawn to the creature. I was very emotionally moved by it, and I just reached forward and touched its hand with mine. When I did that, a current—not an electrical current, but that sort of sensation—moved through my fingers and down my body and out through my leg where it was touching me there. It was like a circuit had been made."

"Did it respond to your gesture?"

"As I put my hand up, it reached forward and we touched."

There. There, that was what I wanted to hear about. "What was it like?"

"It was touch. Very expectant. Incredibly soft skin."

"But skin? Living skin?"

"Oh yes. Cool, soft skin."

I asked Raven to step into the next room, so that I could interview Lorie. "Could you describe where you were in the house that night?"

"I was in the neighboring bedroom with Colleen."

"What happened to you?"

"My door was slightly ajar. I was half awake, and then suddenly fully awake. I heard what sounded like scraping, like maybe a sort of animal like a porcupine or something was crawling down the hall. I became a little bit nervous. And suddenly my door opened much more. I was aware of a small being coming into the room and standing beside my bed."

"In what way were you aware?"

"I saw the silhouette."

"What was it like?"

"A small child. Three to four feet tall. I'm not sure. It was sort of gliding. I knew that it had made the noise. It stood slightly below me and stared. It was a being with a long face and huge eyes. It reminded me of a small deer. Also, very long fingers. I was a bit frightened, but I got mental words from him."

Many of my readers report this mental communication, some describing it as sounding very much like a radio, and others more like thoughts with a spontaneity and speed of execution that makes it hard to perceive them as being self-generated. "How did they sound to you?"

"Like an echo in my head."

"A thought?"

"No. A metallic, echoing sound." Here was a suggestion of technology at work. Could sounds be projected at somebody's head from the outside, I wondered, that would appear to be coming from inside?

"Is this something you ever hear in your regular life?"

"No. Absolutely not."

"What did it say?"

"'Relax, we are not going to do anything with you. Go back to sleep.' It gave me the impression that it had looked in to see who or what was there, and then decided that it wanted me to know that I should retire from the scene because they weren't interested in me."

"What happened then?"

"I felt as if I was sort of paralyzed."

"Physically?"

"Yes."

This sense of paralysis is very characteristic of hypnotic states and can be created even by an amateur hypnotist if he can get his subject into a moderately deep trance. So we have two elements of apparent "technology" in use at this point, one that could have been a simple sound effect, and the other something that has been a part of stage magic for two hundred years.

I have seen the visitors do the incredible, but I have also been aware that many of their feats could be simpler than they look. "Had it moved?"

"Yes. I think it sort of touched my leg. I felt a current, but there was a sudden paralysis. It exited the way it had come. I was paralyzed for five to ten minutes. But shortly after that I went back to sleep."

"Did you have any physical sensation beyond the sense of being unable to move?"

"Drowsiness. Because I went back to sleep."

"Heat or cold?"

"No, but an electrical feeling, as if my body was still vibrating."

"Any odors?"

"Yes. A musty odor. I would liken it to damp. Woodsy."

There was that word again. It is interesting that they both used such a specific description independently. This implies a very identifiable odor, and—more importantly—a real one. Two people might well both imagine a scent, but not the same precise one, not after six years.

At this point in the interview, I asked Raven to rejoin us. "Did either of you think that it was wearing anything?" This was quite important to me. I wanted to know if all the leaping through walls, shape changing, and disappearing had to do with technology or the mind. If technology was the answer, presumably it would have been carrying or wearing something.

Both agreed that it hadn't been wearing anything more than, possibly, a body suit. I had the impression of a naked, damp creature come up from a damp woods, so strange that it seemed to them like an animal, but possessing qualities of wisdom and perhaps of childishness that also gave it human qualities. They'd perceived a combination of great youth and great age. To Lorie, it had referred to itself in the plural, implying that it was not alone.

A complicated picture.

"Was there a sense of nakedness, like you'd feel with a naked human being?"

"No, not at all," Lorie said.

"No," Raven agreed. "In the same way that you don't think of an animal as being naked. It seemed perfectly normal."

When we undress, we feel the nudity acutely, and we telegraph that in dozens of different ways. It was not until we had become culturally complicated enough to feel self-awareness that we became conscious of our nakedness.

I wondered, how could an extraterrestrial, somebody so strange as this, so obviously from another world, possibly go naked in the air and dirt of another planet?

Perhaps the truest answer is that there is presently no way to penetrate the tangled forest of mysteries brought to light by these two women.

"Let me ask you both this. Assume that they're living out in the woods here. You could go out there and interact with them. How do you react to that?"

"Well," Raven said, "the idea of another type of physical contact appeals to me even though it's frightening. My feeling is, after that particular contact, so many things about the way I related to myself changed. I would welcome that to happen again and again."

In fact, Raven has only had this one experience of direct physical contact. And I'm not surprised. It was an absolute peak human experience, in my opinion, probably one of the most unusual things that has ever happened.

"Let's get into the way things about you changed. This is one of the rare times that a human being in anything remotely resembling a normal state of mind has come into physical touch with a visitor. I want to know more about the changes that you experienced. So, Raven, just free associate about them. This is one way to find out one direction more extensive human-visitor contact might go in."

"Basically, when it touched me I had—mentally—the impression that it was asking me, 'What do you want?' My first impression was, go down the hall, because I knew there were other people in the house and I wanted them to be able to see it and have that experience. The second thing was, as I was thinking the thought, to know what you are, I heard myself say aloud, To know what I am. I realized in that moment that this was a connection to a piece of myself. When I woke up the next morning, I was very, very ill. I was having a terrific allergic reaction."

In many ways, I consider this remarkably suggestive and ambiguous statement to be among the most revealing things that anybody has ever said about the visitors. It covers the issue of communication, it refers to one of the most intense physical side-effects, and—above all— there is that veiled reference to the visitor relating to some part of herself.

This is close to being the key mystery of the experience, and why I conceive of it as being so much more complex than the science-fictional "alien contact" idea, with its earthbound concepts of intergalactic empires and governments and such. How could something that can apparently read thoughts even have a governmental structure like ours? How do you choose a jury? Or for that matter, commit a crime?

When you are at the very height of strangeness, when you are so far from your human meanings that you feel as if you are on the other side of the universe, I can assure you from experience that you will encounter yourself. And yet, I think that the visitors are also . . . visitors.

This is as much about finding man as it is about finding them, and will lead the seeker very soon to contemplate the wonder of what is really unfolding on our little dust mote of a planet, as the great being that it has created in its billions of struggling, lonely years, this awakening eye finally opens and gazes outward, this dark reflective eye that is us.

"You were a wreck, Raven."

"I couldn't breathe, my lungs hurt, my eyes were bloodshot, my ears were blocked. But it was the beginning of a recovery of myself. What I mean by that is that it really opened the door to me realizing that it was time to take physical care of myself in a way that I never had. To appreciate my animal nature. It slowed me down in a very positive way. I've always been a very busy person. But what this experience ultimately resulted in was a shift from working for others and doing things for others, to getting in touch with what I wanted my life to stand for. I changed where I lived, who I was seeing romantically, the way I was dealing with other people. Over the next year I shifted every aspect of my life, from what I ate to how I exercised to who I associated with to my job."

As so often happens when the visitors enter our lives, her world exploded. This need not result in terror and confusion: it can be like this, captured richness. "In other words, what you're saying is that the ten or fifteen seconds you spent with this person changed your whole life."

"Yes. It woke me up to a part of myself that I had always been afraid of. It allowed me, in a way I can't exactly explain, to take the power I knew I'd always had and run with it, instead of trying to make it come out in ways that I thought other people would be comfortable or safe with. I just stopped doing that. I took the attitude that, like it or not, this is who I am, and I'm taking my life forward."

"A refocusing of self?"

"A very dramatic refocusing of self."

"And it seems to have come from the presence of this animal nature and from its relationship to your own animal nature—as if it had awakened you to something we're very desensitized to, which is the animal in us and its physical needs—and also its spiritual needs."

"My realization was that I was a spiritual being solidified into physical form. I really got, emotionally, that physical and spiritual are not separated whatsoever."

"Raven, have you had physical contact with the visitors like that again?"

"No."

But those few seconds were not contact with a small little body from another world, they were contact between two huge souls from the unknown. One was this remarkable, enormously realized being with its little damp slip of a body. The other was a woman from Cleveland called Raven.

"Lorie, have you had any physical contact since?"

"Not since then."

In other words, their extraordinary experience did not trigger a long illusory series of exchanges, complete with channeled directions about how to change the world.

I asked them both: "Would you do it again?"

Raven answered instantly: "In a heartbeat."

Lorie was not so quick to reply, but she also said yes.

I had detected in her response a tone I thought might conceal something interesting. "Are they dangerous?"

Raven did not think so, but Lorie had a very different reaction. "Yes. In many ways, they're very clever. Their cleverness raises certain fears in a human such as myself."

Here was a reference to that other side of the visitors, the tough side that I and some of my correspondents had faced. "Let me ask you, if you'd had the chance to kiss him, what would you have done?"

Raven: "I would have done it."

"Where?"

"On the forehead, right between the eyes."

"Lorie?"

"The same."

No, not the same. When I'd said the word "kiss," she'd crossed her legs and closed her fists. I tried to get a little further into this. But I did not wish to question her

directly. She wanted to see the visitors as good. Of course
she did, she had them in her life. But she has also had
some very, very unusual experiences, including a confrontation with a dead relative, of a type that has been
deleted from the UFO stories because it fights the simple
alien contact scenario. "Lorie, I want to shift to you now.
Remember, on the road near the house? Your brother?"

"Yes. I was the last person in my family to see him. In
1971 in New York. He disappeared. There was a big
search, the FBI got involved, but he was never found.
Eight years ago, he was declared dead. He was an artist,
a painter, with a history of personal problems. Alcohol,
drugs. But he was a wonderful person, just too open to
the unkindnesses of the world. I loved him quite a lot. I
was the last person known to see him. On this particular
day, I was walking along the road near your old cottage,
and he was there."

"What do you mean?"

"He was just there. As if he'd walked out of the little house that was up there at the edge of your
woods." There was a small shack there that the kids
had used as a clubhouse.

"Did he seem solid? Ephemeral?"

"Solid. Quite solid. Maybe a sort of translucence."

I have letters from people who have seen dead
friends and relatives with the visitors, and Lorie was the
third to have such an encounter at my cabin. One thing
that is interesting about this is that it is so completely
unremarked in the popular literature on the subject that
it must be getting reported for the most straightforward
of all reasons: it is happening to people. "What did you
think at the moment you saw him?"

"I was shocked. I said, 'Jonathan, what are you doing
here?' And he said, 'I've just come to tell you, sis, you're
in the right place.' I couldn't figure out what he meant
by that."

"What did you think he might have meant?"

"I think perhaps the contact with the visitors has led to change in my life in just about every way. When I first had contact back in the fifties, my life changed, but I wrote it off. I've had a rough life. But from the point when you and I met and we established contact with the visitors, everything changed. It's as if, I was for the first time able to be myself in the world, not having to tolerate a lot of the muck, putting it out of my life."

"You found a husband and all sorts of things."

"Yes. He's recently passed away, but we had six—almost seven—good years together. And then my dear brother Buddy, who was also involved in the theater and nightclubs—he passed away a year before. And I feel the loss, but also that I'm still able to grow."

This explosive urgency to grow, to touch life, to renew, to live more deeply, more fully—it is almost as if, upon coming back from battle, we are hungry to live. "Let's go back to your brother Jonathan. What did he look like when you saw him on the road?"

"He seemed to have on a kind of white robe or toga tied with a natural-colored rope with a tassel. His hair was long—shoulder length. He'd often worn it that way."

"Did he look older or younger than when you'd last seen him?"

"About the same. He certainly hadn't aged seventeen years."

"What happened when it ended?"

"He sort of floated back into the woods."

I know this phenomenon well. It is a very strange thing to see, because it seems as if the being is actually floating on your awareness of it.

"What was the expression on his face?"

"Very tranquil. I was reminded, which I never was

in life, of one of the paintings of the apostles in the Bible."

"Did you have a religious sense connected with this?"

"Yes. Very spiritual. He and I had been a loving brother and sister in life. I was his favorite sibling. I had this very peaceful feeling. I think that's why he came, to give me that. He also said he was fine, and not to worry about him. And I had been worried, for years and years."

I was never able to get Lorie to return in much detail to her feeling of danger. She referred to it, though, in the following way: "I have the feeling that we have to do this right, and that we have to be careful because if we don't we are going to fall."

Again, there was that suggestion of danger, almost as if she was haunted by something so deep that she could express it only indirectly. Or it could be simply a side-effect of confrontation with the unknown.

I went on seeking some kind of satisfactory answer. My mail had reached avalanche proportions by this time, and I began to comb through the letters, seeking that elusive crumb that might bring an answer. That weekend in the fall of 1988 had really changed things for me. For the first time, the visitors had provided some solid information about themselves. We knew what they looked like, how it felt to touch them, a previously unremarked smell, and we knew that they had unusual powers of mind over body. We knew that seeing them in normal consciousness did not mean withering under a demon's glare.

That is where it had stood until the interviews were done in 1994. To the raw information that had been obtained in 1989 was now added the perspective of time, and I had learned something more. As Dora had reported, encounter causes people to make greater demands on their lives. It makes us hungry to live and grow. Who were they, then, these visitors, that they would care enough about us to effect such dramatic change in our individual lives?

This was as much about great issues of species as it was tiny ones of soul. Or perhaps, in eternity, both are equally large.

8

the hidden choir

As I opened letter after letter, I was slowly gaining perspective. By learning what people actually remembered of their encounters—so very different from the stories in the press—a remarkable new picture of the visitors emerged. It was not a sweet picture, but neither was it a terrible one. Rather, it was every bit as contradictory and surprising and various as one would expect from real contact.

When we imagine ourselves going to another planet, we visualize sending a few highly trained astronauts and scientists, bound by elaborate and detailed rules and taking infinite care.

My impression is that the visitors are a much more individualistic bunch. I'd be very surprised to find that they had any sort of elaborate government at all. If anything, it appears that we are being contacted by large numbers of familial groups using a plethora of different approaches under the broad general umbrella of a shared ethic of minimal disturbance of our own freedom of choice.

The slowness and secretiveness of the visitors' approach strongly suggests that they don't want to overwhelm us. That must be a very real danger, judging from the fact that, individually, we are almost always devastated by encounter.

From the publication of *Communion* in 1987 until September 1994, I received 139,914 letters. Between my wife, myself, and our secretary, we read them all. Personally, I have read about forty thousand pieces of mail. We saved a representative sample of about thirty thousand, eight thousand of which have been retyped and mostly scanned into computer-readable format. This was paid for by the Communion Foundation, which is a private foundation funded by me out of earnings on my books. As far as possible, we answered each person, at least thanking them for their effort.

The letters have not been statistically tabulated or professionally analyzed. This awaits both very substantial funds and access to the scientific professionals needed for the work.

We have, however, created some rough statistics. Eighty percent of the letters reflect either positive encounters or encounters where the visitors seemed neutral. Sixty percent specifically mention fear. Twenty percent report negative encounters. Three percent specifically mention hypnosis by UFO researchers, and nine out of ten of these perceived their encounters as negative. (This is probably not an outcome of hypnosis. These people sought help because of their bad experiences.)

In all these years, we have received eighty-two pieces of critical mail, including three letters containing threats. Eight out of ten of the critical letters were from people with religious objections to the idea of the visitors. One man demanded (and got) a refund because he thought *Communion* dull.

About two hundred letters have appeared disorganized and were apparently from people with significant psychological difficulties. However, most witnesses are articulate, concerned people who are very genuinely puzzled about what has happened to them and are seeking knowledge.

I have received letters from many prominent people, including military officers from Australia, Belgium, Russia, the United Kingdom, and the United States. All of these people have been guaranteed total confidentiality, and in cases where it has been asked that no record of correspondence be kept, as was the case with a general who had encounters along with his wife and children, the request has always been honored. Most of my correspondents were writing not to get an answer so much as to clarify their own memories and gain the satisfaction of telling somebody else what had happened to them.

Contrary to the image of witnesses as publicity hounds promoted in the press, they have been remarkably shy of publicity, and I have been careful to protect their privacy in the following overview of what they revealed to me. Correspondents who have been quoted extensively have given their specific permission for this particular material to be used.

We found that people were not reporting the scenario of abduction and manhandling that is so often referred to in the media and UFO publications. The script of being approached by odd little beings, taken aboard a UFO, and subjected to bizarre medical intrusions appears to be rare. Far more commonly, people report interactions at a far higher level of strangeness. However, I do not want to belittle the work that has been done by those who feel that the abduction scenario is true. It would be wrong for me to draw such an encompassing conclusion when we are still so ignorant of the actual nature of our contact. Suffice it to say that it may be only one part of a spectrum of relationship so broad as to be presently difficult to fully classify.

The majority of my correspondents report a lifetime of experiences of one kind or another, and about 30 percent of encounters involve more than one witness. If one member of a family is in contact, it is likely that others will be, too. There are a number of fantastic new dimensions that have hitherto been little acknowledged. The soul is clearly as central to this experience as it is absent from our current scientific view of reality; more than that, actual meetings with dead relatives are common. Children are deeply involved, and sometimes all of these things combine, often in remarkable ways.

A husband and wife are watching television while their preteen child sleeps in another room. The dog becomes nervous and the wife takes him out. As she opens the front door, a large ball of light flies away from the house. Moments later, the child runs into the living room claiming that small figures have just appeared in his room in the company of a relative who had recently passed away under tragic circumstances. The family is shocked, confused, and deeply moved. They write me, then they phone me and we talk for an hour, they pass out of my life.

"They had my dead uncle with them." "My brother was there, and he is dead." "I saw a woman I knew from years ago, who has been long dead." "A man was with them who told me he was dead and asked if that bothered me."

Others see the visitors during brushes with death. "I died on that hospital bed, and when I did I saw a thing like on the cover of your book." "She said she was my mother, and told me that I had to go back, that I could not yet enter the light." "They were in a white tunnel with me." "I saw your visitors after a near-death experience. They were glad to see me, and we all got upset when I had to go back."

There is a flood of letters from kids. So many, many letters from children. Thousands have specifically mentioned that the correspondent is fifteen or under. Often brilliant, sometimes heartbreakingly beautiful, they tell what is in many ways the most amazing part of the story.

More than adults, children, with their much more limited mental development and experience, could be expected to keep to commonplace descriptions if they were making up their stories. But that is very far from the case.

"They play with me on my slide after my mom and dad are asleep." "I do not want to tell my daddy, but I see these people all the time. You are not going to believe it, but they came out of the stove." "They took me on a life raft that floated in the air." "She said she was my gran, but I am afraid it was a great big bug."

A family is preparing for bed when a metallic, cylindrical craft swoops down into the front yard. The parents are terrified, but their child runs toward it. A tall, thin creature touches and reassures them. They also see other figures that look like "trolls in overalls." The wife perceives the tall creature as a man, the husband thinks it is a woman, a perceptual wrinkle that is so consistent that it is one of the few that could be said to be common to the whole experience. The wife asks, "Where are you from?" She gets an impression of a strange, windy desert.

Then they realize that their boy is inside the cylinder. The husband argues for his return, and he eventually is released. Years later, the boy recalls a visit from little people in a strange ship who thought he was very intelligent.

Such are my letters—a totally unexpected outpouring of overwhelming richness, power, beauty, and terror.

The experience refuses to be nailed down. It is neither good nor evil, but like reality, full of twists and turns and moral complications. In general, if there is an overall theme to encounter, it seems to be to chip away at our denial by putting us under pressure. Contact is a high-pressure experience. Many witnesses, like me, end up with post-traumatic stress syndrome. It's almost as if we simply cannot see the visitors unless they shake us up. I think that contact is a little like being waked up from a heavy sleep.

However, I have no letters about people driven mad or seriously hurt, and only one that discusses a death, and that involved misuse of a gun.

The experience is richly varied, but there are also some common factors.

For example, many people see owls that resolve into visitor figures. When beings disappear, as often happens, there follows an odor that most people describe as being like "cigarette smoke" or smoldering cardboard. I have myself smelled this many, many times, even deep in the woods. In addition to myself, a few people have also reported a cinnamon odor, but this appears rare. Generally, no smell at all is mentioned.

Often the scale of contact reported is far beyond our wildest imaginings.

A man awakens to find that he is in the night sky, hundreds of feet above the ground. He is certain that he was neither dreaming nor having an out-of-body experience. Then he finds himself coming up through the floor of a huge room that is filled with long benches. On these benches are hundreds of people, many of whom he knows. "I had the feeling that everybody in town was there."

The descriptions of beings are as contradictory as they are oddly similar. "They had white, chalky skin." "They were gray." "They were dark blue." They looked like bugs, like Greek gods, like some kind of cat people, like Orientals, like ordinary people. "Their arms resembled the legs of grasshoppers." "They looked so tired and old." "She was young and vibrant and she felt so soft—her hands—when she touched me." "He had the appearance of a soldier, very upstanding and strong."

Whether big and dark or more human, the eyes of the visitors always seem to have an extraordinary effect on witnesses. "When I looked into those eyes, I saw eternity." "She was a middle-aged woman, it looked like to me, but she had these golden eyes that took me to my soul." "The eyes were terrible. Lascivious. I had a powerful impression of evil." "He has huge black eyes that communicated total compassion and total gentleness. I fell in love instantly."

There is a lot of fear: "They want to get me, they want to get my children." "Are they evil? Why won't they leave us alone? They are making our life hell."

There is love: "I am scared but when they don't come I am devastated." "I love him and he loves me. How will I explain this to my wife?" "She played with me when I was a baby. As I have grown up, she has grown old. Do they die?"

They see light, "blinding light," "pale light," "green light," "white, chalky light," "light I think was alive," "a blue white light that was scary, like it could see me somehow, see my soul," "black light that made everything seem very pale," and, most often, "blue light," which, incidentally, is also the color traditionally associated with ghosts and the return of the dead.

Often, people awaken to the approach of a ball of

blue light. "It moved fast but stopped instantly." "The movement of the ball of light was weird. One second, it would zoom, then it stops—total stop."

There is lots of precognition. "I dreamed that my husband died. But when we got up, we found out my cousin had died." "They showed me my life as it would be and I have been in a constant state of déjà vu for thirty years." "I have total déjà vu after my experiences. I feel like my life is running on rails."

There is the feeling that enormous change is taking place, and change of mind is often—as in my case—confused with physical disaster. "I really relate to your experience of seeing the world explode. They pointed a wand at the world in my dream, and it blew up very majestically and slowly." And another, "I saw the moon explode, too. I wonder if you know when this will happen?"

They find themselves in odd situations. A man who has had many experiences is working deep in the woods. He awakens to find his coworkers staring at him because he has been sitting there with his eyes wide open, speaking an unknown language. A woman wakes up fighting furiously, sees that there is a small hooded figure beside the bed.

A family hears peculiar noises coming from the woods behind their house. Then a shout of alarm causes them to run to the back door. They observe their teenage boy pinned to the ground by what appears to them to be a six-foot-long praying mantis. With difficulty, they drive it into the woods, but continue to hear the sounds on occasion.

A family with a small estate is troubled by what they think are children hanging about a pond. A few approaches to them reveal that they appear, on close inspection, to be small men. Finally, the grandfather goes out with a shotgun to drive them off. There is a blast, and he is found dead, although his body appears unmarked. During the police investigation that follows, a metallic object is removed from under the skin of his chest. It is taken in evidence, but disappears. The death is ruled cause unknown and remains the only documented death I know of in any way connected with the experience.

There are often minor physical injuries: scoops taken from various parts of the body; tiny triangles, diamonds, or circles etched in the skin; small holes that bleed painlessly; minor burns, like sunburn on chests, on genitals, on faces; dry areas on the skin; dry tear ducts and many different types of allergic reaction.

I got one letter that referred to being placed on a metallic table, then ending up in possession of information relating to the impending end of the world.

This was one of the very few "millennial" letters that I received. Indeed, it had such an odd, hysterical quality about it that I sent the writer a response telling him to stay with the question and beware of getting involved with cults.

It turned out later that the letter was a hoax, its author a reporter who accused me of being the very sort of cult leader I had carefully cautioned him against in my reply, long before I knew his true identity. In his nationally broadcast accusations, he never mentioned the existence of the letter I had sent him. But when I sued him for defamation and gained the right to see his documents, there it was, right at the top. Later, he pleaded no-contest to criminal charges related to his reporting techniques in an unrelated matter and was sentenced to a fine and a probationary prison term.

But the great majority of my letters seemed entirely sincere. There were literally endless reports of awakening surrounded by "tall, thin beings," "short beings," "beings of light," of seeing blue lights hovering in the room, of getting reports from their children of little men coming in the night.

The visitors seemed to be chipping away at our resistance, and a picture emerged of mankind being slowly moved toward contact of a very unexpected kind. The visitors were not simply seeking to meet us, they wanted to become part of our interior life.

When people are engaged by these experiences, most of them do two things. They hide it, and they begin to seek understanding. The great majority do not expect answers. They are looking for supporting facts, and what they hope will be critical crumbs of insight. The ones who ask for help in forming groups or want to join abductee organizations is tiny compared to the number who prefer to deal with it on their own.

Letter after letter included statements like, "you must not reveal my name, but we need help," or, "my children are involved in this, my babies, and you have to keep our name out of it," or, "obviously I am placing my career in your hands but this has been eating at me for years and I've got to tell somebody," or, "we want help in dealing with this situation without ridicule."

People encounter the visitors everywhere, at all times of the day and night. A psychologist, the friend of a friend, wants to talk to me. He describes a close approach to apparent aliens beside a New York City expressway that was full of cars. But none of the other drivers, it seems to him, even noticed.

A year later I get a letter from a reader who apparently did notice. He saw a driver stop, get out of his car, and walk into a circle of "little men" who struck him as being dressed like clowns.

Without knowing of one another's existence, they both describe something like a lighted sign set up over the meeting site, that seemed to be flashing symbols of some sort. The second driver says that when he walked toward the circle of little men, he was warned away.

Just as you don't have to be alone to see the visitors, it doesn't have to be at night, and you can be anywhere: in a car, on a ship, in a plane, the desert, a crowded city.

In general, the press has responded to this outpouring of witnesses with the same dismissive approach as the scientific community and the government. For the most part, the witnesses are ignored or—if they should dare make public claims—ridiculed. I have experienced much persecution because of my public stance, including orchestrated harassment that I will discuss in later chapters. Other witnesses report a similar pattern. Most of the persecution, however, is not organized. Social ostracism by nonwitnesses is still almost as common as acceptance. In the United States, regional differences are significant. In the Northeast, for example, witnesses are far more likely to experience social rejection, as I and my family did, than in the far west.

Mentioning encounters to coworkers can often lead to very negative consequences as well, as is exemplified by the experience of Ed Conroy, whose ability to pursue a career as a journalist came to an end after he published *Report on Communion*, in which he admitted his own contacts.

It is also true, however, that discreet networking often leads to the discovery of other witnesses and interested parties among families and friends, and I have seen many wonderful people discover each other this way. In general, Anne and I have found that witnesses are a good group of people, usually stable, usually fun to know and be with, and we treasure the hundreds of friendships that we've gained through our correspondence. In the early years, we attempted to maintain networks of witnesses, but the ceaseless exploitation of this

by reporters made it impossible to continue without
risking the exposure of peoples' names.

The massive witness presence is a troubling reality to
the skeptics, because they give the lie to skeptical
gospel, as repeated in the March 20, 1994, *New York
Times Magazine* by Philip Klass, the UFO expert of the
Committee for the Scientific Investigation of Claims of
the Paranormal. "'They are little nobodies . . . people
seeking celebrity status."

We may indeed be a bunch of nobodies, but the witnesses are not publicity hounds. The reporter, Steven
Rae, who printed this comment in a story about
Harvard psychiatrist Dr. John Mack, author of
Abduction, knew of the existence of my letters when he
wrote it. He had contacted me through a publicist, and
on November 26, 1993, I had written him, "Of the 99,648
letters I have received as of today, 8,118 have been col-
lected in a database. . . . My correspondents for the most
part demand absolute confidentiality. . . . The great
majority write me just to 'get it off their chest.'" (I mis-
stated the number of letters. Actually, we had well over
120,000 at that point. I had glanced at an old file.)

I also provided him with copies of two sample letters
from witnesses who had given permission for them to
be quoted publicly. He did not refer to the existence of
the letters in his story, preferring to use the authority of
the *Times* to support Klass's assertion.

In his article, he also failed to mention that he had
interviewed me or received a letter from me or seen
samples of witness correspondence. His interview had
centered around an MRI scanning program that had
been undertaken by the Communion Foundation, which
had provided inconclusive results. He had wanted the
name of the doctor involved, but I had promised the
doctor anonymity.

When I tried to question Rae for this book, he did not

return my call. This is typical of the quality of coverage given this phenomenon by the press at the present time.

But the contact process is not going to be interrupted by a press deluded into believing that it is somehow protecting the gullible from error and fakery by taking the stance that it has. To me, this is very sad, because of the wonderful service the press could have performed as contact developed. I have always felt that, had the visitors been met in the first place by peaceful hearts and open minds, the beauty of contact would have emerged first, instead of the terror.

9

the depths

Most of my letters do not describe bad encounters. In general, people are left more in a state of puzzlement than anything else. Most people do not seek or appear to need much help in dealing with their experiences emotionally. However, this is not entirely true. Our rough tabulation showed that about 20 percent of the contact experiences were hard ones. There is no way of telling if there might be buried traumatic memories among the other 80 percent.

Because people like me who get rough treatment tend, as I did, to look for help, UFO researchers have ended up with a self-selected sample of witnesses who have been terrified. This is probably the main reason that the UFO literature concentrates so much on these cases. My own feeling is that even a single report of abuse in all the thousands of cases that have been investigated is cause for concern, and there are far more such cases reported. Some of them must be the results of hysteria or provocative hypnosis by researchers who were themselves frightened. But this cannot be used to explain away all the cases of hard treatment.

After we made the discovery of the Glenrock incident, my desire to finally close the question of whether or not the visitors were evil became intense. To see some cases of bad treatment that were not the result of hypnosis or hysteria, all I had to do was refer to my letters.

One correspondent wrote, "It was looking at me like it was hungry, and I got the idea that it wanted to eat my soul."

I could not help but recall the words of the famous investigator of anomalous experiences, Charles Fort. He'd suggested, toward the end of his life, that our world might be like a barnyard, implying that we are ignorant animals here for the slaughter and incapable of seeing the greater and more terrible meanings that surround us.

Worse, the more the experience directed itself toward the soul, the more intellectually helpless I felt. The soul is a dead concept in Western science and philosophy, an archaic leftover from the middle ages. Of course, most of us still believe in the soul, but what does that matter when thought has failed to meaningfully address its existence for two hundred years? I don't know how to think in terms of the soul. Science offers me no empowerments. Philosophy is lost in a maze of its own making.

Even a short technological lead could grant the visitors a completely inappropriate appearance of magical powers. A few Spaniards—no more culturally or morally advanced than the Indians they subdued—froze vast Aztec armies into helplessness with a combination of horses, guns, and the fact that the Aztecs thought that their appearance meant that the god Quetzalquotl was making his prophesied return.

As I struggled with the notion that the visitors' technology—if it was technology—might conceal frail, imperfect beings much like us, full of greed and fear and doubt, it struck me as highly unwise to assume, as I had at times, that the fact that they address old human mythologies necessarily proves that they are filled with wisdom. If they were indeed wise, I was going to have to see that. I had no intention of ever bringing out the proof unless I could be certain that the visitors would have a positive effect in the human world. I did not want to see them ride roughshod over the religious and cultural institutions we have evolved to enrich our lives. I wanted and demanded respect.

Two of the most compelling "negative" letters I have ever received both came from the same foreign country. I investigated both cases personally and found the two individuals involved to be absolutely honest, normal people. Both have been very specific about demanding anonymity.

The first narrative comes from a middle-aged woman who had a rare conscious encounter. She was at home in the middle of the afternoon and was using a vacuum cleaner when the encounter started. From my own personal experience and observation, it appears that the visitors may use sound to disable witnesses in the initiating phases of an interaction. My speculation has been that the noise of the vacuum cleaner somehow disrupted a sonic attack in this case, leaving the witness unexpectedly conscious when the second phase of the visitors' approach began.

She reported her observations. "This is the most horrifying thing I've ever encountered: I was vacuuming my living room floor at about noon. Suddenly I felt quite ill and thought I was going to vomit, so I sat down on my couch to see if the sick feeling would subside. I then saw that I was not alone. There were three strange little people standing alongside the couch, just looking at me. I froze with fear, as I hadn't even seen anything like this in the movies. Two of these beings looked the same, but one was taller and thinner. I shall now describe them to you:

"The two short, fat ones were about four to four and a half feet tall, with broad faces and black enormous eyes, but only a hint of where a nose or mouth might have been, almost like a pencil drawing. Unlike your visitors, mine had wispy bits of hair at the back of their heads, and they didn't have little blue suits on; they had brown shrouds. The thin hair at the backs of their heads was also brown. These, I instinctively knew, were the workers, and that they were male. The other was female, and about five feet tall. She wore a black shroud and had black wispy hair at the back of her head, and a very elongated face with dark, huge piercing eyes, and once again just a hint of something where a nose or mouth would have been.

"The tall thin one started to speak to me with her mind, and told me I was to go with them. I answered with my own mind that I wouldn't go. Somehow, mind communication seemed perfectly normal at the time, and I felt quite comfortable with communicating that way. This doesn't mean that I wasn't frightened, as I was beside myself with fear. She kept saying 'You must come with us,' and I kept refusing. She then said I could go free, and I got up off of the couch and crawled along my hallway to the front door. When I got there, they pulled me back with their minds until I was on the couch again. They let me go again, and the result was identical, except that this time my husband was standing at the front door; I clung to him, and can always remember how I could smell the wool jumper he was wearing.

"They pulled me out of his arms and back to the

couch and once again told me it was useless to fight, as I would go with them. The two workers seemed to be busy doing something while all this was going on, but I have no idea what. The next thing I was aware of was the sound of my husband's car pulling up. I heard him come through the front door and down the hallway. At this point, I noticed that the visitors were gone. However, when my husband first walked into the room I didn't at first believe it was him. I thought it was another trick. It took about fifteen minutes before I could really believe that they were gone and my husband was really home. My next shock was that it was five-thirty P.M.; I thought it would be at most one-thirty P.M. Where did that time go?"

My correspondent was never able to discover this, despite various efforts at memory recovery. No matter what might have happened during those hours, I was deeply disturbed by this letter. The bullying, the compulsion, the cruel and extremely clever deceits that it revealed on the part of the visitors caused me deep concern.

How could the same sort of gentle creature who touched hands with Raven Dana possibly act like this, even when unobserved? I had no explanation, and even less for this next story, which comes from a man who is well-known in his home country, in contrast to most of us "little nobodies."

He'd had a close UFO sighting some time before, and on this night had arrived home quite late. I will let him describe this encounter in his own words. "I reckon my head had been on the pillow less than thirty seconds when, for want of a better word, it exploded—'it' being my head. The only way I can describe this shocking sensation was that I thought a bomb had blown me to pieces, and that 'I' was nowhere. I ceased to be. After a few seconds the vacuum of what used to be me was

filled by an entity of total evil. This 'evil' thing so terrified me that I started fighting (mentally, physically?)
until I became conscious in my body, unable to move
any limbs. I was cataleptic and, although I was screaming for my wife to wake up and help me, my lips barely
moved and the screams were whispers. Eventually,
maybe a minute or two later, my bodily control
returned, and with it real screams. My wife awoke
immediately and did her best to comfort me, and after
screaming, my second physical sensation was of liquid
dripping from around my ears onto the pillow. I had
rested my head on the pillow while laying on my left
side, undergone the 'experience,' and found myself in
bed lying on my back a few seconds later with the pillow below each ear wet with tears. How much can you
cry in a couple of seconds? How much water can come
out of your eyes in such a short time? Was there some
'lost time' at this point? I don't know.

"After I gained control and began to explain to my
wife what had happened, I was too distraught to look at
the bedroom radio clock. She got out of bed, walked out
to the kitchen and made a cup of coffee for me and tea
for her. She switched on the bedroom light, and we sat
up in bed talking quietly about what may have happened. I became calmer. The whole thing was not a
dream, because I'd never fallen asleep. We both put it
down to a rather violent out-of-body experience, perhaps even an attempted 'possession' by some entity.
Needless to say we were alarmed, but everything was
okay now and we decided to get some sleep and hope-
fully wake up in time for work in the morning. We finished our drinks and the light was still on when we both
said, 'What's that noise?'

"A low humming, and a quick glance at the clock:
two-thirty A.M. The humming quickly turned to a deep,
fast throbbing. Not a plane, not a truck, not a car.

Louder now, and stopping right over the roof of the house, directly above the bedroom. No flashing lights, no glowing—just a very loud sound. We froze; what on earth could be on the roof?! Maybe it was hovering well above the roof—but so loud!

"Before I could volunteer to go outside and see what was going on, all our nice little stories about out-of-body experiences and possession were shattered, as something invisible grabbed my chest and started pulling with amazing force. I felt like my soul, not my body, was being pulled up vertically toward the still loud throbbing noise, and although I thought it would be futile, I screamed out for my wife to lay on top of me. She did this, and the sensation of pulling eased a little. I was screaming and struggling against an 'invisible beam,' with my wife laying full length on top of me in my own bed at two-thirty A.M. What a sight we would have presented if someone had walked in!

"It would have been almost funny, if it hadn't gone on for another two hours. 'They' pulled, I resisted, my wife hung on and the engine throbbed, until finally it went away, and exhausted and badly shaken, even devastated, we fell asleep."

This account was written by a well-known, successful man with two happy teenage children and a thriving twenty-five-year marriage. In reply to my letter asking his permission to use his story, he said, "The experience I went through, and which my wife shared and witnessed, remains the greatest mystery of my life, and far from wanting or needing publicity, I would rather that none of it ever happened, and I am still very careful who I take into my confidence on this matter." He has also discovered that he and two siblings have identical apparent biopsy scars on the same parts of their bodies, and no way to account for them.

I can only comment, at this point, that it is very sad

that witnesses must hide from public exposure or risk the humiliation and harassment that invariably follows the revelation of their names.

Upon reflecting on these and other stories like them, I began to think long and hard about what the public coming of the visitors might be like. I noticed something similar about all my horror stories. While people sometimes report being frightened to find the visitors in their homes, the real horror stories, involving blatantly abusive behavior, center around one, single act, and that is forcible abduction.

With just a few exceptions, these stories involved a person who had in some way resisted going somewhere with the visitors. In these cases, the result had been bullying and insistence.

One thing was clear: the visitors were and are extremely determined. But they have also often been quite responsive to me and others. I wondered if we could ever communicate that we did not appreciate some of their methods. That brought back a recollection of a small moment in the encounter I'd had with them on December 26, 1985, when I had been forcefully dragged out of my cabin. When I screamed that they had no right, a low, now-familiar voice had replied, "We have a right."

This means, at least, that they possess the concept of rights, or they wouldn't have known what I was talking about. That their concept is similar to ours can also be inferred from the fact that they felt it necessary to respond to me as they did. Had they lacked the concept or considered it unimportant, they would surely have remained silent.

Why might they think they have a right? We witnesses gave them no permission to brutalize us.

In human life, compulsion is often used in situations where a given outcome is good for the compelled individual. Usually, this happens when the compelled person cannot understand. For example, parents routinely force children to do a whole host of activities that they would not do on their own.

Did the visitors view us as children, then? Perhaps so. In my case, there were indications of this. They had called me "child," and they induced the return to my babyhood that I reported earlier, apparently to demonstrate that I had taken a first step on that morning that was like the first step of a baby.

Children are not the only ones that we compel. Those of us who have shown themselves to be dangerous to others may be imprisoned; confused or deranged patients may be forcibly kept in hospital.

When ignorance of the benefits of intervention causes an adult to resist it, human society often compels. The sick man might cry out, "you have no right," to which his nurses and doctors would certainly respond, "we do have a right."

Although the vast majority of witnesses are healthy and normal by human definition, I wondered, reading those letters, if the visitors shared that opinion. Soul blindness, I thought, might be regarded by them as an affliction. Now that I have seen into the world of the soul, I regard it as far more than an affliction. It is a disease incalculably worse than cancer, and we are all, to some degree, victims.

As an individual who had seen both the visitors' determination and experienced many benefits from my association with them, on balance I chose a cautious but open-minded approach. I decided that I could not trust them completely and I certainly didn't wish to appear an apologist for bullies, but I also decided, based on the rising degree of civility they were showing to me and my friends, to try and to meet them halfway.

I was supported in this decision by that fact that I

had so many different shadings of reaction among my correspondents. A few appeared to have had encounters just as conscious as the one related above, but with very different results.

"She was standing there beside my bed, and I knew that she was smiling. I could feel it inside myself, although it was dark and I could not see her face. I had an impression of extreme gentleness. She was just so soft when she touched me, like deerskin, almost like smoke. I felt very loved and supported."

Something like this sense of love is as often as not felt even by people—like me, for example—who have had hard encounters. I had been given a lot of rough treatment, but I did not find that I hated the visitors.

Rough encounters may be an attempt to break through the hard shell of denial that seems to encase us. I wonder, for example, how often I'd seen the visitors before my first conscious memories in late 1985? During hypnosis, I shifted with utter and complete spontaneity to the age of nine, and proceeded to remember an encounter that had taken place in the company of my sister and father, where I had seen a whole platoon of ordinary American soldiers lying asleep on little cots, being attended by the same visitor who had come to me in 1985. This had happened on a trip in 1954. What was truly extraordinary was that when Ed Conroy questioned my old friend Michael Ryan for his book, Mike clearly remembered that I'd come back from that trip talking on and on about some soldiers I'd seen.

A substantial number of my correspondents also had dim memories of childhood encounter, and there are apparently many people with repressed memories.

So maybe the violence and the coercion are really an attempt to get us to notice something that we want very badly not to see. If this is true, the ferocity may be a kind of demand for a response. They could be so far outside our expectations—so unreal, as it were—that only the most intense effort on their part will enable us even to become aware of their presence. They may be in the bizarre position of literally swarming through our world—and yet being unable to get us to notice them.

Because of all the ambiguity—good experiences, strange experiences, horrible ones—the visitors come to us out of a cloud of fear and confusion. I know Christians who are dear friends who fear that the visitors are demons. Others consider the presence angelic, and point out that souls like ours, blind to themselves and covered in confusion and guilt, might well regard the agents of goodness as terrifying.

The sense of a shadowy and malign presence, the appearance of government cover-up, and all the ignorance has led to some terrible rumors getting started.

But some of the fear is obviously more sensible than that, and emerges out of the challenge to the worldview that is at the heart of the experience, which, no matter its origin, is among the very most shattering and profound assaults that a person can sustain.

I thought long and hard about what more I needed from the visitors before I went ahead. Through the spring of 1989, I digested the proof and tried to make sense of the horror stories. I agonized. Many times, I woke up in the middle of the night and prayed to God that the whole thing would just end. But it didn't end, it wouldn't end.

Finally, I decided something. If they weren't willing to go away, then they had to do something to convince me that life with them was going to be better than what we have now, and was something that we wanted.

At this point, my experience began to shift. I would be directed to my own deepest fears and see revealed powers of mind that I never dreamed existed. I would learn that the imagination can be a tool of gigantic potency, which we can use to soar into unexpected realms. I would learn that the visitors didn't just want to come close to us, they wanted to come *very* close. This was the beginning of the second phase of my journey with them. Still kicking and screaming and running from every shadow, I was pushed, pulled, and cajoled a little farther. And then I saw it, a distant promise or maybe threat: I saw that they were here for a sharing of self more profound, far-reaching, and world-changing than any we have imagined possible.

I saw, also, that they aren't going to be here forever and we don't have much time before our world starts to come unraveled because of our exploding population.

This might be the last minute, it seemed to me, and the shadows seemed long, and so did the night.

SECTION TWO

Beyond Communion

And he put forth the form of an hand,
and took me by a lock of my head; and the spirit
lifted me up between the earth and the heaven,
and brought me in the visions.

—*Ezekiel 8:3*

SECTION TWO

Beyond Compliance

10

shadows of meaning

In the summer of 1989 an event took place that would signal fundamental change in the evolution of my relationship with the visitors. It came as a result of my desire to see and understand more of what face-to-face contact might be like. Ever since my failure to respond to the three calls that had echoed up from the woods in January of 1988, I had been fundamentally an observer. It was true that I'd seen remarkable things, but I had not tasted deeply of relationship. I wanted to touch them and smell them and taste them. I wanted to spend more than just a few seconds at a time with them. If they couldn't or wouldn't take me to their place of origin, then why not move into my cabin and live with me?

I was beginning to see this as something quite possible. My sense was that the visitors were physical people just like us, but who have evolved a level of mind that allows them to move in and out of physical reality like we enter and leave a room. They seemed to see time from the outside, as we do three-dimensional objects.

Since we cannot comprehend time as a object, we were having a great deal of trouble dealing with them, and I felt that some major contradictions and mysteries had to be resolved before I could go on. I told them this in three ways: I spoke my wishes aloud, I thought them, then I pictured them as best I could.

At first, nothing changed. In fact, nothing seemed to be happening at all. I began to think maybe they could not afford to reveal themselves in the way I had asked because they were too evil to get that close without exposing their secret. If I concluded that they were evil, I decided that I would present my proof along with every horror story I knew and post a warning: stay away.

At about eleven o'clock at night on July 6, 1989, my wife and I were reading in bed, when I came to a passage in Dean Koontz's *Strangers* about a sinister motorcyclist whose headgear had "a tinted visor that came all the way down to his chin." When the main character looked into that black glistening visor, she was swept away in a wave of terror.

To me, the description brought with it a whole secret realm of shadowy memories. It seemed to me that I had seen such a face back in the darks of childhood, and that just this gleaming horror had attacked me in October 1985, an event that, by initially remaining suppressed, had nearly broken my mind a few months before my first consciously remembered encounter in December. In a way, the conscious memories of that month had been a desperate attempt to find my way into the terrors of October and heal a psyche that was disintegrating from the pressure it was under.

In memory I saw what I'd seen then—huge, evil insect eyes and a wand that had pointed at my forehead like a needle flaring with the light of a deadly star.

As with the nine knocks, which had begun to unfold just as I read Dr. Gliedman's argument that reality was not mediated by the mind, an experience related to this passage instantly commenced when I stopped reading, stunned by how much it had scared me.

As I put the book down, I noticed movement in the hallway that directly faced the bed. When I perceived a short, hazy figure, I felt a very real wave of terror. So much for the fearless adventurer.

The figure came racing toward me. It was not a defined shape, but a sort of gray, amorphous presence, moving fast. Rage exploded in my mind and I leaped out of the bed, grabbed the bedside table, and hurled it at the figure with all my might, bellowing, "You'll never get me! You'll never get me!"

Screaming, Anne threw her own book up into the air and jumped away as the table shattered into pieces at our feet.

"What's the matter!"

"They'll never get me! They won't! They sure as hell will not!"

"Who?"

"You didn't see him?"

"Who?"

In an instant I had been plunged into vastly more fear than I'd ever felt before. It had seemed as if the thing wanted to capture me or enter me in some unknown way and dominate my being. I didn't feel a sense of evil, exactly, so much as one of terrific, oppressive power.

As we moved about picking up the shattered remains of the table, Anne expressed real concern about me, and I didn't blame her. Living with me as she did every day, she no longer worried about my sanity. But she now questioned my ability to go on with this, considering that it was obviously still tearing me apart.

That figure had seemed more threatening, I think, than anything I had ever seen in my life. In the moment that it was approaching me, I felt as if a door was opened into a world that I wanted nothing to do with.

Anne had seen no trace of it. "All of a sudden, you just rose up out of bed yelling." Finally, I faced the obvious: I'd had a waking nightmare so powerful that it was a symptom.

In my researches into hallucinatory pathology, I'd watched videos of people who suffered from night terrors. Had a camera been running, my reaction would have looked just the same. But I'd also interviewed such people and read numerous papers about their difficulty, and their terrors did not generally unfold while they were wide awake.

So maybe I'd been dozing. And that, as far as I was concerned, was the end of that. Post-traumatic stress victims suffer from all sorts of sleep disturbance, and nightmares are certainly included.

I was scheduled to spend the next three days at the Omega Foundation in Dutchess County, New York, offering advice to a group of people who wanted answers. It wasn't just a matter of giving a lecture: one of the sessions was to last all day, during which I was expected to pick over the elements of my experience in great detail.

But now I was plunged into doubt about my most basic validity. How could a man who was smashing furniture possibly teach anybody anything about coping with contact?

All I could do was to try to present as objective an overview as I was able. I did not hide what had just happened to me: instead, I used it to illustrate the depth of the fear, how it could spark unexpectedly, producing a waking dream even years after an encounter.

Finally the day was over. I arrived home on Saturday

night fairly miserable. Tomorrow, I had to do it all again.

I found a number of messages on the answering machine. As I listened, I became concerned: they were all from my brother, Richard. Repeatedly, he asked that I telephone him immediately, so I did so at once.

"Something weird happened and I think it involved you."

"In what sense?"

"The *Communion* thing."

"Okay." Had he been abducted? That would be a surprise. "Friday night I woke up because I heard what sounded like a helicopter over the house."

"Does it happen often?"

"Never. Not in all the years I've lived here. I think there might have been light, but the shade was down. The thing is, when I sat up in bed, I saw this little figure standing beside the plant." (There was a large plant in the room that stood under the window at the foot of the bed.) "It just scared the hell out of me, Whitley. It started coming up beside the bed and I grabbed my electric guitar and threw it at it as hard as I could. The thing shot up in the air and out through the top of the window, and I just lay there, scared half to death."

I really cannot express the feelings I had at that moment.

Richard continued. "I had the feeling that it was scared, too, and that I might even have hurt it."

I remember that I was standing beside my bed holding the telephone handset, staring down at the card table that had replaced the smashed nightstand. I sat down, my mind roaring with thoughts, with speculations, questions, my heart breaking at the message of panic and disappointment that had just been delivered to me from another world. "Richard, maybe it was a dream."

"Wait a second, there's more. This morning when I got up I raised the shade and there was a neat circle of glass cut out of the top window and laid to one side, like somebody had used a glass cutter."

"A break, maybe the guitar—"

"No, it didn't hit the window. Anyway, it was a perfect cut except for three missing shards."

"Maybe a prowler—"

"How, in the top of the window? He would've needed a ladder, and anyway, why do it? You couldn't get in from up there. Look Whitley, this has something to do with you, and I'm telling you right now I don't want to be involved in it."

"I'm sorry. I—don't know what to say."

"Well, tell them they got the wrong Strieber. That thing scared the hell out of me and I want no part of it."

"Did you see it—a face?"

"A dark figure three feet tall. It looked hooded. And it shot up in the air like a rocket. Faster than if it had wings."

My breath was literally taken away by the combination of incredible power that the visitors were displaying, and the amazingly detailed knowledge of my life. They knew my brother, exactly where he lived, knew—somehow—that he would react just as I had. "I had the feeling that it was scared, that I might even have hurt it." If they'd called me on the phone in my hand, they could not have transmitted a clearer message.

"What did you do afterward?"

"Lay there in bed scared to death!"

"Did you sleep?"

"Not much! And that's another thing: unlike you, I don't enjoy being terrified."

I went back to the Omega Foundation the next morning and told my audience what had happened, and expressed my shame and frustration at being so incapable of dealing with my experiences.

What would have happened, I wondered, if I'd just stayed still as the figure approached—or if I'd gone outside during the nine knocks, or down to the meadow on the morning of the three cries?

I had asked for total communion, and it had been offered—and look at the mess I'd made. Again. The message delivered through my brother melted my heart and made me feel as if I had fought off a priceless gift.

But it could also be a clever trick, a way of disarming me so that I wouldn't be so hard to handle in the future.

In fact, the agonizing state of unsureness into which I was plunged was and is at the core of relationship with the visitors. To wrestle with a question like this is a sink-or-swim proposition: either it is going to destroy you or it is going to expand your mind. You cannot turn away, you cannot pretend it doesn't exist.

It is this kind of moment—full of unendurable intensities—that offers the real potential for breakthrough.

A few days later Ed Conroy called. He had been on vacation and had just a short time before returned to his apartment. He telephoned me for other reasons, but happened to mention an odd incident that had taken place as he'd unlocked his door. Lying on the mat in his foyer were three shards of glass, neatly placed side by side.

His apartment had been locked, and so he was mystified.

He and my brother barely knew each other and had hardly ever communicated. Unfortunately, it was impossible to match the glass Conroy had found to the window, as it had already been repaired.

I wish that I could somehow express what it means to experience something like this, that fulfills every definition of reality, but that is so far over the edge.

I reflected at this point on all that I had learned so far. It was clear to me that I had to go back to the drawing board. I had asked for deeper communion, but I certainly hadn't expected it to mean some kind of literal melding, which is how the visitors appeared to view it. I'd seen it as a kind of intimate friendship that would reveal us to each other—especially them to me.

But this strange, rushing attack—what did it mean?

My worldview had long ago shifted to accommodate the idea of extraterrestrials. It had shifted again, with the nine knocks, to adjust to the idea that they knew, specifically, that I was here. When I heard the richly emotional tones of the voice from the woods, it changed again. That had been the voice either of a disappointed lover or a disappointed predator and I could not tell which. The other things—the visit to Dora's, the physical display that had happened at the cabin—also made a sort of basic sense. Glenrock had awed me, but its meaning was understandable as an attempt to broaden contact.

But how was I to think about the incredible intimacy implied by this new event? As I fought the being off, I'd experienced terror from the very bottom of my soul. I threw the table because at that second it felt like the devil himself was about to leap right down my throat— so "the devil" had taken his appeal to my brother!

And now there was a new feeling. The damned thing of it was, I felt loved, I felt that there was something good and decent there, and I found myself wanting it to come back, I found myself actually longing to find a way to open myself, to surrender to this . . . gentleness.

This may be what it feels like when a human being gets a taste of nonhuman emotions and the devastatingly intimate friendship that is possible to beings who know their souls better than we know our skin.

I had to face the fact that they weren't just knocking on the side of my house and calling me from the woods, they were also calling me from inside my own life, and they wanted to literally enter me and become part of me.

I saw now a new and incredible aspect of contact: they weren't just here to meet us, to shake hands, to trade histories. They wanted something far deeper, far more intimate than we have even with each other.

I had seen the visceral, instinctive power of my terror and I could not help but believe that there was something valid about it. There must be, there had to be, nothing could be from that far down in a man's guts and not bear an element of truth. But I had also tasted that strange love; I felt the sense of the little being, of its loneliness and its longing to join me, of the loneliness of this great force come from the shadows, and its longing to join us all.

I agonized over the notion that I might have actually hurt somebody from another world. I had read more than one letter that said something like, "I let go with the shotgun, I could not help myself"; "I screamed at them, I kicked at them, I would have shot them if I'd had my gun."

If I had had my shotgun in my hands, I would have unloaded it right at that figure, and that is the truth of Whitley Strieber. I thought, I'm weak, I don't have the strength, I'm not good enough to do this.

But what was "this"? There was nothing relevant either to tradition or to reported encounter experience that would explain what had just happened. I was alone with this one. This was direct communication, a sentence spoken: "you could have hurt me."

The context of this sentence—its grammar, as it were—crossed the boundaries of mind and distance. If this was an invasion, it was happening from the inside out.

One thing was very, very clear: I wasn't even close to getting past my fear, and until that was true, I'd better forget being a lecturer.

July became August, and things stayed quiet. After

I'd thrown the table, the visitors had gone away and I was beginning to think that they would not return to Whitley Strieber. Despite all my fear, I missed them terribly. I found this ambivalence—which is typical of witnesses—mystifying. Part of me loved them, found them fascinating, and wanted every possible moment of contact—until it came. Then that amazing resistance would come boiling up.

In early October, a neighbor came over one weekend to discuss some work that we needed to do on the cooperative road. I had been sitting on the couch listening to a very strange phenomenon: a high-pitched drilling sound coming from under the house. I'd gone into the basement and found that I could hear it clearly by putting my ear on the basement floor.

When the drilling reached a certain frequency, my skin began to feel as if it was tightening, then getting hot. I was disturbed by this and was puzzling over this in the living room when the neighbor arrived. We were sitting and discussing the road as I nervously listened to the drilling. It wasn't a particularly loud sound, and he gave no indication that he noticed it.

Suddenly a thin stream of blood began shooting out of his forehead. For a moment, it looked like a stream of red dye from a water pistol, then it began to flow down his face. We got up immediately; I got him some Kleenex. With Anne's help, we got the bleeding to stop. Eventually we discussed the road, but over the phone.

Later that morning, I went to another neighbor's house with the same mission in mind. My son and his guest came with me. They were eleven at the time, and both wearing shorts, T-shirts, and baseball caps.

We entered the neighbor's house, and there was a brief discussion of the fact that they'd found a large black dog dead on their porch a few days before, and the vet had not been able to determine a cause of death. I noted this in my mind, because numerous witnesses have reported seeing black dogs in connection with their encounters. At that moment, the neighbor's wife walked in saying, "I think the cat's lost, too."

At the moment she uttered the word "cat," my son's companion turned toward us suddenly. Blood was pouring from his nose. His cap, as it happened, was emblazoned with the word CAT in block letters.

Again, I stanched the bleeding. The boy said he'd never had a nosebleed before. I telephoned his parents and they concurred.

A few minutes later, the boy was fine, but Anne and I had had enough for that weekend and we packed up and took the gang back to the city.

Some months later, we would begin hearing soft, repeated thuds from underground back along the ridges behind our house. And after that, there would never again be lights in the sky at night associated with the visitors.

What do I make of this? Well, maybe there are aliens here and maybe they built an underground shelter beneath the ridge. A field a mile from it has been the source of rising lights for years, and in the town of Pine Bush, New York, also near the Hudson Valley, UFOs are routinely photographed and sometimes seen emerging from the ground or disappearing into it. A group from New York has often encountered the visitors in one form or another on a road in that area.

But why all the blood and the strange coincidences? It seemed almost as if the drilling sound had caused the bleeding, and that the coincidences related to the fact that, when you are near the visitors, the meaning of the world itself changes.

So much was beyond my understanding. I was incapable of surrendering enough to meld together with

them. But out of all the fire and discord that had followed their attempt to do this, there emerged a new
level of relationship. I wasn't only curious and afraid,
now I was also full of passion. Despite everything, I
wanted them in my life. I resolved to try to open myself
to what was happening in a new way, hoping that we
would move closer together after all. In a sense, it was
like a developing marriage. You don't marry just the
good side of a person, you marry everything.

I felt so rotten about not making it yet again, and I
decided that I wouldn't blame the visitors for giving up
on me. Sure, they had defects. So do we. But there was
also great vulnerability and great poetry.

I asked: Why can't I surrender to this? And then came
a completely new approach: they dropped me down the
proverbial rabbit hole. I tumbled into the depths of the
unconscious, the depths of time, the depths of everything.

11

the bottom of time

"So he drove out the man; and he placed
at the east of Eden
Cherubims, and a flaming sword which
turned every way,
to keep the way of the tree of life."

—*Genesis 3:24*

To my understanding, the past and the future did not exist except in our minds. The present moment is all there is, and time travel is fiction. I was aware of some elegant physics that suggested that time had more plastic properties than that, but I discounted it.

The visitors, it seemed, had different ideas.

During this period, I was reading in two main areas: physics and the Bible. A man who discovers after a lifetime of doubt that the soul is a definite reality will almost inevitably turn toward books that might somehow operate on behalf of his spiritual welfare. In my young adulthood, I had completely ignored my soul, and now wondered very much what condition it might be in.

I had always believed, tacitly, that the soul was real. But belief is belief; it becomes another and much more urgent matter when something is tangible. At the time, I was reading the Bible to understand the origins of human consciousness, which I feel is recorded in the story of Eden. My interest in physics stemmed from an increasing sense that the visitors might regard what we identify as religion and science as a single discipline. This was based on my deepening understanding of the breathtaking ethic that had actually been present in my experience from the beginning.

They did so much at one time. They were revealing themselves to me as they revealed me to myself. They weren't just showing me new ideas, they were demonstrating a whole new way of being conscious and being alive. They were directing me down a path that led closer and closer to them. And they were operating, always, at the absolute limit of my tolerance. Each confrontation strengthened me, whether it was a failure or not.

Then they shifted gears. They opened a new direction, and breathtaking, awesome new possibilities were presented.

I cannot say that I dreamed the mind-bending journey that I am about to describe, and I have a very specific reason for that. Once, I would have had to assume that the visitors had somehow induced what I am about to relate as a vivid dream. But there was a preliminary event that set it up, that was so incredible and so very curious that I was left with the thought that it must have been meant as a message to me that none of this was a dream.

This happened to two people in a car on an ordinary afternoon, on a crowded New Jersey highway.

It began, however, the night before, a soft September night with summer's end in the air. My son's closest friend was with us at the cabin, and the next day I was to take him down to a diner in New Jersey to meet his father. Two days more and we would pack up for the last time this summer.

Things proceeded normally that night. The kids went to sleep in their bedroom below ours. Instead of going down to the woods, I watched a movie. I had had a busy summer and I was ready for a break. As always, the last thing I did was to check out the house and then set the burglar alarm. At about eleven, Anne and I went to bed.

By midnight, everybody in the house was asleep. I remember no unusual dreams, no disturbances of any kind. However, I woke up at about three because something strange and frightening was happening to me. At first, I thought that I was having a heart seizure. It wasn't painful, but it certainly didn't feel normal. There was a fluttering, buzzing sensation inside my chest that seemed to affect my breathing.

Clutching at my pajamas, I sat straight up in bed. The moment that I moved, I found myself drifting forward with the lazy movement of a bubble.

The next thing I knew, I went down through the floor and into the room below. I glimpsed a man in the room—and then became that man. My son's friend was sitting up, and I was crouching beside the bed talking to him. Quite suddenly, the scene was entirely vivid and normal in every way, except that he was looking at me expectantly and I had no idea what was happening. I could feel that I'd been talking, but didn't know what I'd just said.

My son, in the adjoining bed, was also awake.

I did the only thing I could, which was to stand up, tell them good night, and go back upstairs. I lay in my bed completely perplexed and quite shocked. What in the world was this about? Was there no upper limit to strangeness?

Soon, I went back down and looked in on the boys.

They were both sleeping peacefully. Whatever had been going on, at least it hadn't bothered them.

I spent a sleepless night, worried that if I dropped off, I'd escape myself again. I remember staring up at that dark ceiling and thinking, this is one thing you will never write about, because it is not possible to explain this in any way. But the incredible is at the foundation of contact, and strangeness cannot and must not be edited out in the interest of believability. The whole thing is completely unbelievable from beginning to end, anyway, so why waste time trying to make it credible? It's not and it never will be. But to people who are having these contacts, this won't seem all that odd. We live in a very bizarre corner of reality, we witnesses.

Toward dawn, I guess I did sleep, because the next thing I remember is the radio turning itself on.

I got up and got dressed quickly. I was most interested to hear what the boys would say. I didn't intend to mention anything, and I was curious if they would remember what I'd said, or if they had even perceived anything unusual.

They both recalled the incident and were full of talk about it. But neither boy could remember a single word of what had been said. They didn't seem particularly concerned by it, so I felt that I had no choice but to let it go. I was intensely curious, but from the beginning we'd followed a course of never drawing the children's attention to how very unusual all this was, and I wasn't going to change that rule now.

I tried to analyze the event. It was actually quite interesting, especially in relation to the occasional stories I had read or been sent concerning UFOs that doubled before peoples' eyes and then melded back into a single object. This had happened in a famous French case, and a smattering of readers had reported it as well.

There is a concept in quantum physics called superposition, which describes the indeterminate location of a particle in quantum space. But how could something as large as an entire human body ever follow laws that only functioned at the atomic scale and below? Surely quantum laws did not apply to large-scale objects like, say, me.

We assume that quantum laws stop at a very small scale because the world that we observe around us appears to operate according to a much more obvious physics. You kick the wall and you get a hole. Your foot never goes through it without leaving a mark.

Our floor and our son's ceiling, however, were completely unblemished.

Finally, I decided to just file the whole nutty business away. The hell with becoming a quantum superposition.

And yet, I wondered. What if the body is a quanta? What if its very shape depends upon the mind? I had often tasted a strange, electrical sensation during my experiences, had levitated . . .

What if I wasn't having out-of-body travel at all, what if my body itself was what was changing—and gaining, during these special moments, the power of the visitors? Was Satprem right?

Later that day, I took my son's friend to meet his father at our usual place, a diner on Route 17 in New Jersey. As we drove down the New York State Thruway into gradually more and more crowded areas, I mentioned the previous night again, but the boy still didn't remember what I'd said.

We crossed the New York–New Jersey border and began to pass the almost continuous line of shopping centers, fast food restaurants, and stores that mark the part of Route 17 that goes through New Jersey.

Seventeen is a divided highway and to get to the meeting place it would be necessary for me to take an exit, cross over, and backtrack about three hundred yards to the diner.

We saw his father's truck in the parking lot as we turned onto the exit. There was nothing in the least unusual: we'd done this easily a dozen times over the past few years.

The moment we took the exit, however, something very strange began to unfold. The shopping malls around us disappeared. Suddenly we were going down a ramp that I had not been aware of before. I wasn't too startled; my initial assumption was that I'd taken a wrong turn. A moment later we entered a sunken highway. The roadway was concrete, and the sound in the car became suddenly much less loud. There were high concrete walls, and I could see foliage at the top. The boy said, "Where are we?"

I replied, "I think I took a wrong turn."

He grew a little uneasy, obviously concerned by the radical change that had taken place. Nothing looked familiar to me, either. The road was quiet and empty, which was extremely strange considering where we were. We went beneath an underpass and I saw another ramp ahead. I could see that the boy was really nervous now, and I didn't blame him. I'd been up and down all these roads many times, and I was completely at a loss.

When we reached the exit, we came out into a completely unexpected situation. I had never seen this area before, or any other place remotely like it. The streets were wide and strikingly empty. Although it had been quite hazy and cloudy as we left 17, it now appeared to be sunny, as light dappled down through trees that turned the street into a tunnel.

I pressed the automatic door lock. Although the boy wasn't saying much, I was afraid that he might jump out, because he seemed really upset at this point. I said something like, "I'll get us out of this."

He looked at me with wide eyes, his expression a mix of fear, incredulity, and a trace of spunky humor. He was an admirable young man, and his strength of personality was very much in evidence. "What in hell is going on?" he blurted.

The houses were set back from the street, in lawns heavily planted with shrubs and emerald-green grass. The house I could see most clearly was one story and had no visible roof, which made it look like a huge box. It appeared to be made of tan stone deeply etched with carvings of large serpents. I said, "Do you see that?"

He said, "Yeah."

"What kind of a house is that?"

"They're all like that, Whitley."

"Yeah." I observed another one just the same, then took a turn. The place was sinister, to be frank, and I really did not want to attract the attention of whatever it was that thought images of giant snakes were attractive decorations for a home.

"This sure isn't Jersey," the boy said.

"No, I don't think so." I was getting quite scared. The last thing I wanted to do was to disappear into the Twilight Zone with somebody else's child under my care.

His hand was on the door handle. "What are those places?"

"Don't be scared."

He glanced at me, and there was that brave twinkle in his eye again. "Why not?"

I took another turn, then another, then saw an entrance onto the highway. "I think we're back," I said.

"Okay."

When we went down onto the highway, it was suddenly full of traffic. It was all very familiar—except that it was Route 80, which was about twenty miles from the diner! We'd gone all that distance in just a few minutes, and on back roads.

I returned to 17 and let the boy off with his father. Of course, he excitedly told him the whole story, and they spent a good bit of time looking for the mysterious highway and the bizarre neighborhood. They never found the place, and neither did I, although I went back later and methodically followed maps until I was certain that I had covered every road in the area. I used a pen to mark off streets as I went down them, until I had covered every street on both sides of 17 near the diner. Then I went down to Route 80 and discovered that the entrance ramp we'd used to reach it apparently doesn't exist.

This was one hell of a hard experience to swallow. A year later, I brought it up with the boy and he had a vivid memory of those strange houses. He told me that he and his father had also gone back, but they'd never located a neighborhood remotely like what we had seen. His father did not believe that my stories were anything but mental, and he wanted very much to prove to his son that the whole thing had been imaginary.

So where did we go? Certainly it was somewhere. Two people saw it at the same time, and agreed later on what we had seen. It wasn't that the neighborhood was a little odd. In every detail, it was radically different. I vividly remember the strange serpentine designs on the houses, the lack of windows, the lack of roofs that made the buildings look like boxes. Also, the foliage was so lush, so green.

Had we gone forward in time? If so, what did it mean? Why does the future look like that? What happens here that causes such a radical change? If we went into the future, perhaps the distance we traveled was very far. There is every reason to believe that the earth will still be here in a million years, and even in a thousand million. The sun probably has at least three thousand million years of life-giving energy left.

I was left with a trembling question: What is the future of conscious life on this planet?

Or had we entered some other reality, a world fitted into our own like a Chinese box?

I do not know. Anyway, it all happened in what must be one of the least mysterious places on earth. Route 17 is as ordinary as a hamburger, but it's where I took a drive through Twilight Zone in a cantankerous old Jeep, with a witness.

What was in those buildings? What strange, unnamed events would have unfolded if we'd walked up to one of them, found a door, and knocked?

I can easily imagine nine knocks in reply, evenly spaced in three groups of three. . . .

I was being taught that reality is far larger than we have begun to imagine. The laws of physics accommodate, it would seem, not only the structures we choose to believe, but also other meanings that we haven't even guessed at. We had moved from one world to another. We both saw it. I cannot put it down to imagination. Before it happened, nothing had been said, nobody had been speculating about anything. The only prelude in our lives had been that odd midnight event, the nature of which nobody can remember, but which may well have been related. It almost seemed as if what happened during the day was being somehow planned that night, as if the boy was being told what was going to happen by a part of me to which I don't have conscious access.

Could life be divided into levels, with different relationships unfolding among the same people, and there being little or no conscious contact between the levels? Was this what was happening with Dora's daughter's teacher, for example, or what Raven had meant when she made the mysterious statement that the being she had encountered had seemed somehow to be a part of her?

What is evolution, anyway? If mankind is evolving,

does that mean that a new physical species is appearing to replace us, or that we are ourselves changing? Could it be that our glimpses of other levels of our own lives are a hint of what the much larger scale of mind that is coming will be like? It could be that we are at the edge of discovering that human life is, in effect, a secret society where everybody is a member and nobody knows it—at least, not consciously, and not at the moment.

Our incredible journey very forcefully reminded me that to close the question of the nature of human experience is, given our present state of knowledge, complete folly.

But there was more to come, much more. That afternoon's little excursion was only a foretaste of the visitors' stunning ability to move me among the ages.

It was late on a cool evening about a month later, one of those sweet autumn nights that seem composed of amens. Earlier in the day, it had been windy. Now it was still and quiet. We'd built a fire in the stove and it had burned down. I do not recall what I was doing . . . reading a novel, perhaps listening to music.

This is the first major experience that I have included in this book that is unwitnessed, and it marks the beginning of a departure into a new level of contact which must involve my imagination quite heavily. But I feel that it was involved as a tool, not in the arbitrary way that is usually meant. I did not dream the events that I am about to describe, but rather, I believe, imagined them in a completely new way. It seems to me that the imagination can become a time machine when the images that are being created in the mind exactly parallel actual events in the past. Any of us can do this now, but we don't actually go anywhere. When the grace of the new mind pours up from our depths, among the greatest of our powers will be the ability to make real journeys upon its wings.

Eden came softly, so softly that I noticed almost nothing at first, perhaps a moment of subtle disorientation, like a shiver or the vibration of distant thunder. The first thing I was consciously aware of was that the fire had changed. It was no longer on a grate, and it was spent and burnt and dead, as if it had sputtered out hours before.

The confusion that I felt at that moment was very deep, and the totality of the change made me dissociate from myself. It was suddenly as if I was a companion of myself, linked, but also separate. I appeared to be in a real place but I could not even begin to understand what had happened to me. Because the transition had not been accompanied by any drama, I was completely surprised.

But I had traversed some vast distance, because I was in among tall trees—a deep forest—with hazy sun slanting down from above.

Ahead of me and to the right was a dry stream bed, and the air smelled hot and dusty. In fact, it was quite warm and there was a paradoxical desertlike dryness despite the trees. Then I looked up and saw a tangle of black limbs, stark against a hard sky. I realized that the whole place was dead.

For a moment I sat where I was, looking around me, listening to the silence. Then I felt a flash of panic: Where was the cabin? Had there been a forest fire? I jumped up and began to run. What I thought I was doing was trying to get back home.

The trees around me were huge, mostly conifers, I think, and their limbs were like empty spikes in the hard shafts of sunlight. I went among them at random. There was no path. Then I heard voices ahead, choppy and yet full of warbling intensity. I stopped. Now I was operating under the assumption that I had entered a very special dream state.

I went a little farther, trying to see the people who were talking—or rather, singing. It was a strange mode, an atonal chant sung with some sort of drum. There was such feeling in it, though, such sorrow.

I turned around and around, still trying to find my bearings. I thought I was out on the ridges behind the house—but when had all the trees died? And those voices—they were not like any I'd ever heard before. A loneliness came that was a terrible thing to feel, as if the bottom had dropped out of my heart.

I went closer to the sound of the voices, coming suddenly to a path that looked anciently worn, as if feet had trod it for a thousand years. This path led to a clearing— or rather, an area more sparsely forested.

There was in the center of this space a black, cracked ditch, and clustered alongside it was the most pitiful little group of people I have ever seen. They were tiny and thin, the two men bearded, the three women like prune-faced trolls with heavy eyebrows. Children clung to them, and they really looked to me like little animals, they were so filthy and wretched.

The group of them was singing to the dried stream. They were actually bending down and rising up as if drinking, and chanting in their withered, defeated whine. There was a little mud down in the bottom of the ditch, and there were more children in this mud, taking handfuls of it and pushing it against their open mouths. Their tongues were coated with it.

The sun could certainly have been called a fiery sword. It came swarming up over the gray trees in a thunder of light. A woman kept turning rhythmically and shouting at it, her voice full of babbling rage.

Then they began to come toward me. One of the men wore something stiff and black, like a rough garment made of bark or some kind of matted reed. I think that the rest of them were naked, but they were so brown with filth and scabs that I couldn't tell. They were sick, hideously sick. I could see one woman's teeth right through her cheek, and there were maggots moving in her swollen, purple skin. They brought with them a roar of flies, and I saw that they moved in a cloud of them.

They all stopped at once, as if turned off with a switch. These dark-eyed creatures stared at me, and I realized that the men were carrying stones. One of the women had something that looked like a long Lacrosse stick with a noose on it, which I think might have been a bird or small animal trap.

There was an electric flutter in my body, as if waves of tickling static were going through me. Then one of the men cocked his head to one side and passed his spread hand across his face. He looked so utterly surprised, and his expression was so funny that I think I laughed a little. The woman with the stick reached it toward me. The children were all sniffing toward me, their nostrils dilating.

The woman had an odd sort of a grin on her face, quite menacing. I think that she hoped that I would somehow get caught in her trap. I wondered what I looked like to her—like myself, another of her own kind—or did I have great, black eyes and long, thin arms . . .

The waves of electricity became greater and greater, and by degrees I found myself standing in front of my house. The familiar yard appeared again, cool and dark.

I remember looking up at the sky, at the silver shadow of the Milky Way, and feeling such incredible gratitude that I was home yet again from another deep journey and—above all—that the terrible world I had seen was not my own.

That night, I thought perhaps that I had gone back in time. I would have dismissed it as a dream, and it wouldn't even have been in this book where it obviously stretches credulity to the limit, but I cannot dismiss it because of the other amazing journey I had taken shortly before.

I went somewhere else, physically, with the boy in the Jeep. We both saw plainly that we were not in this world. We weren't in any kind of unusual state of mind. My driving was never impaired, my mind was always alert. And afterward, we both knew for certain that we had been through the Twilight Zone.

This whole sequence suggests that there may be an unguessed-at power of mind present that—if it emerges—could enable us to see our past as it really was and even tunnel into the future, and thus come to a much more true understanding of ourselves than we could ever otherwise possess.

I have no idea if it would be possible to go back beyond the beginning of human consciousness, because none of the journeys I have made in time have involved this. However, if I have actually gone into our own history in a visible form, then others must have, too. So wouldn't there be a record in the past?

Well, maybe there is. What of the gods who march in golden light across history? Who were the beings riding Ezekiel's wheel, and who piloted the vimana aircraft of old India? Who has been behind the apparitions and miracles that have directed us toward the divine?

Could it be that human consciousness has literally bootstrapped itself, reaching backward across the ages to initiate its own history? Is mankind coming to a sort of singularity of consciousness where all moments, in effect, become one? If so, then maybe these journeys are echoes backward from that moment. Maybe all of our history is such an echo.

Two nights later, I dreamed of the people in Eden, and it was in this dream that their identity first occurred to me. Could I have been looking at the burning ejection from the garden? I had always assumed that Adam and Eve were not specific individuals, but rather a realization of individuality, not a specific man and woman, but a discovery of gender. So much is packed into their story: self is discovered, evil and death are discovered, the genders separate, man discovers his individuality, is separated from God, Cain and Abel are born and separated from their mother, and in turn they break apart in violence and murder and discord.

To take the Bible as literal fact, I'd always assumed, is to deny its real truth, to place the arrogance of belief higher than the subtle message of the divine. But this experience recast those thoughts. I began to see the early narrative of the Bible in a completely new light, as a story that at once expressed the truth of creation in a simple and straightforward way, but also resonated with meanings so deep that they seemed to transcend the very words that expressed them.

The Word is not a brain-blasting roar of authority, but a creative, involving whisper. God's relationship to creation is elegant and indirect; we are a small gesture in the gulf of time. I saw how fine is the distinction between the Bible as literal truth and as myth. Maybe a million years of evolution preceded that struggling little family in the dead east of Eden, but they went there, they suffered there, and the memory of their suffering has cast a tremendous shadow across the whole history of Western culture.

In the pain and death of their forest, these people had made a shift: they were not simply *being*, not anymore. They were not looking out like animals, but in like human beings. I saw it in their quizzical, surprised glances, as clear as a chime sounding in the silky dawn, that sharp, distinguishing note of self.

We carry their guilt. That very humanity, after all, was what caused them to lose the thing that the visitors seemed to be indicating to us that we must regain: the ability to surrender, to live with open, innocent eyes, to be as guileless as an animal.

Had I been able to surrender, the approach in July would not have seemed to me like an attack. I saw that I had a new aim: surrender. Give myself up to them—and to my own heart.

It didn't sound easy.

I remained quite interested in the degree of physical reality that I had experienced. The idea of going back in time was incredibly romantic to me. To think that it might be possible to walk yet the stones of the Acropolis, or to be in the throng at the Mount . . .

So I did some research. Could Eden have been a real place? I found that there is a certain event that might have signaled the actual death of a real Eden.

Roughly eighteen thousand years ago, as the last ice age was in its death-throes, the region of the eastern Mediterranean had a very different climate. For well over a hundred thousand years it had been a verdant subtropical forest filled with fruits and berries and edible tubers. In those days, the prevailing jet stream in the upper atmosphere insured a continuous flow of moist air across the Mediterranean basin. The sea itself was smaller and forests stretched from the verdant mountains of the Levant down into valleys now lost beneath its waves.

It must have been an easy life in that world, a life wrapped in eternity. By the shores of the sea and in the many streams and rivers, there would have been abundant and easy fishing. The land would have supplied everything, much like Polynesia, and there would have been among the people the same innocence and nakedness that European explorers found in the South Seas.

But the climate changed, and we know now that there was probably an abrupt shift in the flow of the

Gulf Stream that either brought about or was caused by a parallel shift in the atmospheric jet stream. Over a matter of just a few short years the eternal forest died, and the people who depended on it must have suffered agonies attempting to survive. Some would have migrated, others remained and tried to eke a living from the earth. The fiery sword of the sun would have beaten down on them; they would have sought some reason for the random violence that had struck them from above.

So Eden was probably a very real place—and our expulsion was an artifact of climate. Back then, it was the pressure of this overwhelming change that had caused us to discover ourselves, that had compelled us to evolve. The same was true now, in my own private world, as the devastating pressure put on me by the visitors compelled me to change in what seemed to be quite fundamental ways.

I no longer believed that time was frozen; to my own personal observation, it seemed to be functioning much like a fluid.

The visitors had now completely shattered my model of self and universe. I no longer trusted my own assumptions, not any of them. I didn't know what I was or where I was in space or in time; they had freed me, in this sense, from the slavery of expectation.

It was as if they had given me new eyes, to see new things, hidden things. I didn't know it, but by demolishing my understanding of the world, they were beginning to answer some great questions about it.

They were responding to my request for total communion. And as usual, their plans were a lot bigger even than my greatest expectations.

12

michael's gift

A month passed without the visitors, then another. In the third month, I began to be uneasy. Six months and I was miserable.

For a year, the visitors withdrew from my life. Surely they wanted the proof to be published. *Communion* was drifting into the past. My fifteen minutes of fame were over.

I almost decided to just go ahead and write the book. But I agonized. I couldn't get rid of the fear that I was helping something evil. I went into the woods, I meditated nightly, I read, I spoke to them in my mind—but the only response was silence.

Maybe I'd asked for too much. Or maybe I'd asked demons to smile and they couldn't, so they'd gone away.

Nineteen-ninety passed, then 1991 came and went. I got contacted by congressional staffers who were investigating the intelligence community in some way that

appeared related to the Roswell incident and started
having to answer all kinds of questions about my
sources in my novel *Majestic*.

I was getting really uneasy, and pleading with the visitors for help in this thing. Even though they were silent,
my letters kept me connected to their living presence, and
they were certainly very active in other lives. This was
when I saw that they were starting to go to children in a
major way. And they were really active: the letters were
coming in an avalanche from all over the world.

Contact was roaring ahead without me. They were
trying so hard, and the people they were touching were
trying just as hard. What a battle I was witnessing, as
thousands of human beings struggled with the
unknown. Every time I got a letter from a child, I was
reminded that the greatest miracle in all of this might
well be us.

But I remained frozen. Were they evil or good? Until
I knew the final, absolute answer to that question, I
decided that I would keep my proof to myself.

In the summer of 1991, when swarms of UFOs
appeared over Mexico City, I thought that they were
about to announce themselves. But the story barely
made the American papers. For this sort of thing to
work, it would have to take place over New York or
Washington, and happen in such a way that prolonged
and detailed media coverage could take place.

But why would it happen? There was still no
medium of contact. Most of my letters were asking me
what was going on. People had no idea what to do—no
more than I did.

Finally, after two long years, the unexpected happened once again. The key to the new way of thinking I
was seeking was handed to me by a dying man. He
brought me as close to the visitors as I had ever been, he
gave me a clear look into an even deeper, even more

hidden part of our world than I had found thus far and—what is most critical—in a few electrifying seconds he completely revised my understanding of good and evil, the meaning of death and—for me—the meaning of man.

Over the course of this book, I have referred a number of times to there being a relationship between the visitors, the soul, and death. Like everybody alive, I have wondered if death means anything. I've seen how our most potent religions relate to death. Some, like the ancient Egyptian religion and Tibetan Buddhism, even provide detailed instructions regarding the soul's outward journey. But to a man whose deepest core beliefs stopped at the observable edge, the fact that the visitors could open the doors that they did had come into my life with the power of an earthquake.

Then I met Michael Talbot.

Long before we became good friends, we were acquaintances. We had been introduced at a writer's convention in the early eighties. He was in his twenties then, an intense and deeply humorous man, obviously brilliant, obviously a little put off by the swirling mass of other writers at the convention. I was intrigued by him and, as I am always eager to see young writers come along, encouraged him to send me his new book.

I get dozens of manuscripts and generally read about twenty pages of each. If the book hasn't grabbed me by then, I read at random to see if it picks up. Ninety-nine out of a hundred times, the book does not work for me.

Michael's book, *A Delicate Dependency*, worked. In fact, it was splendid. I wrote him that I would never forget it, and I was pleased when my comments appeared in the frontispiece.

It was a vampire story, and one of the best I'd read in years. With hindsight, I think that it is one of the best that has been written.

I got back into touch with Michael, and there followed a friendship that slowly moved from the casual to the more serious. A less good man might have been embittered by the life he had led. He had eventually had the troubling experience of discovering that the fact that *A Delicate Dependency* was indeed a very fine book didn't mean that it wouldn't be ignored in literary circles. In our culture, literary success does not depend on good writing, and his book is probably one of the best lost novels of our generation—and, among horror stories, the best.

As we got to know each other better, I discovered that Michael was fascinated by science and had some experiences that had convinced him that our understanding of the universe and our place in it is very limited. In his brilliant book *The Holographic Universe*, he wrote, "There is evidence to suggest that our world and everything in it—from snowflakes to maple trees to falling stars and spinning electrons—are only ghostly images, projections from a level of reality so beyond our own that it is literally beyond both space and time."

This was Michael's poetic and yet accurate way of expressing the significance of what physicists call string theory, which postulates that all subatomic particles are actually short vibrating strings of energy embedded in higher dimensions and that what we call "reality" is in hyperspace no more substantial than a vibration.

This means, of course, that the physical world may be much more amenable to twisting, bending, and shaping than it seems. That solid old chair might not be so solid, and the mind might be full of doors where we now see brick walls.

Michael did not believe in the ordinary world. He saw magic as a misunderstood physics. The reason *A Delicate Dependency* was such a masterpiece was that he was so genuinely uneasy about life's possibilities.

Vampires and werewolves—what he referred to as "folkloric beings"— weren't entirely impossible in Michael's world.

In *The Holographic Universe* he wrote, "Once, while deep in thought about a novel I was working on about werewolves, I noticed that the ghostly image of a werewolf's body had formed around my own body." He hastened to explain that he didn't feel that he'd actually become a werewolf, but then added, "The holographic image that enveloped my body was real enough that when I lifted my arm I could actually see the individual hairs in the fur and the way the canine nails protruded from the wolfish hand that encased my own hand."

We had many a wide-ranging conversation about the nature of being and the true function of the imagination. I see imagination as an unused tool of enormous power and look upon it as one of the keys to the evolution of the human mind. Michael was also fascinated with its uses, and when one day he called me and said he had cancer, he added rather sardonically that he would find out now whether or not visualization really worked.

When I'd described the *Communion* encounter to him in February 1986, his eyes lit up and he said, "You've broken through . . . damn you!" We laughed, and I promised to introduce him to the visitors. At the time, of course, I hardly thought that such a thing was possible. Little did I know.

Michael and I didn't see much of each other for some years, so his call in 1992 came as quite a shock. He'd apparently known about his disease for some time at that point, and when I went to see him he was a profoundly altered man. Of course, I feared AIDS. He scoffed. "I wish I had AIDS. This is worse than AIDS."

He was pallid and thin and had a chronic cold. The moment I walked into his apartment—the moment our eyes met—I saw the shadow upon him. He was so young, not even forty! Where had the leukemia come from? What had happened to him?

There was nothing in his life that could explain it, no exposure to the usual cast of caustics; he didn't even smoke. I read up about his version of the disease and found that it could be stopped by chemotherapy, but that it usually came back, and when it did, it was generally terminal.

Michael was on his journey, and it didn't seem at all like my family deaths, with their sense of appropriateness and lives completed. He was fifteen years younger than I, a writer just approaching his best period, a brilliant and vital human being.

He was not reconciled to death, not at all. In fact, he was bitter. He felt as if something had cheated him. And why not—he was right.

He took his chemotherapy, and a remission was achieved. He got better, a lot better. In fact, he seemed to come entirely back to normal. The old raconteur reappeared and the old sense of humor— sardonic, droll— came back. Michael's attitude was, "I'm cured." I wasn't sure if he'd read any medical texts about his type of leukemia, and I had no way of knowing what his doctor was telling him. How do you tell a young man that he has a terminal illness? How?

The Holographic Universe had been published in 1991, and he hadn't let me read any of it beforehand, but when I finally got a copy of the book, I had devoured it in a single sitting. The first half was a very clear analysis of recent brain research, primarily that of a man who was a distant acquaintance of mine, Karl Pribram. I'd had some fascinating conversations with Pribram at the World Affairs Conference at the University of Colorado, before I ceased to be invited back for being the dreaded *Communion* man. Pribram postulated that the brain was essentially holographic in nature: that is to say, that its activities were more like the functioning of an interdependent ecology than a machine made up of separate parts. Michael used this, and the idea that matter is a wave in hyperspace, as the springboard for what was basically a general theory of the occult.

Ever the storyteller, he peopled the second half of his book with a fabulous series of well-documented mysteries. Michael was exceedingly well-read, with strong concentrations in physics, brain science, and the unexplained. His opinion was that mankind wasn't really at home with the universe or comfortable with reality because we lacked final understanding. Because a unified theory of matter eludes us, he felt, we cannot explain even the most ordinary facts about our world—let alone the extraordinary ones that so interested him.

He told tales of people who had been lost in time and related fairy folklore that included journeys through time. He thought perhaps that an afterimage of the past might somehow linger, hanging ghostly in the meadows and fens of the fairy country. He told of people who had slipped backward in time, of a group who had been passed by a company of Roman soldiers while in the Levant, of two women who had blundered into pre-Revolutionary France while on a visit to Marie Antoinette's Petit Trianon at Versailles, of others who had heard in 1951 the sounds of a battle that had taken place nine years earlier.

I was not too surprised by this part of his book, given my own similar journeys.

He told stories of the mind altering the body, stories that haunted me as I read the book, in view of his condition. The most remarkable of these stories concerned an incident of mass psychokinesis that occurred in France in the eighteenth century. Michael knew all about obscure topics like the Jansenists, a now-forgotten sect of religious hysterics that was enormously important in the Paris of the early eighteenth century.

I used to play a game with him where I would utter some word, and he would proceed to discourse on it. "Demon" brought the most cogent explanation of how and why the Greek word "daimon," or inner self, became the name of a monster from hell during the fear-choked and ignorant middle ages. "Jansenist" brought the marvelous tale of the "convulsionaires," who were so numerous in Paris in 1733 that it took three thousand volunteers just to guide them about in the streets and make sure that dogs and little boys didn't harass them.

It seems that an abbé of the puritanical sect known as the Jansenists, Francois de Paris, died and was buried in Paris in 1727. In *The Holographic Universe*, Michael wrote, "Because of the abbé's saintly reputation, worshipers began to gather at his tomb, and from the beginning a host of miraculous healings were reported." These included cures for cancer, deafness, arthritis, fevers—the list was long. "The mourners also started to experience strange involuntary spasms or convulsions and to undergo the most amazing contortions of their limbs." The seizures proved to be contagious, and spread until "the streets were packed with men, women, and children, all twisting and writhing as if caught up in a surreal enchantment."

The convulsionaires acquired supernormal abilities. "One member of the Paris Parliament . . . witnessed enough miracles to fill four thick volumes on the subject." The affair went on for years and years, and the incredible abilities of the participants were witnessed by thousands of people, as a matter of routine.

Some examples: "A twenty year old convulsionaire named Jean Maulet leaned against a stone wall while a volunteer from the crowd delivered a hundred blows to her stomach with a thirty-pound hammer." Twenty-five blows with the same hammer then collapsed the wall. In another instance a young woman convulsionaire had got bent into a backward arc. Convulsionaires often pleaded to be tortured because it relieved the pain of the convulsion, and in this case, she had herself raised to a great height with a fifty-pound stone lashed to her midriff and then dropped. Then she had the stone hoisted up and dropped on her stomach again and again, all the while screaming to be hit harder.

When the convulsion ended, she got up and went home.

Convulsionaires "could not be hurt by the blows of metal rods, chains, or timbers. The strongest men could not choke them. Some were crucified and afterward showed no trace of wounds. Most mind-boggling of all, they could not even be cut or punctured with knives, swords, or hatchets!" Convulsionaires became clairvoyant. Some could read with their eyes closed. There were instances of levitation. "One of the levitators . . . was so forcibly lifted into the air during his convulsions that even when witnesses tried to hold him down they could not succeed in keeping him from rising up and off the ground."

The convulsionaires have been forgotten by our pedantic and narrow age, but in their time they were a tremendous cause célèbre, so much so that Louis XIV had the abbé's cemetery walled up. Voltaire commented, "God was forbidden, by order of the King, to work any miracles there."

In the summer of 1994, I made a personal pilgrimage to the little church of St. Medard in Paris where the abbé is buried. At the church, I found the cemetery still walled up! The abbé's grave was such a wellspring of the unknown, that the Age of Reason simply closed it—and it remains closed.

However, just because a thing happened in the past

is no excuse to bury it. What it means—it and many other documented but unexplained anomalies—is that we are unconsciously editing the laws of physics in order to make our world appear as it does. The visitors can walk through walls, they can fly, they can disappear at will, change form.

Michael wrote of the convulsionaires, in part, I think, because of his own feelings about this, but most especially because of his illness. Not long after *The Holographic Universe* was published, I received a call from him: "The tumor's back, but it's not going to get me. I just don't see it."

I knew that the odds were now dreadful, but I couldn't say this, not in the face of his touching hope. He went for more chemotherapy. He had a small chance of getting another remission, a short one.

I saw him two weeks after the treatment, and he looked wonderful. His book was doing fairly well, and he was getting some radio time and a few reviews. But the book pressed the envelope of the real. It made a convincing case that the mechanistic model of the large-scale universe so beloved of intellectuals and scientists was fatally incomplete, and so it was shunned in many important review media.

Like so many other genuine intellectual achievements, it was rejected by those who want to believe that we already understand the universe—we little band of recently risen animals, barking at our visitors with voices as yet hardly changed from the days when we lived in the forest.

Michael phoned me and asked me to get the visitors to help him with his cancer. Hearing his words, realizing that they meant that the chemotherapy must be failing, my heart almost broke in two. Many's the night I'd spent praying for the desperate people who have sent me letters. "Please, Mr. Strieber, I have stage-three

Hodgkins and three kids and no husband, please get them to save me." "My friend has AIDS, he's suffering in agony, call the visitors, get them to come." "I need medicine from the other world or I am going to die."

These letters always torment me, because I cannot control the visitor experience, but there is a feeling that, if only I knew the right terms, I could somehow help.

I asked for help for Michael, just sat in the middle of a dark room in the night and asked and asked and asked in my mind and heart—pleaded, begged, demanded, cajoled, promised . . . and all the while had the certain feeling that this is not about curing the living; that insofar as it is about death, it is about dying well.

About a month after I pleaded on behalf of Michael's body, I got a letter from him. In it he described an experience of waking up to a pack of wolves in his bedroom. They leaped on him and he thought that they were death come, that he was finished. But they did not eat him, they seemed to be eating the tumor itself, that wild colony lodged in his blood, licking it, devouring it. He felt a little stronger, perhaps, but he was by no means cured. In fact, the tumor was getting worse.

I decided to organize a weekend at the cabin on his behalf. I was no longer asking the visitors to come to him and cure him. I asked them to help him face death.

All together, there were twelve of us. In the group were Lorie Barnes, two friends connected with Congress, Raven Dana and her boyfriend, and Ed and Dora and their children, and a fascinating witness from California who'd apparently had a cure in connection with her contact experiences.

What a lovely weekend we had. It was August and we went out to a local farm and got all kinds of vegetables—about five different types of squash, kale, radishes, all sorts of things. This farm is a wonderful place, owned by an ancient but incredibly healthy man called Ralph. He's been farming organically since before fertilizers and pesticides were in use, brushes his teeth with a stick, and is twice as full of life as most twelve year olds. Even his vegetables are jolly, and he'd made a sign on his front lawn out of squash that said "Hi," although I'm sure that he had no idea what sort of customers it would soon attract.

We also bought some peach pies and had a feast. That evening, Michael and Lorie Barnes worked a Ouija board, which proceeded to tell Michael that he'd been called "Lydia" in a past life. So we started singing "Lydia the Tattooed Lady," and Michael said, "I wish I was a Lydia now, one that didn't have cancer."

That night me and one of the government people, who is also a psychic, took turns giving readings. It's not something I do often, because I have no way of telling whether or not it's real, but I enjoy it. This lady, who is an expert at remote viewing—finding errant submarines and such—was really "on" that night. She was very sweet to Michael, but it was also obvious that she didn't see him lasting long.

So I got to feeling pretty sad. For his part, Michael was cheerful. In view of his condition, I did not try one of the rigorous journeys to the cave. Instead, we went down to the stone circle and sat together for a time. It was good in the soft night under the stars, in the last of summer.

Later I got Michael to read to us from *The Holographic Universe*, and he chose sections about all that is available in the cosmic hologram, access to the future and the past, to other realities, to the hidden world of the soul. Very quickly, it seemed, midnight chimed and we retired.

I was awakened at about five in the morning, very suddenly. It was the gray hour just before dawn. I've long felt an affinity for the dawn, and I thought of walking out into the woods until sunrise.

Then I realized that I was in a deliciously light, tingly state, and I began to hope that they'd come. I sat there feeling the state growing, eager for it to develop fully. But it didn't. Instead, it turned off so abruptly that I gasped from the sudden sense of returning weight.

For a moment I was disappointed, but then I heard a voice downstairs. At the new cabin, the front door is directly under our bedroom, and the back stairs lead down from a hall right behind the head of the bed.

The voice was calling quietly. I couldn't hear the exact words, but I knew that it was Michael. Assuming that he was in some way uncomfortable, I went to attend to his needs.

Halfway down the stairs, I saw him walk across the family room and pause, rather tentatively, before the front door. This was a full-pane double French door with a very sheer curtain. It was easy to see through this curtain, especially because the predawn sky outside was lighter than the room.

There was a shadow out there. I could see it clearly. It shocked me, because the likelihood of a stranger appearing at our door in this rather isolated area at five in the morning was vanishingly small. Then I saw that the figure was very thin, and seemed to have a huge head.

The idea that this was a visitor certainly hadn't crossed Michael's mind—he was laughing, of all things, and in a rather condescending way. But as I went a little farther down the steps and heard the voice on the other side of the door, I realized that something extraordinary was happening. I didn't catch the words, but the voice had a familiar low tone, deeper than any normal voice.

I stood on the stairs about three feet behind Michael. He didn't acknowledge me. Various suggestions sped through my mind: how to calm him down, how to let him know I was there so he wouldn't be so scared—all sorts of boy scout scripts. Then I heard him say, "Are you trying to sell those vegetables?"

It stunned me practically senseless. Then I saw that the visitor was holding a big paper shopping bag full of squash.

When I realized that Michael thought he was dealing with a bag lady or a beggar, I became embarrassed, whereupon there followed the most hilarious moment in my whole experience with the visitors.

"Don't you realize that could be the creator of mankind," I hissed, wildly overstating the case in order to make him act more dignified.

Barely glancing at me, he muttered, "She's dead broke."

"She can't be dead broke," I said, "she owns the world!"

"I'd give you three dollars for the squash," he said through the door, "but I don't have my wallet."

Had it been me at that door, I would have been trembling with fear, struggling to push the thin curtain aside so I could get a better look, asking all sorts of questions.

But, my God, remembering back, I recall how very human she seemed. A human woman wearing a shabby little gray dress, with a thin wisp of white hair and two gigantic black eyes that wrapped halfway around her head. But a word like "human," it seems to me, crosses many boundaries. Maybe Satprem's friend Mother actually made the transition she and Sri Aurobindo struggled with for so long.

Certainly, I felt as if I was in the presence of greatness in the form of a mother.

Suddenly sticklike, Michael jerked toward the door. His face pressed against it so hard that I heard the glass begin to crack. It's a cheap door, just a big piece of glass with a wooden frame over it to make it look as if it was mullioned. "Oh, God," I said.

She was also up against the door. He was holding the curtain back, and I could see long, skeletal arms, the big head—and the bag of squash dangling from her hand.

It seemed like a young man gently kissing his grandmother, or a little boy and a little girl too shy to touch without the barrier of glass. Or mother and son, or sister and brother. There was a profound sense of relationship, of all relationship.

Then she began to speak, her voice rumbling, and Michael raised his hands and pressed them against the glass, as if he was a tramp peering in the window of a palace.

I don't remember anything after that. My next clear memory is of waking up. The first thing I thought was, Michael is going to be one hell of an excited guy.

I dressed and sailed downstairs, expecting to find him sputtering with wonder.

Half an hour later he came stumbling up from the basement, having just woken up. He got some coffee, picked up the paper, and started reading. "Morning, Michael," I said.

"Morning."

I waited. And waited. I was just about to decide that I'd had a rather intense dream when he looked up and said, "You know, I had a kind of an odd dream last night." He smiled. "You were in it."

I stopped him and went to Lorie Barnes, who was sitting out on the back porch, and told her what had happened. Then I asked her to come in and listen with me to Michael's dream. We did it discreetly. I didn't want to affect his memory in any way. I was half expecting to hear him blurt out something totally unrelated.

"It was one of those dreams where you think you've woken up even though you're still dreaming. I opened my eyes and I was, like, vibrating. It was wonderful, it felt delicious. So I floated up out of bed and up the stairs, and there was this old woman at the door. She was a bag lady selling vegetables door-to-door."

"What did she look like?"

"Deformed. Really more than that. A mutated face, really. It sort of kept trying to turn into a nightmare. But I was laughing at her. I told her I didn't have my wallet. Then you came down the stairs and started whispering to me that she was the creator of the universe or something."

"I was there."

"In my dream you were."

"Do you remember anything specific about her?"

"An old woman with huge eyes. Thin. Wispy white hair."

"Clothes?"

"Homemade and very cheap."

"I was actually there, Michael. It was no dream."

He laughed and would not be convinced that it hadn't been a dream. Lorie said, "Whitley told me every detail before you did."

Michael simply laughed the harder. I really didn't know what to make of it all. Had it been a shared dream? I can't imagine that I could ever have dreamed that a visitor would show up on my doorstep with a bag of squash. Such a thing wasn't in the lexicon of my imagination.

I told him, "Somewhere along the line I got the impression that she personally conceived of the human race—the woman whose portrait is on the cover of *Communion*. Who was here this morning."

"It was a dream. And I doubt that particular creation myth. Anyway, the visitors are imaginal. They're projections of the psyche. They aren't aliens."

"Why are you so sure?"

He just shrugged and went on with his paper.

To this day, I can't draw a final conclusion about what happened that morning. But there were subtle signs that something very real had transpired. First, the curtain on the front door was still pushed aside and needed adjustment, and there were smears on both sides of the glass. Second, when I'd gone down to the store to get the paper, I'd noticed that Ralph's squash "Hi" had been disturbed. About ten squash had been taken, causing half the "h" and all of the "i" to disappear.

The weekend ended quietly. Summer also ended, school started, and Anne and Andrew moved back to New York. Some time in the autumn, I realized that I hadn't heard from Michael in weeks. I called him. The news was not good. His tumor was getting aggressive and he was very sick. He told me that he'd almost died the week before. I thought to myself, Whitley, you jerk, why aren't you with him? What's the matter with you? So I said that I loved him. He said that he loved me too, and then that he was going to miss me. It hurt like hell to hear that, and I began crying, I couldn't stop myself. Michael cried too. I was talking to him for the last time, I knew it well. "Michael," I said, "I think you're so damn wonderful."

"Yeah," he replied, "I have to agree. What a waste."

Suddenly our tears were pained laughter, but I felt such rage that this marvelous young man was going.

I couldn't get myself to hang up the phone. There was a silence, a howling silence. "Michael," I said.

Then he said, speaking carefully, "I'm working on a new book. I've just about got the proposal put together and I'm going to take it out in a couple of weeks."

The conversation was a torment, and I was as relieved as I was anguished when it finally ended. I tried to get myself to face the fact that Michael was going. A few weeks ago he'd been so hopeful. I wish that I could report that the visitors had cured him, or welcomed his soul into a new life. But it wasn't quite like that.

This time of passing, as it turned out, was to be used as a lesson of primary importance.

One weekend night about a month later, Anne and my son and I were together at the cabin and I was meditating in the guest room, sitting in the midnight dark trying to keep my mind empty and concentrate my attention on my body. Suddenly, I felt a presence in the inky blackness. This presence was really strong, and my impression was one of dreadful evil.

An instant later I saw something on the floor before me—a thing like a giant salamander, so black that it was visible only as a thick, squirming darkness against the shadowy floor. It undulated, moving away from me. The means of locomotion was primitive in the extreme, and the thing seemed to exude a quality of dread.

Then I saw that there was a glowing thread connected to it—and to me. I looked down, appalled: the thread in its jaws was unreeling out of my chest.

I got out of there fast. As I left, I turned on lights and shut doors behind me. Almost running, I went down the hall to our bedroom and got under the covers with Anne. I thought, you idiot. Talk about an overactive imagination! Try hyperactive.

But there was a part of me that said that it wasn't imagination, that the creature had been something quite real, something from the other set of meanings.

I'd long since learned to sleep even when the visitors were obviously moving about in the house, but this time I didn't dare. There was no sense of trust at all. That thing had been evil.

I lay there in misery, tossing and turning. I tried to read but I couldn't concentrate, tried to pray but the words kept getting lost. I felt unanchored, spiritually and physically. Also, there was a pain inside my chest that felt like a burn. The impulse was to pull at the skin, to get it open and get to the wound. Not for the first time, I worried that I'd finally scared myself so badly that I was having a heart attack.

Around me, the house seemed to whisper and sigh. It was as if the walls had turned to shadows, and I was exposed directly to the darkness and mystery of the woods. I tried to come to grips with my fear, but the idea of confronting it by returning to meditation was too much. I held on to my wife and eventually fell asleep in her arms. Together, we rode the reaches of the night.

It was just before dawn when I woke up. I felt awful. I was still terribly afraid, literally trembling in the thin light. I was also sweating and thirsty and got up to get a drink. What had happened to me during that meditation had the flavor of reality about it, as if some monster I had dreamed up for a story was actually lurking around in the house. I had the sense it had gained control of a part of me.

The religious beliefs instilled in me in childhood predispose me to concepts like heaven and hell. Had I been raised differently and had different beliefs, I might not have thought that I had been touched by something from hell. But the sense of the demon was powerful.

I remember standing in the bathroom staring into the shadowy face in the mirror and wishing that I'd somehow been given a life different from the one I was living. As I was staggering back to bed, I thought: go meditate and do it well, or you're never going to be able to face this again.

To endure the fear, I knew from long experience that I had to embrace it.

No sooner had I turned down that hall on my way to the guest bedroom where I meditate, than I saw around me great billows of glowing smoke. The effect was simply incredible: for a moment I thought that the house had exploded. But there was silence, and the smoke wasn't roiling, but rather moving very slowly, like a cloud mass.

Out of the center of the smoke there came a hand that glowed a soft electric blue. As if it was finding its way along a string, this hand touched my chest, then my own right hand, and for a few moments I grasped its clammy coolness, feeling static crawl along my palm, as if the hand was made of some kind of charged material.

Without warning, Michael's voice burst into the center of my brain, and it was howling, pleading, not wanting to go, not understanding why. My mind almost closed down, such was the terror I felt and the anguish—a grinding, cutting anguish of soul.

I remember telling him that it wouldn't last forever, that there would be deliverance.

Then our hands separated. An instant later, the hall was the hall again. Sunlight was starting in the windows, soft and new.

Clutching my chest, I sank down. I wept bitterly, full of anguish that Michael must have died and that he had somehow been transported into hell, that his beautiful life must have contained some hidden wrong. Such was my torment that I lay on the hall floor, my knees up to my chest, my arms around my head. I lay there and cried and prayed to God that Michael be saved, that this terrible thing not come upon him.

And then there came into me a tremendous peace, as if every cell in my body had suddenly surrendered. I saw good and evil as one, I saw angels and demons as different aspects of the same vast compassion, and knew that hell is only what we make it, and that mercy is everywhere, in the air, the heart, the old light that sings us through from babyhood.

Before that moment, I was in the habit of hating the people who oppressed me. I would wish evil things on them, I would pray against them. But now I saw that such prayers are not wanted, that there is a love that is literally without qualification, and that it is immediately present, here and now, always. This open, free and encompassing love is part of the soul. It is part of my soul, and I can touch it if I want, I can live in it, I can feel it all the time.

The darkness had taught me, had drawn me into a new and deeper view, had shown me what the love that is spoken of by Christ and Buddha truly is. I saw the true meaning of compassion: that it is the courage to give what is most needed, no matter how much it hurts. The screaming of Dora's child took on new and resonant meaning for me, as did the suffering of the world and, in the end, also the awful silence of God in the face of our bloody history.

I saw beyond good and evil, thanks to Michael, and I saw that my attempt to classify the visitors as one or the other was just an illusion and was the reason they had withdrawn from me. I realized that the visitors viewed good and evil as tools of the soul.

Michael had put me back on the road at last.

I saw the true meaning of "love thine enemies," that the enemy makes the victory sweet as certainly as the light depends on the darkness to be seen. If there was no evil, good would be invisible; if I was not an imperfect creature, why even be alive? I'd have no goal, if God had given me wings to begin with.

Two days later I got a call from one of his friends. My name was on a list of those to be informed in the event of his death. After some struggle, he had passed quietly. It had happened two days before.

This was the gift that Michael Talbot gave me.

13

what the darkness said

After Michael died, I spent two months in turmoil, trying to make the new vision of reality that he had shown me become clear. I was out of direct touch with the visitors, but the journeys through time obsessed me. I saw such an amazing array of powers just beyond my grasp, just on the other side of the wall of fear.

Because of Michael, new insights began to build. I saw that the visitors are our friends because they are also our enemies, and I began to see that there might be a deeper, more essentially fruitful impulse behind their slow emergence among us than I had understood before. I now saw them—and our possible relationship with them—as being beyond good and evil. And so I also saw that they were neither angels nor demons. They were telling me that they, too, were imperfect, and when I saw that I glimpsed a grand potential for partnership. For the first time, I began to see why they were actually here.

If we learned, as they had, to live beyond time, we could attain the same level of capability in the physical world that I was observing in them. Then we would come jointly to the greatest work, which lies along the pathless path of eternity. At least, that was my rather idealistic notion.

One thing that had become clear was that they didn't want slaves or genes or souls or anything remotely like that, or they would have taken them. You don't get wooed by somebody who is attacking you, and we were being very carefully wooed. The visitors were here to become a couple with us, and they were acting much more like an impatient, imperfect, and overeager lover would act than like a predator.

Virtually the day I realized this, everything changed.

I had rarely had encounters in the city, and I was quite surprised when I heard noises downstairs that sounded suspiciously familiar. We were at our new apartment in Brooklyn Heights, which was in a brownstone. We were the owner's only tenants, so it was usually very quiet. These quick, stealthy footfalls I was hearing were remarkably precise. They were followed by a creak on the steps. Whoever it was, they were on their way up.

Despite that telltale precision, my first thought was that we had a burglar. As I don't have a pistol permit for New York City and hadn't any weapons there, I was scared half to death.

I got up and went into the hallway. Nothing. I went into my wife's study, which was adjacent to the bedroom. Nothing. I searched the whole apartment, upstairs and down, going through the familiar old routine of looking in closets, but the place was empty.

I trudged back up to bed and was just on the point of going through the door to the bedroom when I had one hell of a shock: I was jumped from behind. I staggered, I shouted—and then I realized that I had one of the visitors on my back.

My heart started hammering. Love, fear, even desire rushed through me. My breath came fast.

I staggered along with this person clutching my hips with his or her thighs, the head turned to one side so I could see it down behind my right shoulder. Two thin arms were protruding in front of me, pinning my own arms to my sides. They were more than strong, they felt like steel. Struggle got no results at all. The one thing I could do was to bend my forearms so I could touch the wrists. They were hard inside, soft on the surface, as if made of bone covered by deerskin. There was no feeling of muscle or fat. But that did not make them weak, believe me.

The person was heavy, too, weighing easily forty or fifty pounds. I lurched along the hall calling, "Anne, Anne," and being swept by amazing waves of feeling. This felt like the kind of embrace that you might get from a child who loves you and has missed you terribly—or from somebody who can no longer contain their passion and just sort of explodes. And I was exploding, too. I wanted to hug this person and kiss them and somehow make up for all the years of struggle that they'd been through.

My emotions were incredibly powerful, and I felt that the same thing was going on behind me. The legs were squeezing, the head was pressing against me, the hands were twisting around like snakes and touching my fingers. There was none of the sense of vibration or electricity that others have reported, and that I had felt while being touched in December 1985.

The skin was neither especially warm nor especially cold, and I at once noticed a very peculiar property: when I ran my thumb down toward the end of a finger, there was a subtle undertone of resistance that felt like dragging your fingernail down a blackboard. Drawing my thumb back, the sensation was silken.

I began to form the impression that this was a young woman, and that she was the same individual who had called to me from the woods a few years before. It was a distinctly different person, I think, from the one whom I saw with Michael, a much less awesome, more accessible person. There was a tremendous feeling of presence, and a sense of fierce, possessive love. I felt wanted and needed and desired, and I was frantic to respond more fully. But I couldn't, not in this ridiculous position. I was gasping, trying to talk around uncontrollable sobs, staggering, trying also to get into the bedroom and wake Anne up, also to turn around. I was being assailed by a dozen incredible sensations: the extreme pleasure of physical touch, because I had begun vibrating with a marvelous sensation everywhere we were in contact. The fingers twining in mine moved with breathtaking delicacy.

Then she was gone and I went loping into the bedroom, my arms windmilling.

Anne sat up in bed. I said, "Did you see it?" She answered, "What, what?" I thought—damnit, not again—and raced downstairs, hoping she was still in the house. The front door was open, and I dashed down the final stairway to the sidewalk.

The street was empty—except for me in my pajamas peering along the lines of parked cars.

I returned to the bedroom and removed my pajamas. We examined them, but there was nothing unusual on the cloth—no stains or anything. Nothing had been left behind on the floor, either.

I lay back on the bed and told Anne the story. She is the quiet center of my whole experience, and I rely on her to provide perspective. If not for Anne, *Communion* would never have been written around the questions that are its core. She has borne her strange isolation from direct experience with great patience, and we have both concluded that her role is to keep me from going mad by pulling me back from the edge.

I was so sad about what had happened. Why couldn't the woman have stayed? Why couldn't we just become friends and have done with it? Total communion was obviously beyond my reach. Anyway, what if it meant I'd somehow leave my relationship with Anne? That could not be, that would devastate us both. As so often, we slept in each other's arms that night. And then there were other nights, many of them, and I began to think that it was over at last.

Summer came, and my dear old cat Sadie got seriously sick with thyroid problems. She'd lived in my lap for about ten years. We'd written everything from *Warday* on together. She even went with me to the visitors once, which I reported in *Transformation*, to my oft-televised embarrassment.

This gets me to the way our cats react. The Siamese, who is an active, concerned cat, does not like the visitors. Sadie, who was about the most peaceful creature I ever met (even when she caught mice, she just nibbled), regarded them the same way she did anybody else who entered the house: she went for the lap. Because of the peace that was in her, she had no trouble accepting them except at the most stressful times.

I worked only at the cabin and was often there during this period. After the incident, I was encouraged to start going out to the woods again. I was drawn to an old Indian burial ground, seemingly by the visitor's direction, and I was now meditating there regularly. After my experience with Michael, I wanted to indicate to the visitors that I hoped to find out more about their relationship with death. Anne's only comment was, "Don't make them think you want to be killed."

That didn't worry me. In all my letters, the only one in which a death was involved was the one where the man went down to the lake with the shotgun. Nobody has reported a permanent kidnapping, a serious injury, even a serious sickness, unless you want to count allergies.

In July 1992, I was walking about half a mile behind the house in the afternoon when I noticed what looked like about a twelve-year-old boy sitting against a big tree. He had something between his fingers, and I assumed it was a local kid out sneaking a smoke. The woods were quite dry, so I strolled over and said, "Better be sure you put that out when you're finished."

Then I realized that he was wearing a tan jumpsuit. I saw that his eyes were deep set, and his skin was . . . old. And it wasn't a cigarette, it was a little silver wand, and here came my old friend fear.

He opened his mouth slightly. Still looking straight ahead, he growled. It sounded nothing at all like you or I would sound if we were trying to imitate an animal. This was a real growl. Suddenly he didn't seem human at all and I was alone way out in the woods with him and he was growling and he had that wand and I took off.

At first I only moved quickly, but when I was out of his sight, I ran. To this day, I do not know if he was a real child or something else.

Feeling happy to be home and safe, I spent the afternoon sitting in the sun and dreaming about time travel, which had become my constant reverie. One by one, I was exploring each fascinating puzzle that the possibility raised. For example, if I learn to do it in the future, why haven't I come back and taught myself how? Unless, of course, that's what all of this is about.

As night fell, I began to think more about the person I'd seen. I had this desire to involve myself with the visitors physically, and I wished that I'd at least touched his hand or his cheek or something. But hadn't he had little spiked teeth? No, surely not. As the sun drops, the imagination rises.

Although Anne never sees the visitors, she is almost always the one who is aware that they are coming. At dinner she said, "They're here."

"They're always here."

"No, this time they're really here. You'll have a busy night."

I ate my supper in silence. Afterward we watched a baseball game. At about eleven, I stepped out on the back porch. It was a starry night, as I recall, and the woods were very dark and very silent.

I could go out there for the gray people, whose cantankerousness, whose passion, whose magic were all very familiar to me. But that growling . . . tonight the answer was no.

Instead, I went to my meditation place in the guest room. I had been meditating there ever since we built the new cabin, using it as a place to go when the weather was bad. I sat down in the middle of this room, which would soon be the scene of so much, and prepared myself by directing my attention to my body's sensation.

A moment later, thoughts began to flow.

I reflected that I'd felt lonely since the incident in Brooklyn, but not like an unrequited lover. The loneliness was much greater than that; it had an enormously poignant quality to it, as if it reflected, even more than a hollow place in the heart, one in the ages.

Because of the way we are, trapped in linear time and enslaved to our narrow view of the physical, the visitors cannot really share with us the way they want to, which is in every possible way. A great deal of the strangeness of the relationship, I suspect, has to do with our ability to see only a small part of what is actually unfolding between us.

They were displaying themselves to us in all their
glory and horror, and they obviously wanted all of
mankind back. But we could not give everything,
because we do not know all that we have. Until we
come to know ourselves as history has truly made us
and see into the soul's greater world, both sides are in a
sense lost to each other.

This was the reason for the sorrow I had felt while in
that electrifying embrace. I had the feeling, afterward,
that they have been waiting and waiting for us, but that
time is growing short and they cannot wait forever.

Finally, I forced myself to clear my mind, to discipline myself to prayer. "Total communion," I said, "give
me total communion." I prayed to God for it, I sought
the way in the Christian spirit of giving, and by the
ancient wisdom: "Know thyself."

The meditation seemed a particularly strong one. After
my prayers, my mind opened to crystalline clarity. My
whole body seemed to vibrate with an inner electricity.

After I'd been there for about fifteen minutes, there
came a terrific thud on the roof. It sent a shock of fright
right through me, because it sounded exactly like a
rather heavy body—forty or fifty pounds—had dropped
down out of the sky. I could even hear small creaks as it
seemed to settle into position, adjusting itself to the
slant.

After a moment there was another, then a third. In
all, there were seven. They formed a ring around me,
with the roof between us.

I was very, very excited. I talked aloud, inviting them
in. I did overtone chanting. I tried projecting thoughts, I
said what I wanted in my mind and repeated it aloud.

Nothing happened, so I simply cleared my mind and
waited, keeping my attention focused on my body as I
had learned in the Gurdjieff Foundation. After about
half an hour, there was another great clatter on the roof

and then silence. They'd come, they'd left, and that seemed to be the end of it. I was reminded of the opera Philip Glass did based on experiences like mine, *10,000 Airplanes on the Roof.*

The next night I decided that I had to go out to the woods. Maybe I was finally going to get an answer to my question. Maybe somebody would come running at me again, and this time we would fall into each other, and the marriage of being that seemed to be the next step would finally take place.

I was so scared as I left the house that I literally had trouble walking. I moved stiffly along like a robot with a flashlight, trying to keep up enough saliva so my mouth wouldn't dry up. It takes about fifteen minutes on the path to get to the burial ground.

Part of me was excited, because I had observed in the past that every time the fear level rose and I challenged it, I ended up with a deeper relationship.

This has been absolutely fundamental to my contact. The more fear I can handle, the more I am given, and the more my understanding deepens.

When I'd first started out in the woods, I'd carried a powerful flashlight, but it had gradually become my habit to take the smallest one possible. For the same reason, I had avoided night vision equipment. This was not about equipping oneself against fear, it was about accepting it.

Two large logs had been laid in an "X" in the center of the burial ground, and the path to it was marked by Indian-style trail markers that I assumed had been made by the visitors, so it was easy to find even with a very small light.

For a time, as I sat in the burial ground, nothing happened. But soon I started hearing a sound. It wasn't in the least stealthy: it sounded like an acrobatic troupe crashing in the bushes.

It was much too loud for deer, and too large for coons and such. For a moment I thought I saw something, but when I shone my flashlight there was nothing there. I began to hear wheezing sounds somewhat like the blow of a deer, but much louder.

So that was it. Deer.

But then the crashing began to move. It came out into the clearing, resolved into footsteps, then went whispering off through the grass. As the invisible figures passed by, the wheezing began to sound very much like a person of small stature sneezing with an allergy attack.

I waited for a while, but nothing more happened. My mind was whirling with impressions and thoughts. Things might have taken yet another turn: unless I was wrong, I had been hearing people who could not be seen. And the one—perfectly visible—whom I'd walked up to the day before yesterday had been small.

After silence returned to the woods, I went back to the house. I thought about vivid dreams I'd been having, of going down a long road in what appeared to be another world, of passing through a strange desert beneath an orange sky, traveling as if the journey was forever . . .

Could I ever go to another world? Surely people who could arrange these apparent traversals of time could take you more-or-less anywhere.

The next night it rained and I meditated upstairs. There was so much banging on the roof that I decided to stay in the room at night for a while rather than go to the woods.

However, I also went up during the day and examined the whole roof, looking for any signs of animal infestation. There aren't any places something could hide, and no trees overhang it. Nevertheless, I set a ladder up the following evening and prepared myself with my most powerful flashlight. I wanted to absolutely exclude the animal possibility.

At midnight I entered the room, and a few moments later there were three thuds, and then a drumming sound, exactly like somebody was impatiently drumming his fingers on the roof peak.

I dashed outside, swarmed up the ladder, and shone the light. The roof appeared empty. I went up and walked the peak. No animals, and there wasn't any place to hide. Birds, then? They'd have to be really big birds, and travel in flocks, and drum their claws, and fly at night. But there are no such birds.

Anne had also heard the sounds, so she listened to my stomping to see if I could duplicate them. It turned out that my movements didn't make nearly as much noise downstairs as theirs did. To make thumping like we heard, a 190-pound man had to really crash around. So maybe they were heavier than I thought or could alter their weight.

One of the reasons I was being so careful was that I had noticed that the noises did not have the accuracy that I was used to from the visitors. I didn't care to spend my evenings communing with possums.

I climbed down off the roof and went into the room. Even as I walked in, I knew that possums weren't the problem. A moment later there was a terrific lot of noise on the roof, like a crowd jostling for position. I sat down and an instant later felt something come bursting into my mind—also physically, bursting into me . . . hard to describe . . . like being touched on the inside.

Pictures began to flash in front of my eyes, of everybody I had ever known, even people I'd met only briefly. I saw faces I hadn't seen in years, kids I'd toddled with, college friends, old clients of my father's, clients and coworkers from my business years, men, women, children.

It was almost as if something were chasing me through my memories . . . and I was running.

Down so very deep that I was almost unable to sense it, a hidden part of me was trying to escape this. There was terror down there, as well there should have been, because I shortly began to realize that what I was seeing here were the wrongs I had done these people.

Now, this was new. In all the years I had been doing this, there had never been any apparent reference to things I'd done that I considered wrong. But this felt like there was a pack of wolves inside me, and they were sniffing out the things about Whitley that he really would prefer to hide.

Not wolves, sweet angels.

No, more complicated, more . . . human.

I felt like something was present that knew me far better than I knew myself—or rather, than I was willing to tell myself.

I was getting frantic, but I couldn't make it stop. On we went, reviewing my life.

We came to a certain face—one that I really hadn't wanted to see. With this person, I had done wrong.

The roof erupted in thuds, like they were stomping with rage. Then they came roaring down around me right through the beams, a crowd of racing shadows, shabby and stinking of sweat. I could see that they looked human, but they were crouching, they backed into the corners, they acted like I was the wild wolf.

Attracted by the sounds, the cats came in. They were stressed but also curious, and presented an odd, almost funny appearance. They were flat on their bellies, their tails all puffed up behind them, slinking toward me out of the lighted hall, yowling as they came. It was extremely bizarre behavior, and seeing them did it for me: I ran. The Siamese dashed between my legs, shot downstairs, and began racing around the house wildly.

Then the visitors all trooped down the stairs, some of them jumping up and down on the runners, others leaping off the landing and dropping with soft thuds.

They moved fast and I didn't see much. They banged against furniture in the living room; they acted furious. For a moment I thought they were going to break the place up. Anne certainly participated this time. She was sitting up in bed in our room at the end of the hall, and her eyes were wide. "They're noisy," she said.

Sadie started hollering. I had to force myself to go downstairs, but I got her. I saw nothing unusual. Sadie was on medication because of her thyroid, and I was worried that the excitement might hurt her, so I took her to bed. Anne said, "I told you they were coming."

"They're gone," I replied.

"It sounded like they were moving the furniture."

"I think they were mad. I think I'm in trouble."

"You're in trouble."

The cats got nested under the covers and the four of us finally settled down. I had spent years with severe sleep disturbances because of the visitors, but time had taught me to trust myself and my family to them, and I had no trouble sleeping, even though we were obviously right in the middle of a big experience. As hard as many of my encounters have been, what had happened to me has also been very, very extraordinary, and I am more than grateful for it. I loved the visitors for it, and with love was coming—more slowly—trust.

About two hours later I woke up to familiar, machinelike jabs to my shoulder. Once I probably would have leaped out of bed, but no more. This had happened too often, and too often there was nothing there. So I wasn't really expecting to see anybody when I opened my eyes.

I was absolutely stunned.

They were right there, and they were glaring at me. I

reacted like I might have to a coiled snake, to see human
faces staring at me from a position about three feet
above the bed. There was light around them, and I could
see that they were all men, small, wearing gray tunics
except for one, whose tunic was white. The tunics had
short sleeves and were cinched with black belts. Their
arms were thin, their hands seemed rather big. Behind
them, where the raftered ceiling should have been, there
was a black, starless maw. Something about that darkness really frightened me. It would not be for another
two years that I would come to understand its shocking
meaning. All I knew then was that it was oppressive
and lonely and big, and where was my familiar ceiling?
Reality seemed plastic indeed.

The faces of these people were terrible to see. Their
eyes were normally shaped but as dark as lampblack,
and their stares were amazingly ferocious. I could literally feel their minds pushing and probing me, and they
took me straight to where I did not want to go.

I thought, my God, I will never commit another sin as
long as I live. Despite my anguish and shame, I managed to look back into the faces. It was a hell of a hard
thing, to force myself not to turn away from those penetrating, enraged eyes.

It lasted for a moment, then another. I still remember
finding behind their anger, a strange, nameless emotion—something like love, but totally absent any sense
of possession.

They left abruptly, rushing away in a crowd. I threw
off the covers, my automatic impulse to run after them.
But long experience told me that I would not find them,
no matter where I looked.

I stayed up for a while after they left. Sadie and Coe
were uneasy and only slowly calmed down enough to
go back to sleep. Meanwhile, I meditated and thought.

The visitors had never reacted to me like this before,

and, frankly, I had not considered that the condition of my conscience would be an issue for them. But it certainly was. This could not be more clear.

I really had a lot to think about. Could it be that the state of my soul had been what was preventing me from achieving total communion all along? But I wasn't that bad, surely not.

Or was I? Sometimes I think that the most invisible thing in the world is sin. People hide their sins foremost from themselves, and I was no exception.

How do you free yourself from sin if, for example, the person you sinned against has died? How do you free yourself?

On that fairly dismal thought, I drifted asleep. But this had been too much. Trust or no trust, this was not going to be a night of sound sleep.

My eyes were closed, and maybe I'd been sleeping very lightly, when I heard rustling.

Were they back? No, it was the cats. No, the cats were both under the covers.

When I opened my eyes I saw dark shapes against the beams of the ceiling, which seemed to be back to normal. I thought, now what? I turned on my bedside lamp and proceeded to receive the single worst shock of a life that has sustained some fairly severe shocks.

Hanging from the ceiling were four tremendous spiders. Their bodies were gleaming black and striped in irregular bright yellow. Structurally, they were hourglass spiders. The only problem was that they were easily a foot long and their legs spanned perhaps two feet.

Then I noticed that something strange was going on under the covers. I ripped back the sheets and saw two cats literally frozen in terror, hissing and hissing. Spiders must have a smell. I'm sure they do. I couldn't detect it, but I assume that the cats could and did, and they felt that it was, in this case, unusually strong.

The next thing I knew I was out of that bed and on my way as far as I could go barefoot in pajamas. But Anne was still back there and Anne was sound asleep.

I was afraid that the things were going to fall on us. On her. She'd married me because she'd wanted an interesting life, but this was obviously more than anybody would have bargained for. Above her, the spiders were working, weaving what I would describe as curved hutches made of silk.

They were, in short, settling in.

"Honey," I whispered. "I think—"

What did I think?

I thought I was being punished is what I thought. Contrition? I begged them to forgive me. I would have howled contrition but I was afraid I'd upset the spiders.

Then they were gone, just like that. I grabbed Anne, I started kissing her, and then I noticed that the cats were still panicked. What was I—stupid? I'd seen things disappear before. What if they weren't gone?

As far as I know, they're still waiting . . . for the day I die.

"Go and sin no more," the priest used to say at the end of confession. I wish I'd listened.

I spent the rest of the night reading the Bible and trying to figure out how one might truly repair a sin. Dawn came, clear and pure, and Anne got up and we had breakfast. I didn't tell her what had happened. Why bother her with a story like that? Did I think that the spiders were real? No. I thought that they were created by my imagination with the help of the people who had been there earlier. Directed imagination.

But what about the cats? The visitors are quite capable of producing little side-effects like that.

What I assume they did was to extract from my mind the most frightening possible image and translate it into the appearance of reality, probably using hypnosis. For skilled mental manipulators like the visitors, this sort of thing would be easy. Maybe the condition of the cats was hypnosis, too.

At least, I hope so.

I tried to make sense of things, but not by attempting to understand the visitors. Instead, I went back along my own train of questions. What had I asked them that had led us to this particular point?

I had asked about their connection with the dead. So what were they saying? Were they also the judges of the dead?

I finally said to Anne, "I've seen demons."

She responded, "Here?"

"A nightmare. Mother of all nightmares."

We sat out in the garden together, and the morning breeze played in the wind chimes. She liked to count the frogs that were coming up to our little pond, and we enjoyed the peace of its life.

And then I saw it: this communication wasn't about getting forgiveness, it was like the journey to Eden, a lesson in the consequences of guilt.

To be with the visitors, I had to be free. But freedom did not involve suppressing what I had done that was wrong. Pretending is a waste of time; the actions are engraved on the past.

Like everybody, I'd sometimes wounded people in ways that were never going to heal. The message was clear: live with your sins, taste them, bear them, face what you have done and what you are. That is the direction of freedom.

14

glimpses of a new world

At this moment of great personal challenge, the visitors disappeared from my life yet again. Dark, hard days followed. I was left in a black state, feeling that the things I'd done wrong had somehow irretrievably ruined my soul. Also, my outside life was unraveling. My book sales were continuing a fatal downward synergy that had started with the false accusation on television that I was a cult leader. I was in the middle of a sad period where numerous friends and relatives were dying, and the many small persecutions visited upon any man who makes controversial claims were depressing me. The congressional investigation I have alluded to seemed to be causing me to come under some sort of surveillance, and we began to experience strange intrusions at our cabin. The intelligence community had intruded into my life before, and I really did not want them back.

The visitors' abandonment seemed calculated to leave me in the worst possible state of guilt as well, to add as much weight as possible during a difficult time. I understood this process from my studies of ancient initiatory religions: this stripping of the individual of his self-value, followed by a descent into his own underworld.

Weren't they a little late? It seemed to me that I'd been wandering around in the underworld for years.

The long, dreary autumn of 1992 wound down to Christmas. My boy was growing up and suddenly there was a wonderful young man coming down to the tree with a gentle smile on his face. Where was my child, his eyes radiant with excitement, looking in wonder at Santa's bounty?

With only one child, the growing up is like the falling of a curtain. I have always loved children, and I had enjoyed Andrew and his friends enormously during their childhood. Our young man was setting out now, and the toys that had been miracles were left to the dust.

Each Christmas, I remembered December 26, 1985. I longed to heal the past, to go outside on the night of the nine knocks, to walk down the path to the woods on the morning of the three cries, to open myself heart and soul the evening I had thrown the table.

I wanted another chance, and this time surely I was ready.

Absolutely nothing happened over Christmas 1992, but one morning in late January 1993, I had a personal vision of remarkable power.

I was half asleep, just at dawn, when I noticed a pleasant sense of movement, then of speed. A moment later I was rushing upward. Above me was a sky of startlingly clear blue. As I went higher, it slowly faded to blackness, then became filled with stars. But they were very different from the familiar constellations. First, they were clustered in hundreds of groups across the sky, and they were not only full of rich and delicious color—golds and greens and yellows and reds and many more—they radiated with a light that seemed to caress my heart, and to be filled with singing.

Then my vision expanded more and I saw the earth behind me and it was shining in the most extraordinary way, not with the light of the sun, but with what I felt at once was the light of souls.

Far above me, there was an area where the light of earth seemed to be touching the light from elsewhere, and space somehow did not seem so large. There was a green hue dancing against the black.

This blackness was really appalling. It seemed emptier—much emptier—than any normal dark. I knew it from the night the seven visitors had appeared, and it was just as terrible now, a dark from beyond the edge of the universe. By contrast, the clusters of stars were far warmer and more alive—a real joy to see—than normal stars. There were also many fewer of them than normal, and I felt then that what I was seeing were not stars at all. In fact, the ordinary stars were not there. I was seeing the glow of the souls that cling to other inhabited planets: this was not the atomic light of suns, it was the living glory of the conscious universe.

In physical reality, the universe seems rather aimless—a place where life struggles to survive and the stars slowly expend their energy as the empty ages pass.

There was no such sense of meaninglessness in this view of the universe. Here, the light was alive. The glow around me was composed of conscious being in mass and multitude, and I saw that surrounding earth is a huge, organic presence that represents the final, superconscious, and ecstatic limit of life. This was why we exist. It is where we go when we die, and it contains not just humanity, but an entire mirror of every single thing that has ever been touched by the transformative power of death.

I knew, and it did not frighten me at all, that I had entered the world of the dead. During the moments that I had relived my first steps back in 1988, I recalled that the light of the sun had seemed to be talking to me. Now I knew that it wasn't the light of the sun.

As if it had finally noticed and embraced me, there flooded into me a most vibrant and delicious sensation. My sins were gone, and I saw that I had been my own judge all along; the visitors had only pointed this out. With new clarity I understood advice given me long ago by a beloved teacher and nun: give your sins to God.

In the end, this is where I would take my flawed soul, to this glory.

As the shock of the moment wore off, such an unimaginable vastness of detail flooded me that I could not keep up with it. I felt then that every single instant, every single perception, no matter how tiny, still existed in the extraordinary weave of souls that surrounds the earth. The least movement took me flowing down the streets of a life, the cries, the sweat, the struggle. The tiny journey I had made into past time now seemed almost superfluous.

It wasn't penultimate moments, mostly. For the most part it was an immense, incredibly alive tapestry of small living details—the gleam of light upon a child's hair, a pencil falling, a man burning leaves, children leaping back and forth across a stick, the cry of a boy who had found a comb, the spiking sting of a bullet's penetration.

From below there arose a murmuring, continuous voice, the prayers of the living—tortured, groaning, like in flavor to the sighing night wind or the great groan of the sea.

With the voices of souls there came also the tastes and smells of the past, the scent of cooking, the fall of snow, and the sights—Rome of ancient days all painted and glorious, a bloody whip upon a hook, a great foundation built on pain; cries, singing, the whole agony of women's birthgiving and all the fears of the ages, the delicious coziness of babyhood and the gleam of a ball thrown high into the light, the calling of a lost boy on a road.

I also saw a thing that I had not expected, that not all souls persist, that the immortal potential is more fragile than we have dared to face. I saw the souls of the dying coming forth—a man saying, "I just checked out" in a shaky voice, a tiny baby bouncing off life like a spark. But I also saw people die without anything coming out. Where did their souls go? Could a soul be killed by an evil life? Maybe hell is the terrible moment when a soul realizes that it has forfeited its immortality. Would not such a death hang forever in eternity, a kind of captured end?

My relatives and friends seemed to gather near, my father and my mother, Michael, and all the others who had gone in recent years, and the peace that flowed from them entered my heart, and I knew that I had come here in search of strength, and strength was being given me.

I felt the huge height, saw dawn overspreading the land below, and began dashing straight down at breakneck speed.

For a moment I hung in midair, amazed to see a plane coming up. I watched an American Airlines jet climb into the sky, saw its gleaming wings tremble, heard its piercing roar, saw a pilot with dark glasses sitting in the cockpit.

Then I was in bed again—and the sound of the jet was dwindling away to the west. There was a yearning in me that was terrible to bear as I sensed my own beloved dead going back without me. But I also saw something else: that the evil I had perceived in myself was as much a part of my potential as my good. It was not something to be rejected, but rather transformed. There was a limit, though, that was exemplified by those empty bodies, which I now realized had referred in some nameless way to empty places in the sky. I cannot put into words how this looked, except to say that there was a sort of rueful, poignant dimming here and there in the living tapestry, as if the souls not there will be missing—and missed—forever. Even so, the light of man shone bright, but the places of the souls lost to the tapestry of heaven are like the skeletons of leaves.

When I got up, it was a sunny morning. Anne was making coffee, Coe and Sadie were at the foot of the bed, and I was late. Anne reminded me, when I told her of this vision and how it had led me to a new understanding of sin, that among the things I have heard the visitors say were the words "have joy."

If one could pass beyond guilt, one would come to see sin as integral to the process of resurrection, and look upon the chance to bear one's mistakes as one of life's most valuable gifts. That was why the residue of evil appeared so beautiful, and why the living dark that I saw cannot ever prevail.

Now I saw what I had received from Michael Talbot in a deeper way. The work of demons is certainly evil, but one can transform it in oneself. In learning to work with one's dark side, one also finds that the old Greek meaning of the word "daimon" still has currency: evil is a great teacher. It is not for nothing that the tree of Eden is called the tree of knowledge of good and evil.

The journey into one's sins is a tremendous education. Knowing oneself is not simply a matter of intellectual understanding, it is a compassionate embrace of one's own fractured soul.

You find that your soul is being etched deeply by every tiniest act, that you are a kind of work of art, your own essential creation: the way your soul looks is how you have lived. It is this that we live for, to add the beauty of our years to the tapestry, and go back and work again if it is not done, to transform the little chip of stone that is oneself into something that can fly.

The deeper mankind goes into his dark heart, the closer he will also get to the stars. We know what's out there. The light of souls permeates us: I saw it. To the babies, it speaks directly—which is why, I think, that we have amnesia about our early years.

But that's changing. The veil between the worlds is growing thin. We're on a journey of discovery, not only as individuals, but as an unfolding creation. By emerging, the visitors will disrupt and profoundly change everything and we know it, and that is what all the denial and the resistance is about.

I searched through the *Tao te Ching* and the Gospels, to which the visitors had years ago directed me. I found a particular sequence of words taken from both that seemed to offer an exceptional enlargement of meaning: "From before time and space, tao. It is beyond being. How to see this? Look inside." "In Him was life, and the life was the light of men." And then their shocking, summarizing admonition: "Have joy."

15

in the nature of joy

One hot August night in 1993 I dragged myself in for the midnight meditation yet again, not expecting anything much.

A moment later, from overhead: wham. I almost jumped out of my skin. It had been twelve full months, the longest absence ever.

Again there was that sense of being overwhelmed by a terribly alive presence. It surrounded me like an alien skin, touching me—and my body proceeded to betray me. My soul had been planning to stay, but my body couldn't bear the sense of threat and got out of there fast.

In a year I'd forgotten just how powerful their effect was, how physically vulnerable it could make you feel. The sense of a person being right there when nobody can be seen is very hard to endure, especially when that shocking insight is present. Instead of concentrating on

all my complicated intellectual material, I would have
been better off just relaxing, but I was already in our
bedroom by the time I regained control.

I was furious with myself. I assumed that my leaving
like that would signal the end of the encounter, and this
after a whole year of waiting. I said, "I'm glad you're
back." I'd had a real feeling that somebody was physically there. I was on our bed at this point and suddenly
heard movement, creaking floorboards. I waved my
arms around, trying to feel whom I could not see. Then
I asked if I could smell them, smell their skin, seeking
as always to engage my primitive senses as much as
possible. I said, "I will fear you less if I can smell you."
There was an immediate response: the sense of presence disappeared.

At three I was awakened by a slap to my leg. I
opened my eyes to observe a shadowy figure standing
beside the bed. It scared the hell out of me. While I
could no longer imagine the visitors hurting me, the figure was so real that it didn't even occur to me that it was
a visitor until he hopped onto the foot of the bed and
leaned against the bedstead and I saw how small he
really was, and realized that he was in a white tunic.

I could see that it was a man, small like the ones from
the year before had been. His face was pretty shadowy,
lit only by the glow from my alarm system controls. But
my impression was of pale skin and rather heavy fea-
tures, perhaps even a little paunchy. He had black hair. I
started to grab Anne's shoulder but was stopped by a
quick gesture.

Other husbands and wives were involved together,
and she'd put ten years of her life into this. But I was
torn. I also didn't want him to leave. "Who are you?"

The way he was slumped, he looked like a dead
body, almost, or a doll. One time many years ago they'd
brought a sort of cardboard doll into the room, and I

thought—but no, I could hear him breathing. I felt like he wanted me to come closer. Despite his strange, slumped emptiness, it was beginning to seem like the most normal, most casual meeting.

I threw off the covers and sat up. As I went closer, I realized that his stillness had to do with fear. He wasn't stiff or shaking like I would be, but there was something in the posture that spoke volumes about another hidden reality of contact. The visitors, it would seem, may well be as scared as we are. This fragile little man was certainly scared—and why not, with a demonstrably unpredictable giant creeping toward him in the dark?

He was completely real, and there was no question at all that he was somebody from another meaning. I crawled toward him until I was sitting on my knees right beside him. He was just a little slip of a thing. I don't think he was even three feet tall. I doubt if he weighed fifty pounds, his ability to pound on roofs notwithstanding.

I said, "Hi."

Never looking at me, he slowly held up a knobby little hand. I took it—cool and quite oily—and inhaled the scent of the skin. It seemed human to me: a strong, sweet scent, untroubled by soap. For the first time in all these years, I was finally touching one of the visitors just as Raven had. His hand lay in mine like a cool little bird, absolutely still. I wanted to hug him, I was so glad. Apparently he detected this wish, because his hand shot out of mine as fast as a flash of light. I think that the thought of being enclosed in my arms was too much for him.

"I'm sorry," I said. I gazed at him. He was so incredibly still. Except when he had moved his hands, he might as well have been stone.

Then I realized that he was looking straight at me. The face was frozen, but not the eyes. It was just as if the barely visible pupils contained a substance, it was so penetrating. I felt him come into me, felt him go down inside me, felt something starting to bloom—a flower opening, a fire starting.

An unconscious fear reflex threw us both back. I threw myself toward the head of the bed; he disappeared in a flash. Then I was flat on my back and I blacked out like I'd been injected with a drug.

All the next day, I read and thought. I talked it out with Anne.

The next night at midnight, I went into the room, expecting nothing. I assumed that I'd failed again and was facing another year of work.

But he was there, a little bundle of darkness sitting in a corner. He obviously did not bathe, and his skin was human enough to smell like I might have encountered him in a warm subway car.

I sat down near him. My mind was just whizzing with thoughts, with questions, with really incredible joy. I wanted to turn on the light but the thought brought a soft sound from him, like a groan of tired annoyance. It didn't matter. I could see him well enough from the light coming along the hall.

I was so excited. I wanted to talk, but he seemed to straighten his posture, and I got the feeling that I was to calm down and meditate. I disciplined myself to it—and at once fearful images started coming. I saw one of the huge spiders. I saw a wolf. I saw the dark thing that had connected me to Michael. Somehow, though, these images did not frighten me. On the contrary, the spider looked kindly, the wolf sweet, and the dark thing seemed to exude a sardonic sense of humor. They were still dark, evil images, but something had changed about the way I saw them, something very deep.

When I opened my eyes what seemed like a few moments later, an hour had passed. He was gone from the room, so I got up and staggered off to bed, my legs tingling.

I spent the next week in glory. He came every night at midnight. By day I read the *Tao te Ching* and the Gospels and struggled with my deteriorating business affairs. I was inspired to reread John in the original Greek, as I had not done since college days. I sought to contemplate the logos anew.

At midnight I would go into the room and he would be there. He explored my mind, and I found that he could go down all the way to the old dragons at the bottom of my consciousness, and all I would feel was joy, joy, joy.

Soon Anne and I began to notice movement around the house during the day, to hear doors closing in the basement or upstairs, and to smell his presence.

Incredibly, he appeared to be living with us. We did not speak much about him because we didn't want to scare him off, and we did not ever talk about him on the phone or to other people.

I, of course, prowled around the house trying to get a look at him during the day, but he would not allow that.

We began to find the guest bed unmade at odd times, usually when we'd been gone.

We got used to him being around, but he never again came as close to me as he had on those first few nights. Usually at night in the room, he would be above me. He could float in the air, he could disappear in an instant, he could walk through walls, he could enter my mind.

I was getting used to this last process. What had seemed so terrible a few years ago now came to seem sensual and incredibly educational, and I started to worry that he would leave when he got to the end of me.

The first thing he did was to establish a much more rigorous regime of inner work. He began waking me up at three and again at six. We meditated for an hour at midnight, another at three, a third at six. In spite of this, I felt no sense of sleep deprivation. In fact, my body began to feel wonderfully light.

He started leaving little bits of candy in my basement library, in front of books that he wanted to bring to my attention. He never spoke, although I talked to him all the time. My Siamese didn't react to him much, and I wondered how Sadie would have handled the situation. She had passed away earlier in the summer, and we'd spread her ashes in the garden.

I asked him to indicate a book that was really important to the work we were doing together. Soon he placed three small, white candies—just ordinary little candies, half-sucked—in front of *Life Between Life* by Dr. Joel Whitton and Joe Fisher.

I sucked the remains of the candies and read the book, which was about what existence might be like for souls destined to reincarnate, while they reside between lives. It was in this book that I was introduced to the concept of the bardo, the space just beyond death. I was interested to see that the soul in the bardo confronts the Mirror of Karma, which Christians conceive of as the judgment.

I had the odd feeling that this man was not a visitor at all, but a man who was in some way alive and dead at the same time. I began to think of him as a spark of the great tapestry I had seen that had somehow taken on physical form without going through the process of birth.

Maybe that's what all the fairies and silkies of Celtic lore are, and the sylphs and even the gods of old times. I could see that I must also be, in one sense, living in the bardo before I was dead. I had certainly looked into the Mirror of Karma.

I kept working and meditating with him. It was a wonderful, incredible period in my life, and I wish dearly that I could share him with every single soul in the world. My hope is that contact will lead to friendships like this for everybody who seeks them.

As I came to my peace, I began to see with more clarity. I sought to free myself as he was free. I was fascinated with his physical abilities. I'd seen him disappear. He levitated at will. When he left, he'd shoot off through a wall.

I came to think that classical physics must be a way the mind has of ordering what is really a hyperquantum reality. Classical physics, which expects the stone to drop when it is released, does not allow the body to levitate and makes all walls solid, may not be a final reality at all.

It certainly isn't for him. Maybe, as more and more of us see the visitors with our own eyes, we will come to perceive the world more as Michael Talbot thought we should, in ranges and probabilities rather than definite, seemingly immutable structures.

Then our vision of the universe will, I suspect, change. We will see it in its greater truth, its meaning arrayed in constellations of souls. Maturity will no longer seal us away from the truth; even as adults, we will continue to hear the voice of the light.

It was not until November that we finally stopped meditating three times a night. We'd done it for about six weeks.

Autumn was early in 1993, and by Christmas there were terrific snowstorms.

December 26, 1993, the eighth anniversary of my first remembered encounter, came and went. But it didn't matter. I was a new man, I was living in glory. Night after night, I went up to the room, and he was almost always there.

I finally discovered some physical limitations. When the temperature dropped below about twenty degrees, for example, he would not come unless he was already in the house. Also, he slept during the day and he was extremely shy about it. Sometimes, he used the room. Once, I went in with a camera when he might have been there. He wasn't, at least not visibly, but his bed has never been slept in again, and I have quit trying to take unwanted pictures.

How I loved him. I had never loved anybody else like this. I didn't know his name, I rarely saw him, I'd never heard him speak. But he knew me vastly better than anybody else ever had.

I took joy in this, and somehow even the fact that the knowledge was a one-way street didn't disturb me. He was a teacher, a real one, not the sort of egocentric fake that usually treads the path of enlightenment. By any human standard, he was totally enlightened.

One night he stood close behind me for an hour while I meditated. I was able to listen carefully to his breathing, and it was fascinating. Not once in all that time did it change or vary in any way. Not a sigh, not a deep breath, a cough. Just in and out, in and out, with the sort of absolute precision that I associated with the gray people.

They are masters of illusion. I have seen that with my own eyes, and I wondered if perhaps he—but no, he seemed completely real.

Another time he put his hand on my head and slowly worked his finger into my skull. I felt him reaching down inside me physically and spiritually and in ways that I cannot put into words. It was among the most lovely and also the very most difficult things that has ever happened to me.

In February an old school friend of mine, Oliver Heard, came up to New York on business and spent a night with us. Because it is also our guest room, Oliver would sleep where all this had been happening. I wondered what would transpire, as it was clear to Anne and I that our visitor was in the house.

Oliver is not a believer, and we'd never discussed the *Communion* question much. Most of my old friends had taken the whole thing in stride, assuming it to be some kind of elaborate fantasy or possibly a practical joke.

The countryside was sere with old snow, and it was very cold. We went to bed about midnight. Half an hour later, I happened to notice a light on downstairs and went to turn it out. Passing Oliver's room, I heard his fan roaring. Since it was ten degrees below zero outside, I looked in on him.

I was appalled to find that the guest room was at least ninety. My poor guest was asleep with the fan roaring at full blast and the windows opened. I cut off the heat in that part of the house, finished checking around, and returned to bed.

Spending the day with Oliver and others who weren't interested in the visitors, talking politics, my friend from the bardo had come to seem far away.

I wondered if I ought to go down and meditate in the living room. But I was tired, and I decided to sleep.

A few minutes later, there came a rattle of newspapers. Had it come from downstairs, or from Oliver's room? I got up and checked on him again. His room was still boiling, but he was dead asleep. I returned to our room.

More sounds, and now it was clear that they came from downstairs. I sat up in bed, concerned. Then a low voice drifted up from the family room below, struggling mightily to form words: "It's me."

The shock of hearing him speak—of having him suddenly enter what had until that moment been a separate part of life that was mine alone—caused me to revert back all the way to my original state of fear and I went rushing through the house with a gun in my hand.

I was halfway through the living room when I came to my senses, yelled out an apology, and dashed upstairs. He was in our bedroom, but he jumped up to the roof as soon as I arrived, and this despite the cold.

I went down in the meditational position and thought frantically how sorry I was, how I was aware that I had made a mistake, how we could go on, could try again. I felt his chagrin and his bitter disappointment, and I found myself saying, "I will let you, I will manage it, only please, please come back."

He did not come back.

I know why he didn't: as I was then, I could not quite reach the surrendered openness that I needed to really enter the relationship.

He offered me something truly new, and I think that same offer is made to us all. To surrender by becoming strong, to transform our evil by understanding it, to become a species whose consciousness transcends the boundaries of the world, to gain control over the very form that physical reality takes, to ride the winds of time—all of these things are possible to us. We have only to go into the night and take the hand that reaches down to us from the dark unknown.

And thus ends the communication from the visitors. Beginning with their proof and proceeding through a series of multiple-witness encounters, they have made a compelling case on behalf of increased contact. I have also used my own subjective experiences to illustrate some possible potentials and goals of relationship with them, and what it might be like to live together in the same house.

They have not really answered the questions of who and what they are, and my guess is that they cannot, because our present level of comprehension will so filter the information that there will not be enough of its truth left with us. Were they to answer these questions now, I think it probable that we would get nothing out of it but more confusion. Clearly though, we would do well to table our prior assumptions about aliens. This might be about aliens in some way, but that is not the whole story.

In this section of the book, I have made every effort to name every witness I possibly could. I have made exceptions to this rule only in the cases of children and individuals who have specifically requested anonymity.

In the next section, I will follow a different procedure. Because it deals with the government and because people have jeopardized their careers to contribute to it, I will in general not name any names except those of the dead and people whose statements are already public knowledge.

However, I am in possession of all the identities of the people quoted and mentioned herein and have spoken personally with most of them.

SECTION THREE

The Official Story

Of all the causes which conspire to blind
Man's erring judgment, and misguide the mind,
What the weak head with strongest bias rules,
Is pride, the never-failing vice of fools.

—*Alexander Pope,*
"An Essay on Criticism"

16

the horror stories

There is a great deal of very understandable interest in what the government knows and does not know about the visitors. As I stated at the beginning of this book, the contact process probably failed to reach the government in the early fifties, and I doubt that it is going to be much of a factor in the future.

Previously, it has been assumed that official acknowledgment would somehow validate the reality of contact, but the proof that is already available is sufficient to do that for anybody who does not need an additional push to be forced out of denial.

Over these next few chapters, I would like to try to cast some light on the confusion and horror stories that abound in this experience, and identify those aspects of the negative cloud that surrounds the contact process that have been intentionally created by people hoping to protect their secret failures by disabling it.

Because the visitors have established a direct link with the people, the press can continue with its failed approach, the government can do what it wishes, and science can indulge itself fully in institutional and individual denial: none of it matters. When the visitors enter a person's life, that individual gains access to all he needs to begin a relationship, without reference to established institutions.

Should encounter become sufficiently extensive, it is even possible that new or genuinely renewed institutions will eventually emerge as human society responds to the challenge. Every aspect of the new institutions would reflect the ethics of encounter, which so clearly stress the value of the individual and the importance of the soul. Under such a scenario, government's objective would be to use the minimum of power and communicate the maximum of freedom to the individual, to give us the widest possible playing field for personal realization. Science would become too rigorous to be tempted any more into the trap that has ensnared it—of editing its observations to protect its theories—and would finally come to terms with the concept that the physical world is vastly more extensive than it has yet understood. The press would be too ethically motivated to function as it does now, which is to recast everything that happens in terms of black and white, with strong emphasis on the black, in order to capture our attention with false shocks and illusory fears. Instead, it would try to report accurately on the real world, disseminate facts, and identify true questions.

To have working public institutions is not a hopeless ideal. As, one by one, we become resensitized to our souls and see with our own eyes how the way we live affects what we become, the fierce, compassionate, and determined ethics displayed by the visitors will spread among us, even to the official world. The secret government, which is now acting in a routinely unethical manner, the sensation-seeking press, the denying scientists—all will look to their souls, and when they do that, they will try to repair the damage they are now doing themselves and others. My hope is that this deeply personal process will be part of the revitalization of the human world that contact demands.

As soon as government saw that it could neither understand the visitors nor predict their actions, it began to lie. Later, it also spread fear.

The lies started shortly after the first sightings were reported in 1947. They were carried by the press into society at large, until they came to be supported by a culture of denial and an industry of fear. This fear translated itself into horror films and scary stories in the fifties, then evolved through the sixties and seventies into a scenario of alien terror so spectacularly awful and so detailed that it began to seem real.

While the fact that encounters can be abusive and frightening cannot be responsibly ignored, it is also true that these problems must be addressed directly if they are going to be solved. Reworking them into what is essentially a sort of folklore is not going to do anything but make it harder to understand what is real and what is not.

Horror stories were not the only early response to contact. From the beginning there was also a positive current running through the popular culture, from *The Day the Earth Stood Still* in 1951, in which benevolent aliens warn the world about the dangers of nuclear war, to Steven Spielberg's enormous personal statement on behalf of a productive view.

Without quite realizing what we were doing, we have been debating, as a culture, whether or not to open our lives to the visitors ever since they first appeared. And the debate has now come to a point of decision. The people in power don't want to do it because they fear that they will be made redundant. However, the great majority of us, it appears, are ready.

As a result of the publicity engine that was cranked up because of the popularity of *Communion* and *Transformation*, many of the horror stories began to be amplified and even to enter general belief. I saw that I had a responsibility to investigate.

I decided to do the same thing with these stories that I had with the visitors themselves. Rather than hiding from them and trying to ignore them, I went after them and tried to understand. My objective was not to disprove them and gloss over the difficult parts of encounter. My objective was to obtain an accurate picture of what was true and what was not.

The first thing that I discovered was that the great majority of the horror stories began with a single source: a physicist called Paul Bennewitz.

In the late seventies, he and Dr. Leo Sprinkle, an early abduction researcher, were examining the case of a young woman who remembered seeing horrific cattle mutilations during a close encounter. Her stories, in fact, suggested the presence of an evil deeper than is known in human life. Frankly, it suggested that there may be very real demons abroad.

As he listened to her story, Dr. Bennewitz became convinced that she had been implanted with a device that evil-soaked aliens could use to track her and control her mind and that the communications medium must be extra-low frequency radio, or ELF. He then built equipment designed to test for such radio impulses, and believed that he found part of an ELF harmonic emanating from her body.

At the same time, the United States was secretly working on various devices intended to mediate the operation of the human mind with ELF. In part, this technology had grown out of a concept called the "Neurophone," which had originally been developed to aid the deaf by sending electrical impulses directly to the brain.

Dr. Bennewitz was apparently also the first to claim that the aliens involved came in two shapes: small, gray creatures with huge black eyes who were extremely dangerous, and tall blond ones who were much more positive toward us, but in many ways even stranger.

By 1980, Dr. Bennewitz was involved in a one-man effort to warn mankind that the United States was engaged in an alliance with an evil alien power, from which it was obtaining technology in return for delivering human beings for hideous physical experiments and mind control.

The Bennewitz stories remained deeply buried in UFO literature until the late eighties when John Lear, the son of the creator of the Lear Jet, emerged as an advocate. Mr. Lear was a sincere and persuasive man. Like most of the others I met who were brokering fear, he appeared to be very honestly terrified.

He produced a group of papers allegedly written by an alien called 'O. H. Krill,' that suggested the presence of an extraterrestrial base underneath a mesa in New Mexico, and went into some detail about this and about the objectives of the alleged aliens.

As public interest rose, more new claimants surfaced and more such documents appeared. A whole subtext of secret government-alien complicity emerged, suggesting that the United States was engaged in trading access to members of the public for alien technology, and that people were being badly used in this process.

Probably the most careful of the fear merchants is Linda Moulton Howe, who is a leading expert on the mysterious cattle mutilation phenomenon. But she has only to tell the truth to get a scare. Cattle are surgically destroyed in odd ways, often with their blood being drained, their sexual organs neatly excised, and other peculiar effects, such as their hearts being removed through small holes. I might add that the extraordinary exactness of the incisions reported is to me very suggestive that the visitors might be involved.

The mutilations are fearful, but is that because they seem by our standards to be so strange, or because there is something intrinsically horrible occurring? Certainly, the cattle do not die pleasantly. It even appears, to an extent, that an effort might be made to actually induce fear in them, and some of the fear merchants speculate that the visitors feed on fear.

But then again, we routinely terrify cattle, and even do things that seem calculated to induce terror in them, without actually trying to. When I was ten my father was involved in a small way in the cattle business, and I went to see a slaughterhouse in operation. The bellowing terror of the cattle as they go down the ramp to the slaughtering floor is something to hear. They know what is happening to them; they smell the death, they hear the screaming of the beasts ahead in line. But nobody is trying to scare them. In fact, nobody cares whether they are scared or not. The objective of a slaughterhouse has nothing to do with the feelings of the cattle. It's not about their fear, it's about their meat.

So the visitors do no worse to cattle than we do, and appear to do less of it. To what use they might put the cattle, I cannot speculate, and therein lies an appropriate source of caution. Until we do understand what is being done to them, we cannot sensibly conclude more than that some visitors, like us, slaughter cattle. An ameliorating factor might be that they are showing a certain concern for the way we have structured our world by attacking this particular species in this way, and not—say—our pets.

It is also true, however, that many witnesses have received a message against the slaughter of animals for food, and as a result have become vegetarians.

Mind control, the government allowing abductions in return for alien technology, gene and fetus theft, cattle mutilations, underground bases—these are the primary horror stories. There are others, even more bizarre, that involve aliens boiling human body parts in vats and such, but I won't go into them except to say that none of my readers have mentioned observing this sort of activity, nor have I. I have, however, been accused of claiming that I observed witnesses' disembodied heads aboard flying saucers. I neither observed this nor made such a claim.

There is a detailed description of the location and the topography surrounding the alleged alien base in the Lear document. The document states, "The base is $2^1/_2$ miles northwest of Dulce [New Mexico], and almost overlooks the town. There is a level highway 36-feet wide going into the area. It is a government road. One can see telemetry trailers and buildings that are five-sided with a dome. Next to the dome, a black limousine was noted—a CIA vehicle. These limos will run you off the road if you try to get into the area."

In the fall of 1989, Edward Conroy and Dora Ruffner, on assignment from the Communion Letter, visited the Jicarilla Apache Reservation that surrounds Dulce.

Their first discovery was that few, if any, UFO investigators had ever been there and Jicarilla Apache officials in Dulce were hardly aware of the stories.

In reality, there is no thirty-six-foot wide highway into the area of the Archuleta Mesa, which turns out to be more like a ridge than a classic table mesa. There are no telemetry trailers, no buildings at all. There is no indication that there has ever been a highway in the area, and there are no ruins of buildings.

However, the document also states that the Jicarilla Reservation has, since 1976, been one of the areas hardest hit by cattle mutilations. It turned out that the reservation newspaper, the *Jicarilla Chieftain*, did record mutilation reports in 1978 and 1979. On May 8, 1978, the *Chieftain* reported that a bull had been found with its sex organs removed, with an incision made around its anus and the blood drained. The article continued, "according to reliable sources, many people have viewed mysterious objects in the area at the time the mutilation occurred." A photograph of strange markings found in the mud near a mutilated cow was published with a cut line reading "Unusual Landing Gear." New Mexico's official cattle mutilation investigator characterized the destruction as a predator attack of no special consequence. New Mexico's coyotes must be unique in nature, considering that they have landing gear that leaves marks that can be photographed by a newspaper, and can surgically excise the anuses, eyes, and hearts of their prey.

Dora and Ed engaged Jicarilla Apache officials in conversation about the possibility of there being an alien base under the mesa that had, as the report stated, "been in operation since 1948."

The Jicarilla creation myth holds that the tribe itself emerged from the underground and were not created by God but by supernatural beings who live inside the earth.

It would thus appear that the "alien base" claim is rumor grafted onto a local creation story, supported by the fact that there were indeed a few cattle mutilations in the area during a time when it was supposed to have been among the "hardest hit."

What we are seeing is the updating of a myth surrounded by just enough evidence to trick even a careful researcher into accepting it all.

Or are we? Unfortunately, the story as it emerged would also be an excellent way of concealing the presence of a base. Given that there would be inevitable rumors, it would make sense to place the base in an area where real activities would be blended with local folklore. If the Jicarilla told stories of alien comings and goings, they would do it in the context of their own mythology and be unbothered by the fact that their "spirit" creators were still under the mesa where they were supposed to have been for ages.

Assuming that there was a sudden upsurge in public interest, it would then make sense to further conceal the base by actually publishing a document claiming its existence—but doing so in a way that does not stand up to scrutiny. So people like Dora and Ed would go out and find that the claimed surface installations didn't really exist, and that the whole story could simply be a confused retelling of the local creation myth.

The fact is that there is unlikely to be any way to make a final determination. However, that isn't really the issue. What is at issue is why the document even exists, and who created it. No matter the existence of the base, the document is a devilishly clever piece of propaganda. It wasn't concocted by John Lear out of his imagination. It took careful research; there is a remarkable design that to even quite careful scrutiny yields only more questions. The document further claims something that is consistent with all the other horror stories: it suggests that the government is closely allied to evil aliens who are doing dreadful things to humankind.

And this, I suspect, is what is meant to slip in along with the truths and clever mirror-images of truth that it conveys.

Let's discuss the matter a little further.

William Cooper, another UFO researcher, also allegedly claims that this supposed secret alliance between aliens and the United States government involves a technology trade and exchange of "ambassadors."

As Lear's stories emerge in part out of Dr. Bennewitz's ideas, Cooper's material appears related to tales told by Richard Doty, a former Air Force noncom assigned, according to his claims, to the Office of Special Investigations, the Air Force's intelligence arm.

I interviewed Mr. Doty after his retirement, although he apparently told this story while on active duty as well. In my interview, Mr. Doty repeated the same tale that he had told many times, of the capture of a living alien, whom, he said, was a mechanic or engineer aboard a UFO. This being, he continued, had not been able to talk until Air Force surgeons had rebuilt his vocal chords, which was done in 1949. He stated that he had seen videotapes of the alien and is the originator of a now-famous story that aliens like strawberry ice cream. This tale, played out on national television, was at one point used to ridicule the whole idea of encounter. In earlier versions of Doty's tale, the videotape was described as film, but that was before videotape was invented.

I can recall a college friend and his father, an Air Force pilot, telling a version of this same story back in 1963 or 1964.

There are severe problems with the story. For one thing, the operation to remove the human larynx was not developed until the mid-fifties, and laryngeal reconstruction was still a difficult process in 1994. The claim that Air Force surgeons could have successfully reconstructed nonhuman laryngeal anatomy in the forties is probably without merit. There is also the story about a simplistic assumption that the visitors are culturally similar to us, with its tales of engineers and spacefaring alien "crews." But even a superficial examination of the evidence reveals a situation that is so radically strange that the existence of any familiar social structures among the visitors would appear to be most unlikely.

This is, I think, a story, probably invented in the early fifties, to give the impression to people who discovered the truth that the Air Force was in better control of the situation than it was. And indeed, this motive may underlie much of the disinformation. Bear in mind that, in the early fifties, opinions about the existence of aliens were very different. The government had not yet fixed on a policy of general public denial. Even the *New York Times*, in recent years absolutely opposed to the faintest suggestion that extraterrestrials may be present, was neutral.

Internally, there must have been considerable concern in the Air Force. After all, aircraft had appeared with capabilities that were vastly in advance of our own. If these were Russian craft, they were set to win the cold war. And if they were extraterrestrial, then where did the aliens stand: Were they, perhaps, cold warriors as well?

Between the first sightings in 1947 and the wave that took place over Washington in 1952, the Air Force must have realized how helpless it would be if a landing took place.

This was probably when the stories that the government had secret contact with aliens got started. Had they landed, an impression could have been created that our leadership had some understanding of the situation. The president would have had the opportunity to speak from seeming authority, thus staving off panic.

Each time over the past forty years that there has been a new wave of sightings or closer contact reported, the stories have reappeared in slightly updated form, but have always reflected the cold war thinking of their originators. Secrecy, clandestine bases, spies, infiltration:

these are the dominant themes. Dr. Bennewitz was reportedly told that the two types of alien were engaged in a sort of cold war of their own: they were fighting for control of the human soul.

Whatever the actual truth, even the situation as it is known is probably too complicated to reflect a good guys–bad guys cold war in the sky.

Another of Bennewitz's theories involved devices being implanted in the unfortunate witness he had studied. Memories of this happening are reported by huge numbers of people. I personally have detailed memories of something being inserted into my nose, and many of my correspondents have nosebleeds after their encounters. There is a substantial body of documented evidence of strange injuries and scars connected with encounter memories.

The Communion Foundation, with the assistance of an interested radiologist, had MRI scans done of twelve individuals who claimed that they had experienced nasal intrusions. I also received an MRI scan, but not under the program.

In two cases, anomalies were found. One woman and one man had septums that showed minor scarring and some deviation that could have been associated with injury from an object entering the nose, but which also might have been caused in other ways. The man also had a few "unknown bright objects" in his brain, which are seen in about 1 percent of MRI scans, and, if extensive, appear related to neuromuscular diseases.

I know the case of the man quite well, because he was me.

It is also true that there are electromagnetic effects reported around close encounter witnesses; indeed this is a major part of the profile that emerged from Dr. Kenneth Ring's study of them, as described in his book *The Omega Project* which was also supported by the

Communion Foundation. Close encounter witnesses often become demonstrably electrosensitive after their encounters, as has happened to me.

What about mind control, the concept that so terrified Dr. Bennewitz? I think it's possible that some sort of esoteric control might be involved, and that complex instruction sets can be used. In my own experience of this, I could, at any time, have simply stopped. I could have refused to do what I was being asked to do. There was absolutely no sense of compulsion at all, and I was completely aware of the existence of the instruction set in my mind.

But couldn't such a thing be unconscious? What about the gentleman who sent me the letter from Glenrock? Was his action entirely coincidental, something that it just popped into his head to do seven years after the event?

Caution, as I have said before, is the byword. Informed caution and ignorant fear, however, are two very different responses to the unknown, and I believe that much of the disinformation examined above is designed to spread fearful lies on the back of some very strange facts.

Beyond the motive of creating the false impression that the government has more knowledge than it does, is the usefulness of the fear itself. If people are afraid, they can be controlled.

Spreading false fear along with an impression that government understands will make people flock to established authorities for help the moment the visitors emerge. If one thinks about it for a moment, one quickly realizes that a whole mechanism is in place for this.

So, let's say that the visitors do appear. They repeat, over New York City, the same overflight sequence that occurred over Mexico City. Extensive television coverage cannot be debunked; stories about light reflecting off flocks of seagulls and temperature inversions cannot convince anybody, because the video is too detailed. It becomes impossible to deny that they are real.

The media would enter a feeding frenzy of ratings and circulation. Instantly, all the scary stories would leap to the front pages, along with the notions that witnesses are brutalized, that fetuses are stolen, that the very soul is in danger.

People would be clawing the walls of the military bases, seeking help. The whole governmental infrastructure would remain intact, kept in operation by a public desperate for protection.

There is thus a powerful motive for government to spread stories that it knows more than it does and to make these stories fearful.

However, while there is obviously compulsion of witnesses taking place, in sum, the visitor experience appears not to be physically dangerous. This does not mean that it isn't dangerous in other ways. Obviously, it is extremely provocative and should be addressed with great care.

My readers usually express confusion rather than terror. At times, they also express anger, and I don't blame them. I feel exactly the same way. If asked in the first place, I probably would have gone with the visitors on my own. Their whole approach, indeed, seems calculated to generate maximum fear, albeit with minimum real harm. From all I have observed, I believe that this is a sound, if painful, approach on their part. I feel that it will lead in the end to communion with them far more profound, and more useful to us, that we could otherwise expect.

Fear or no fear, compulsion or not, implants or no implants, to be driven to such anger that you cannot find value in the adventure and must seek constant support would appear to require much more than exposure to the visitors. It also requires exposure to fear-oriented counselors and horror stories and hypnosis and—in the end—submission to control from people who are probably far more ignorant of the situation and less capable of turning it to useful advantage than the close-encounter witnesses themselves.

17

it gets personal

In late August 1994 I received a letter from a friend, Linda Jordan, who had inexplicably dropped out of my life in 1992. She wrote, "I've been very concerned about your family's welfare, and I've certainly taken a more cautious stance about certain subjects." She and I had last seen each other over breakfast in 1992, after which she ceased contact with me. She continued, "Something very strange went on during that breakfast which I'll relate to you now. We had just begun to eat when a man and woman came in together. They took the table just behind us. Your back was toward them, therefore they were out of your view. The woman's back was toward me (I never saw her face, but she had short, dark hair), and the man was seated facing me. He was in his late forties or early fifties with black, wavy, slicked-back hair, not tall, wearing a dull brown suit." She went on to say, "This man was staring intently at me. It was not a 'flirting' stare."

For the next half hour, the intent stare continued, with Linda too frightened to tell me. I remember how preoccupied she seemed, as if her mind was elsewhere. In all that time, Linda wrote, the woman the man was with never moved, never turned to look in the direction he was fixedly and remorselessly staring.

"Then," Linda continued, "to top it all off, he pulled out a video camera, continued his intimidating stare, slowly put it up to his face and aimed it directly at me. The woman just sat there like a robot, not moving at all. I was really spooked about the whole thing, and just couldn't bring myself to tell you."

They left, according to Linda, about five minutes before we did. She went through the lobby of the hotel trying to see if she could find them so that she could get a look at the woman's face, but was unsuccessful.

I feel that this man fits the description of a gentleman who called himself Colonel Russell when he entered my life in 1983 when I was doing research on a novel called *Black Magic* that involved the use of ELF as a medium of mind control. The remarkable black hair was a distinguishing characteristic, and even more so that odd, piercing stare.

At that time, this man made what appeared to me to be an attempt to recruit me for some intelligence agency or another. His contact with me had come after I had asked for and received help from the Air Force Office of Public Information, which had enabled me to visit a Minuteman Missile Wing and observe its nonclassified operations. During that visit, I told the press officers all about my book and described my interest in ELF in some detail. A few weeks later, the colonel called and we met over lunch. When I rejected his offer of recruitment, he was most unpleasant about it.

I refused to help him because I feel that the clandestine recruitment of writers and electronic journalists is probably illegal under the First Amendment. In any case it raises freedom of speech issues that are certainly not amenable to easy resolution. During our conversations he implied to me that many people in the media are recruited. In the December 17–24, 1994, issue of the *London Spectator*, it was revealed that the British Secret Service had a long history of involvement with writers, and the KGB engaged in this activity as well. I feel sure that Colonel Russell was telling me nothing less than the truth when he bragged about the degree to which American writers and journalists had been recruited by his service, presumably the CIA.

In 1992 when he seems to have shown up again, I was just beginning to work with congressional investigators who were exploring whether or not the intelligence community had been failing to report activities relating to the presence of possible extraterrestrials to Congress and had been warned that surveillance and intimidation might result.

On July 1, 1989, UFO researcher William Moore made a speech to the MUFON convention in Las Vegas, in which he said that he had, to an extent, cooperated with officials in the disinforming of Dr. Bennewitz regarding ELF in the early eighties. He had done this in an effort to ingratiate himself with them. Moore said that he had been approached in September 1980 by a member of the intelligence community who offered him information about UFOs in return for help in the Bennewitz case. According to Moore, the liaison was to be Richard Doty, who was then on active duty. What was asked of him was that he supply information about Bennewitz's ELF-related research, which was apparently very disturbing to the intelligence community.

By mid-1982, Moore claimed, Bennewitz was an emotional wreck because he had been fed horror stories about evil grays, mind control, and underground alien

bases that had absolutely terrified him. The poor man
had armed himself, installed extra locks on his doors,
and believed that aliens were entering his house by
coming through the walls. He thought that they were
injecting him with chemicals.

Initially, I bought guns and installed an alarm system as well, and I didn't need any disinformation to
induce me to do these things. My own fears were quite
sufficient.

Moore also said that he felt that the whole body of
horror stories being fed to Bennewitz was false, because
he watched the disinformation process literally from
within, as it was being applied.

It would seem, however, from the parallels
between what others have reported in their own lives
and what was secretly told to Bennewitz (and remained
obscure for many years thereafter), that there is a mixture of truth and falsehood involved. In any case, by
1983, Dr. Bennewitz was understandably having a difficult time.

It is noteworthy that an interest in ELF brought the
intelligence community tumbling head over heels into
my life just as it did his. But does that mean that ELF is
really being studied as a form of mind control or that
aliens are involved?

What we know is that Bennewitz's and my ELF
research drew significant intelligence interest back in the
early eighties. In Bennewitz's case, he suffered terribly.
In my case, they tried to involve me in complicity with
them.

In September 1987, I received a very provocative letter, doubly disturbing because it was mailed to my cabin
by a person unknown to me. I had been extremely careful to keep the address private, so this implied an
aggressive effort to search me out.

It remains one of only two that I have gotten from

members of the public at the cabin. The author had included his telephone number, and I called him. We had a forty-minute conversation during which he spoke with authority and passion about evil "grays" and tall, appealing "blonds." The tale he told me, involving an invasion by horrific gray-skinned aliens who were seeking to "improve" their species with human genetic material was strikingly similar to what had been fed to Paul Bennewitz and has emerged out of some witness hypnosis.

However, by that time, I'd had enough experience with the visitors to know, at least, that the gray-blond imagery probably reflected our own cold war mentality much more than it did the actual structure of what was out there.

Attempting to have a two-sided discussion, I offered the idea that, if there are aliens about, they must surely be more complex than he claimed. After all, one can find every shading of good and evil right here on earth. If human life is this complicated, why would more advanced alien cultures have taken on the cartoonlike simplicity of a made-up tale? To characterize two entire species as if they were simply single individuals, one good and the other evil, struck me as absurd, and I told him this.

He did not care to hear my opinion. He was not interested in disagreements. "We have a war to win, here, and you've ended up on the frontline."

I thought: he sounds like a soldier, a cold warrior in full cry after a new space-age enemy.

He claimed that the visitors were not only aliens but also from "another reality," and that public acceptance of their reality would be the "open sesame" that would enable them to complete their invasion. The government was engaged in a subtle holding action, he claimed, seeking to stave them off by spreading denial and isolating "enablers" like me as one would a Typhoid Mary.

The image of evil aliens invading us using mind control simply does not fit the complicated and ambiguous reality of contact as it is actually being experienced. In addition, it seems absurd to imagine that it would take a species as advanced as the visitors fifty years just to prepare their invasion. Had evil aliens actually arrived here in 1947, the invasion would have also been concluded in 1947, probably in a matter of days.

When I confronted him with this, he became defensive. "We've made efforts to ward them off."

"How? With bug spray? Fly swatters?"

"You have a sense of humor." His tone of voice strongly suggested that he did not.

"I just don't think you're in touch with reality."

When I said that, I meant something very specific, and time has only served to make me more sure that my early intuition was correct.

Because the experience is so strange, it has a tendency to mold itself to fit whatever expectation a witness may bring to it. When the mind perceives something that doesn't make sense, it imposes its own sense. Random shadows become the Man in the Moon. A flimsy accusation against a feared man becomes indistinguishable from proof of guilt.

The contact experience is full of such failures of mind—my own included. For example, for a time my experience melted into something that fit my Christian background, and I saw the gray beings as demons and the blond ones as angels. As easily, I made my vision change so that I viewed them as a military force from another world. I'd seen them setting up an empire here; I'd also seen them as psychological parasites from another dimension, who depend upon our belief to enter our reality; I'd once decided, based on the structure of the cattle mutilations, that they were indeed bizarre creatures who eat fear the way we eat food. From the precision of movement and sound that I observed, I concluded for a time that they were machines and spun out a whole scenario based on the idea of physicist Dr. John Von Neumann that an intelligent species might populate the universe by sending out devices capable of reconstructing itself in every detail when a suitable planet was found. Because the first visitor I recalled encountering seemed female, I viewed her for a long period as a postindustrial vision of the mother goddess. When I conceived of the visitors as an outgrowth of the old Celtic fairy mythology, they also took on that appearance.

It is not that the visitors are chameleons. What changes is not what we see, but how they appear to us.

This is why I think that when the cold warriors of the early fifties looked at the visitors, they saw a structure that fit their expectations: they saw good guys fighting bad guys, with the spoils of victory being control over the human race. Because the cold warriors were also of the Judeo-Christian tradition, the visitors further focused in their minds into an updated version of the angels-demons scenario.

My guess is that some version of this scenario has become official policy, and thus I doubt very much that the most utterly secret view of the visitors held within our government's bureaucracy actually reflects reality.

Understanding what they really are, in the final and absolute sense, will be among the greatest of all intellectual accomplishments. Until that time, the only sensible response to them remains one of open-minded prudence.

When it became obvious that I was not exactly

sweating blood over the terror tale that my caller was telling me, he became angry. He was obviously not used to disagreement, and questions infuriated him. I am a stubborn man and when I feel that somebody is trying to push me around, I tend not to go anywhere. His voice rose, he became strident. I finally concluded the conversation, as it was obvious that there was nothing to be gained from it. But I was shaken. This call had a big-time fanatic taste to it. I had visions of this gentleman arriving back here in the woods some night armed with kindling and a stake. I wanted to walk these woods being scared half to death by little men, not human fanatics with blood in their eyes.

So I decided I'd better get a handle on him. I needed a picture of him and knowledge of his whereabouts so that I could inform the local police that I had acquired my first lunatic. I did not, at that point, relate his rantings in any way to official policy.

The man's telephone number and address were in Dallas, and my brother, who is an attorney, introduced me to a Dallas detective who did work for law firms. He soon determined that the address was a mail drop, and that his calls were also being taken by a phone at the mail drop and automatically forwarded.

He was able to discover that the forwarded number went to yet another mail drop with another phone.

Now came a very major surprise. This second number was being forwarded to a Defense Department exchange located in Colorado.

The detective was quite disturbed to find that the Defense Department was involved, but I was about knocked flat. The Lear documents were just then surfacing, and this guy had talked about evil grays . . . I thought: they're trying to disinform me into the madhouse. I did not discover until later that this had already been attempted with Bennewitz.

Maybe if the scenario hadn't been so one-dimensional and so unlike my actual experiences, I would have gotten scared, like I was probably supposed to, instead of angry, which was what did happen.

I kept trying to follow the matter up. I called in my few pitiful political markers trying to find out who was on the other side of that Department of Defense exchange.

In the end, I discovered that the final destination of the calls was the home of a scientist, a physicist, who lived in the foothills of the Rockies near Boulder. When I called this final number directly and asked for the individual who had been telephoning me from behind so many safeguards, my request was met with a very long silence. Finally, the male voice on the other end asked, "Who is this?" It was not the voice I'd spoken to when calling the first number.

I said my name and repeated my request.

"How did you get this number?"

"This is the number he gave me."

"No. This is not that number."

"Why are you doing this? What's all this secrecy about? Why are you hiding behind a DoD screen?"

I found myself listening to a dial tone. I re-placed the call, but the line was busy. Two days later, it rang with no response. The day after that, it was listed as disconnected.

The detective then reappeared in my life. He had been threatened by the Boulder police, who said that they were going to charge him with impersonating an officer. How they came up with this idea, or why they even bothered him, we never found out. There were no charges filed, of course, but their sudden appearance out of nowhere does suggest that somebody may have been talking to them behind the scenes.

Matters remained unchanged for a couple of months,

when it came time for me to attend the World Affairs Conference at the University of Colorado in Boulder. While I was there, I planned also to visit the address in the foothills where the mysterious scientist lived. I found it easily enough, but the house proved to be empty. So I went down the road and knocked on a door of the nearest neighbor. I asked the lady who appeared, "Who lives there?"

She said that she did not know his name. I asked her if she had ever spoken with him. "No, he's very private."

"Any movement at night?"

At that point, a voice called to her from inside the house, and she shut the door in my face. I rang the bell, but nobody came. The neighborhood was extremely quiet and I became uneasy. I returned to the university area and did not try again to visit the house.

Some months later there was a terrible fire in the foothills above Boulder. Along with fifty-two others, the physicist's home was destroyed. By an apparent coincidence, I discovered from a report in a local newspaper that he moved to my area of upstate New York. By that time, though, I was too scared of the government to try to contact him.

Some really new thinking is going to be necessary if we are ever going to get past the tendency of the experience to mold itself to our expectations. I suspect that the government has had enough contact to trigger this process, but has not understood that what it is observing is constructed out of its own fears and expectations. They really believe that there is a cold war in the sky, I suspect, and that we must somehow ally ourselves with the good, familiar-looking blonds or we will be parasitized by the evil, ugly grays. And then there are awful lizard-men who enter the picture, but there seems to be little served by discussing them.

We need to reconstruct our whole attitude and

abandon the many camps that divide us now. There should be only one camp: all of us, this little band of creatures called mankind, standing together in an unsure world. It is out of such a stance that the truth will be gained, not out of the darkness, confusion, and superstition that seem currently to animate official thinking.

18

blood on mars

The first time that I came across a possible hidden government policy devoted to concealing evidence of extraterrestrials was in 1984. Although it apparently had nothing to do with the visitor encounters that began to unfold the next year, it appears perfectly possible that my immediate and powerful impulse toward disclosure encouraged the visitors to come closer to me.

In the early summer of 1984, Dr. John Gliedman, whom I had then known for about a year, telephoned me with an interesting proposition. Knowing of my interest in scientific anomalies, he wanted me to meet a most unusual man, Richard Hoagland. "Hoagland is an old friend of Margot's," he told me, referring to his wife, National Public Radio reporter and author Margot Adler. "He's on to something I think you'll find fascinating." So I met Hoagland, who showed me a fuzzy picture of what appeared to be a gigantic face staring up from a desert plain.

My first thought was that aerial archaeology had uncovered an incredible find in the Sahara or the Gobi or somewhere. When Hoagland told me that the picture, taken by the Viking Orbiter, was of Mars, I was quite surprised. He explained that the image had been discovered some years before by two NASA scientists, Vince DiPietro and Greg Molnaar, and examined by them using imaging techniques that were then state-of-the-art, but which were now surpassed by more accurate and detailed systems.

Even so, the results were startling, and I was certainly fascinated. Staring up from Mars's Cydonia plain was the haunting image of what appeared to be a human face. I was already aware that some of the critical tests on board the Viking Lander that had been designed to detect the presence of life in the soil of the red planet had returned a positive result. The planetary science community had ignored these results on the assumption that they couldn't be right because they didn't fit expectations. They were explained away, with some small plausibility, as unanticipated chemical reactions.

But I didn't expect that to be the response to this artifact, because I was well aware of NASA's early expectations regarding the possibility of finding extraterrestrial remains as we expanded into the solar system and of the policies it planned to follow when this happened.

In 1960 NASA had cooperated with the Brookings Institution to publish a report that said, "Many cosmologists and astronomers think it very likely that there is intelligent life in many other solar systems . . . artifacts left at some point in time by these life forms might possibly be discovered through our space activities." Carl Sagan had theorized in a 1963 paper that probability theory suggests that our solar system is likely to have been visited an average of once every ten thousand years by space-traveling civilizations.

So I thought that NASA would be ecstatic that these images had been uncovered in the mountain of data sent back by the Viking Orbiter.

NASA, as it turned out, would not deal with the pictures. They had rejected them as a trick of light. This perplexed me, since the importance attached to finding the remains of a nonhuman culture obviously mandated taking every chance that presented itself, no matter how long the odds.

In the years between 1960 and 1984, however, a great deal had changed at NASA. The most important evolution was that the space shuttle program had brought the agency into direct and extensive cooperation with the military.

In the 1960s, the notion that alien visits had probably taken place in the past was a commonplace of science. If artifacts had turned up, nobody would have been surprised. On the contrary, they would have felt the same elation that I experienced when I gazed at the Mars face.

By 1984, however, virtually the entire planetary science community was marching to the military band: we are alone here, we have always been alone, and there are no artifacts of intelligent visitation remaining from the past. Sagan, once a reasoned supporter of the simple mathematical probabilities involved, was now a fierce public exponent of the idea that—while artifacts might be found somewhere sometime—nothing under present study, no matter how compelling the evidence, qualified. He went to some quite startling lengths to debunk the Mars face—lengths to which, in fact, a scientist would not generally go and that seemed to me more related to propaganda than scientific discourse.

In the June 2, 1985, issue of *Parade Magazine*, Sagan appealed to the public in an effort to reduce interest in the face, and thus decrease pressure on NASA to explore it further. Sagan's strategy in abandoning scientific discourse at this point was correct, if his object was to discourage study. Public interest was the only thing that might compel NASA to do otherwise, since pressure from the scientific community would be in the opposite direction, as planetary scientists sought to protect cherished theories by avoiding observation of anything that might challenge them.

His article includes side-by-side photographs of the face, which appear to reveal that, at one sun angle, it is nothing more than a range of low hills. However, the two images reproduced were apparently not taken on an as-is basis from NASA's original output. Instead, the image that makes the face look like hills seems to have been processed by a special method called false-color imaging, in such a way that the normal shadows disappeared.

Of course, I realized then, as I do now, that there is a case to be made that the Mars face and its accompanying artifacts are natural formations. However, even if the case for an artificial origin was less strong than it is, a rational scientific community would be rabid to explore it, simply because even a long chance of finding an alien artifact is obviously worth substantial resources. The stakes are so high that the resolution of this question in an open, public context is the single most important reason to continue to explore Mars.

As that face stared up at me from the Cydonia plain, my imagination embraced the NASA of the past—that grand and so gloriously American organization, full of vigor and excitement—that had taken us to the moon and laid plans to go to Mars.

Hoagland explained to me that NASA would not do any more imaging on the face. He and the small group of scientists who had been drawn to the mysterious picture wanted to do more work, but they needed money.

Dr. Gliedman thought that I might agree to give a dona-
tion. He was right, and I was soon involved with the
group, which was known as the Mars Anomalies
Research Society, Inc.

On the committee were Dr. David C. Webb, who had
been a member of Reagan's National Commission on
Space, physicist John Brandenburg, Vince DiPietro, who
was one of the original imagers, writer Dan Drasin,
astronaut and planetologist Dr. Brian O'Leary, imaging
specialist Dr. Mark Carlotto, Randy Pozos, and Dr.
Gliedman. Dr. O'Leary is the original Mars astronaut,
and, if our Mars exploration program had not been
abandoned in favor of military objectives, he would
have been to the red planet and back by now.

Dr. Carlotto, who was a contractor for an intelligence
agency involved in reconnaissance, was in possession
of imaging equipment so advanced and so secret that
many of its controls had to be shielded from the eyes of
committee members without proper clearances. The
primary purpose of the equipment was to transform
satellite pictures into clear and accurate images with
high detail content. The fact that the Mars face was
reimaged on the best equipment known to man in 1985
and came out looking even more like a sculpture has
been efficiently suppressed. However, the results of
studies made with the TASC Corporation's equipment
were routinely used in the most sensitive of reconnaissance projects. Except for what he did on the face,
Carlotto's work was routinely assumed to be completely accurate.

My specific role was to finance the new analysis of
the data and subsequent study that Drs. O'Leary and
Carlotto undertook.

On December 13, 1986, the group met at Carlotto's
lab in Boston. At that meeting they reimaged the face
from the original Viking data. The picture that resulted

has become known worldwide, but Dr. Carlotto's reputation and the power of the equipment that was used to obtain the picture have been ignored by the press. Even though the public has apparently only been allowed to see false-color images compared to normal-contrast ones in the mass media, interest in the face has stayed high.

I did not attend the Boston meeting, because by that time I was struggling with the *Communion* experience and had withdrawn from direct participation in the committee out of concern that my connection with the UFO subculture would embarrass the other members and compromise the already tenuous standing of the project in the scientific community. The fact that "UFO zealots," in Dr. Sagan's words, are excited by the face was and is a major bar to science taking a serious interest. It should be remembered that my encounters started after I became interested in the face, not before.

I received in the mail a copy of the image that O'Leary and Carlotto had derived from the Viking telemetry. Staring up at me from the distant past and the depth of mystery was the strangest single thing I had ever seen, stranger far than the original Viking image, even stranger than the face of the alien I had peered into the year before. This was truly an enigma from another place and time: the face was no longer shadowy and tentative, it was quite clear. It glared up, teeth bared, as if raging at the very heavens.

Drs. O'Leary and Carlotto eventually published a paper in the *Journal of the British Interplanetary Society* that makes an impeccable case for the face being worthy of serious scientific investigations. This duly peer-reviewed monograph drew the interest of additional open-minded scientists to the face, and they were hopeful that the Mars Observer that was scheduled to go Mars orbital in late 1993 would provide much more detailed imagery.

Their hopes were dealt a blow by the apparent

destruction of the spacecraft just as it was making its orbital insertion maneuver, but NASA had already gone to such extraordinary lengths to keep the data it sent back secret that it probably wouldn't have mattered anyway.

To make certain that public access to all images from Mars would be strictly controlled, NASA secretly altered its long-standing policy of openness. By so doing, it defied its most fundamental public mandate, which is to operate as openly as possible. This is why we went live to the moon, and why America used to brag that space exploration in a free society should be open, in contrast to the Soviet Union's secretive approach.

Shifting to a more Sovietlike approach (ironically, as the Soviet Union collapsed) NASA granted a private company, Malin Space Science Systems, complete authority over all Mars Observer data returns. It did this through a legal fiction that Malin actually "owned" the pictures. In other words, these pictures, paid for in full by the American people, were to be first examined by Dr. Michael Malin, the owner of this company, and then released, if at all, only on his say-so.

Dr. Malin, of course, is a violent opponent of even photographing the face again. He appears to have been intended, in effect, to operate as a censor. But the public pays for NASA, and the public has an absolute right to know everything that NASA discovers, whenever possible at the moment the discoveries are being made. NASA's attempt to violate this principle would appear to be a fundamental repudiation of its public trust.

In the weeks before the Mars Observer was slated to go into orbit, public pressure to release all the images became stronger and stronger. But, like both of the Soviet Prometheus probes before it, which also had the potential to reimage the face, the Mars Observer ceased to report right before it arrived. There was suspicion that NASA may have aborted the mission rather than continue it and risk being forced by an outraged public to photograph the face. Others speculated that the mission continued in secret, that the people NASA had working on it were fired and a shadowy intelligence-gathering organization, the National Reconnaissance Office, allowed to take over.

I normally receive letters and electronic mail from ham operators quite soon after they hear any unusual telemetry from space. As of the late summer of 1994, I am fairly sure that the Mars Observer had not started reporting again on any of its publicly known frequencies. However, the National Reconnaissance Office possesses the capability to control the mission from the intelligence installation at the Goldstone tracking station, which can be patched into a 200-foot deep-space dish antenna and bypass all civilian information channels. Whether the Observer can communicate on unlisted frequencies or not I was unable to determine.

What, between 1960 and 1995, has transformed NASA from the enthusiastically public agency it was when it was founded into the secretive bureaucracy that exists today? Why was it so intent on controlling what we were allowed to see of Mars that it was willing to go to extraordinary, possibly even illegal lengths, to censor the pictures even before the Mars Observer apparently failed?

The reason may well be that the data from Cydonia strongly suggests that the face is not natural and if the Observer had confirmed the existence of artifacts on Mars, hard questions might soon begin to be asked about what is happening here on earth.

NASA's lack of openness does not end with the Mars mission. In February of 1992, Representative Howard Wolpe of Michigan discovered and released an internal NASA blueprint outlining how to evade the Freedom of

Information Act. This memorandum revealed that NASA employees were encouraged to destroy drafts of documents where possible, to print rather than use handwriting that is more easily identifiable, to avoid putting cross-references in documents and use stick-on notes that can easily be removed rather than annotating in margins.

Do we understand so much about our world that we only waste valuable public resources by studying things like the Mars face? Is the scientific community's narrow—and very recent—vision of mankind as an evolutionary isolate really true?

The Mars Committee and its various offshoots have struggled consistently over the years on behalf of the public interest. Their work is presented with great documentary force in Dr. Stanley V. McDaniel's 1993 book, *The McDaniel Report*, published by North Atlantic Books of Berkeley, California. This report should be required reading for anybody who cares about the future of public science.

As I write, the battle rages. NASA is, in 1994, attempting to make censorship of incoming data a permanent part of the exploration process—in other words, to institutionalize compromise of the public trust while appearing to serve it.

Frankly, the battle will end only when the treasure that our nation lavishes on space exploration is being expended by a new scientific organization that is staffed by open-minded and adventurous researchers and divorced from the military and the intelligence community. Ideally, it would be exclusively devoted to the free, open, and genuinely scientific exploration of the vast cosmic unknown, and everything it found would be available to all.

19

communion and the
intelligence community

About two years after I published *Communion*, I
received a phone call from my uncle, Colonel Edward
Strieber, who was a retired Air Force officer. He was a
brilliant and unusual man, for whom I had great respect
and love. I might add, at this point, that I have been
around him and other Air Force personnel all of my life,
and the criticisms directed at that organization in this
book do not extend to the courageous people who maintain our national defense, but to the bureaucracy which,
to a far greater extent than would seem wise, controls it.

My uncle told me that he was very proud of my having written *Communion*, and rather pointedly mentioned
that he had spent much of his career at Wright-Patterson

Air Force Base. I had learned about the significance of that base early on. It was where the debris from the Roswell UFO crash had been sent.

This crash had taken place near Roswell, New Mexico, in 1947, and had been the cause of much speculation as it had originally been admitted by the Air Force that it involved an extraterrestrial craft. Subsequently, General Roger Remy of the 8th Air Force changed that story and said that it was the remains of a radar target. However, in 1979, Major Jesse Marcel, who had originally gathered the debris for the Air Force, made public statements on videotape and in interviews with William Moore and Charles Berlitz for their book *The Roswell Incident* that the debris had some extraordinary properties, such as being as thin as cellophane but bulletproof, which could not be explained. In 1994 the Air Force, at congressional prodding, published another statement about the debris, this time claiming that it was the remains of a Project Mogul balloon that was being secretly used in an effort to detect sound waves from any possible Soviet nuclear test. This statement, carefully reported on the front page of the *New York Times*, fails to mention either that Major Marcel described the debris publicly as being of unknown origin in 1979, or that he was involved from 1948 in the very project that used the Mogul balloons and was certainly in a position to know the difference between their appearance and that of the debris he had recovered. The *Times* failed to mention Marcel—in fact, it failed to do any original research into the story at all and regurgitated the Air Force statement uncritically. The story was also picked up by the Associated Press, which added a touch of humor.

Even back in 1988 when my uncle called me, I already knew that something was wrong with the Air Force's public posture of denial in regard to the Roswell incident, because I had come into brief contact with a Dr. Robert Sarbacher while I was working on *Communion*, his name having been mentioned in *The Roswell Incident* as the author of a letter stating, quite simply, that he'd worked with debris from recovered flying saucers. His letter said, "I still do not know why the high order of classification has been given and why the denial of the existence of these devices."

In 1986 I searched Dr. Sarbacher out and had a telephone conversation with him, during which he stated that the debris he had worked on had some very unusual properties. "That fabric we obtained at Roswell had molecular welds so small you couldn't even identify what they were until the sixties, when the microscopes to do it became available." He understood that defense contractors were using this information in making seamless coatings that would cover "radar-proof" planes—which later emerged as Stealth aircraft. I also asked him if he had seen the material. He told me that he had seen it, examined it, and studied it. Was it of nonhuman origin? He answered: "What I can be certain about is that it was not produced by any technology that we were aware of in 1947. Or now." He said this in 1986.

Later, I sent him a detailed description of my experiences via UPS overnight. I didn't hear anything for a while, then received a telephone call from UPS. They could not deliver because the recipient was deceased. The UPS driver had been told that he had fallen off his boat and drowned.

Because I obviously could not obtain written confirmation from Dr. Sarbacher of what he had said to me on the telephone, I published only quotes from his letter in *Communion*. In view of the much more substantial evidence I now possess of the active involvement of the intelligence community at this point, however, I feel justified in repeating his remarks even though I kept no written record. He knew that he was speaking for public attribution, because I told him this at the time.

My uncle informed me that he had knowledge of the Majestic project. He spoke of the delivery of alien materials, artifacts, and biological remains to Wright Field from the Roswell Army Air Base in the summer of 1947. He felt sure that the existence of these materials and what to do about them had been debated at the highest levels of the government. At that time another officer who had personally handled the biological remains at Wright also told me of his experience. He said that the bodies he had observed had a "vegitative" quality, and that the internal organs were unformed. I asked how they could have lived. He said, "We thought they were possibly fakes. But not of this world. Certainly not."

In 1991, after I had written *Majestic,* my uncle put me into contact with a general—an old and trusted friend of his—who knew even more. This general, Arthur Exon, is the cousin of Senator Exon, who himself has been interested over the years in UFO-related subjects. The general appeared to me to have more knowledge of the debates my uncle had referred to, and seemed to think that President Truman, Secretary Forestall, and others had been involved.

Roughly a year after the publication of *Majestic,* I received a telephone call from a gentleman associated in an official capacity with the Congress, whose work related to budgetary matters and brought him into substantial contact with the intelligence community. My first reaction was to assume that this was another intelligence officer, and I came close to just hanging up on him. I asked for and received a detailed statement about his background and present employment. To my amazement, when I checked his credentials, it developed that he actually existed, and they were real. I asked friends in Washington about him and discovered that he was well respected and powerful in his area of expertise. As I got to know him and the people working with him, I gradually became more comfortable, but I never entirely lost a sense of caution, despite the fact that I became friends with him, and we have enjoyed many good times together. I have learned to respect his fierce integrity and dedication to the public good. It developed that he was part of a relatively informal investigation being conducted by his group and Senate staffers into whether or not the intelligence community has engaged in illegal activities in relation to UFOs.

There were two areas that concerned them. The first was that disinformation might have been spread by governmental organizations within the United States, illegally propagandizing the American people. Their major concern, however, was that there may be substantial secret activities being funded that have not been properly disclosed to Congress.

If this is true, it means that everything that the intelligence community does in this area is fundamentally against the law. The group had questions for me, and we set up a meeting for two weeks after the initial call. We met for lunch in New York, and there followed a three-hour conversation during which I was bombarded with questions about my sources in *Majestic*. I asked questions, too. Were there real aliens here? They thought something was being kept from Congress but did not know if this was it. But they were in a position to know with certainty exactly which classified programs had been reported to the Congress.

Later, I asked the leading member of this group what he thought the intelligence community might be hiding. His response was interesting. He explained that the U.S. government is the most complex human organization that has ever been created and that its operations are in many cases too intricate and too bound up in "need to know" secrecy for any single individual to understand. The illusion of policy can even emerge out of the complexity of the interactions between various individuals and agencies.

There are so many nooks and crannies, so many different power centers, so many secrets. The UFO matter could easily involve thousands of people and huge sums of money and hardly even cause a ripple, because no single individual or group, isolated within the context of its own secrets, would ever be aware of the true scale of overall activities. Rivalries, such as that between the CIA and the FBI or those between the various armed services, would further complicate matters by causing additional walls of secrecy and deception to be raised internally.

I was well aware of how fierce these rivalries could be. I once stumbled on an "unofficial" CIA operation that was disclosed to the FBI and broken up because it was taking place, in part, within the continental United States. Because my father had once had a relationship with the FBI, the CIA officers involved jumped to the conclusion that I had exposed them. Their fury toward me was absolutely amazing.

To make matters worse, government organizations tend to be vulnerable to infiltration from outside groups with missions of their own. An example of this sort of thing that involves the CIA has been in the news recently. One reason that has been advanced for the CIA's astonishing failure to predict the collapse of the Soviet Union has been the apparent fact that many low-level Soviet analysts were fundamentalist Christians who believed that the battle of Armageddon was going to be touched off by a Soviet-American conflict over the Middle East. So they simply failed to accept the evidence. The Soviet Union couldn't collapse because it didn't fit God's plan.

I asked my new informants if an organization as complicated as the intelligence and military infrastructure could possibly keep secrets. They responded that it was an excellent keeper of secrets, because the "need to know" concept compartmentalizes things so thoroughly.

I spoke with a reporter who specializes in the CIA. He explained that secrets not only get kept well, they also get lost. As individuals with clearance in a certain area retire, it is conceivable that files could become legally inaccessible to anybody on active duty. He felt that many things had been intentionally hidden in this manner, behind complicated walls of secrecy that will only be penetrated when and if massive declassification is undertaken.

After I had known the congressional staffers long enough to be comfortable, I began putting them into touch with various figures who had been involved at Roswell, as well as other military and intelligence personnel I felt might be helpful to them.

The investigation proceeded through the early nineties, always at a low level, always on a relatively informal basis. I heard subpoena powers mentioned a few times but never saw them exercised in pursuit of information.

One thing they concluded was that some of the suspicious projects were being funded by a mixture of public and private money, making them very hard to track. When they told me this, I could not help remembering a remark made to me by Jim Canaan, a reporter for *Air Force Magazine*. He said that the Joint Chiefs had told him that objects of unknown origin are tracked at the edge of space every year, that some are probably spy aircraft owned by foreign countries, some are debris, some of natural origin, and some private aircraft. What sort of private plane would be flying at—

say—a hundred thousand feet? The Pope, perhaps, on his way to a conference with St. Peter? To me, these are very serious issues. If gigantic private funding is somehow involved in UFO-related activities, this presents some pretty appalling implications. Who would be doing it, and how could private resources provide such enormous funds?

In my investigations into this area, I had intimations that shadowy secret societies were involved. However, I was never able to establish a link.

Before I began to give the staffers the names of my *Majestic* sources, I wrote material for them about the UFO community, offered them access to encounter witnesses, and developed character studies for them of various UFO researchers whom they asked me about.

During later conversations, the one I dealt with most frequently expressed a more developed concern that federal agencies might have illegally propagandized the public about UFOs. Again, his concern had two levels. The first was that the intelligence community might, for reasons of its own, be using UFO groups as conduits for stories designed to obscure secret activities, such as the flight of secret aircraft, and this would not be legal because Congress had not been informed of any aircraft with the flight characteristics being reported. The second flowed from the first. It was that the community could be using friendly scientists and media people to make certain that the public simply dismissed the whole UFO issue. If UFOs were, in fact, unexplained, this was an illegal activity.

He wanted to know why so many individuals with former or active military or official connections—people like Robert Lazar, Philip Klass, Richard Doty, and William Cooper—would all be involved in what might be disinformation. He agreed with me that the inner structure of the Dulce papers suggested the work of skilled disinformers and commented that "They're very good at what they do. The disinformation that I have seen is very well done, and it works."

Over the months that followed, I think that I questioned him almost as much as he did me. I learned, gradually, that he was quite certain that something was wrong with the way the intelligence community was reporting its knowledge about UFOs to Congress, and he felt that it was an important problem.

He also came to my cabin many times, usually arriving in the company of a person who worked within the intelligence community. To my knowledge, they never had an encounter with the visitors there. In 1991 and 1992, I noted that a small airplane would fly at high altitude in circles around the property in the predawn hours after encounters had taken place. It came once while they were present, but they did not think that anything had happened to them during the night.

One interesting thing that I obtained indirectly as a result of my conversations with these people was the idea that the defense contractor E. G. and G. Rotron might be in some way involved with witnesses. In early 1993, I had seen a fragment of an interview with a Rotron official that seemed to confirm not only that aliens existed, but that Rotron was working on defense projects relating to their presence.

The name of Rotron struck me, because I had heard it before under peculiar circumstances.

In late 1992, we'd been getting unpleasant telephone calls at our cabin, hang-ups in the middle of the night, sometimes accompanied by scary, sneering laughter. I'd been the only one to pick them up, and I really didn't want my wife or son to have to endure them.

So I called the telephone company's nuisance bureau and they suggested the installation of caller ID. It had only been available in our area for a short time, and I hadn't known about it. So I got caller ID at the cabin. A couple of weeks later, another of the calls came in, this one at about eleven at night. I looked on the caller ID, and there was a local number. I telephoned it, but there was no answer.

The next morning, I phoned again. This time a receptionist's voice said, "E. G. and G. Rotron." They have a facility in nearby Woodstock, New York.

I said, "My name is Whitley Strieber and somebody's been making nuisance calls to me from this number. I've got it on caller ID." There was a long silence, then another voice came on the line, a heavy, old-sounding male voice. I repeated my complaint. He said, "We'll look into it, and please accept our apologies." The calls did not recur.

In the autumn of 1993 I was signing books at a shop in Albany, New York. A man approached and said he had a story to tell me. A friend of his had experienced a visitor encounter. A few nights afterward, he'd been eating at a local diner when he'd been approached by two people, a man and a woman. They had told him that they knew of his encounter, and they would like to pay him a hundred dollars to go to a government facility and be examined. He agreed, only to find when they got him in the car that he was to have a hood put over his head. Because of his curiosity, however, he eventually agreed to this as well.

Once inside a building, he was unhooded and given a physical examination, which was apparently quite ordinary in nature. Then he was once again hooded and returned to the diner.

He spent some time working to find the location where he'd been taken. As he is very familiar with this area, he was eventually able to retrace the car's movements. When he had finished, he found himself at the Rotron facility in Woodstock. He had, of course, not the faintest idea about the Rotron connection that I had uncovered. Indeed, I got his name only because of a chance meeting.

Rotron is a public company, so I obtained copies of the annual reports, 10-K documents, and other official filings in order to learn more about its structure and known operations. It is a broadly based manufacturer of scientific and technical instruments, and also provides numerous different kinds of support services to commercial, industrial, and government entities. It has annual sales in excess of $2 billion. Some of its more substantial areas of operations involve support of the Department of Energy in relation to nuclear site cleanup and the providing of technical services both to private industry and government. It is the Base Operations Contractor for NASA at the Kennedy Space Center. In 1993, its Technical Services Division was reorganized into operating groups: Defense Materials, Management Systems, Special Services, and the Washington Analytical Services Center. As its defense-related activities decline, the company has been trying to move into nongovernment markets.

In my analysis of the company, I found that it had three very large shareholders: Invesco PLC, the University of California, and FMR Corporation. Among the three of them, they held about 16 percent of shares. Invesco is an investment company, and its holding reflects a profit motive. I did not examine the rationale for the University of California holding, and I was not able to obtain any information about FMR Corporation.

In addition to the small Woodstock facility, Rotron has extensive operations in Colorado; a facility on Mound Road in Miamisburg, Ohio, in the middle of the area once held by the archaic mound-builder Indian culture; as well as operations at Area 51 and supporting operations in Las Vegas.

I was not able to discover specific public information that linked Rotron to the UFO phenomenon, so I researched the local newspapers to see if there were any stories about the Woodstock facility.

It turned out that there had been so much nighttime truck traffic at one point that the company had been convinced after a long dispute to build a wall of trees so that the lights wouldn't bother the facility's neighbors. The local story is that there is an enormous classified records-keeping facility there and that the trucks bring secret files that date from before the computer era.

The Iron Mountain Records Storage Facility is a few miles away in Rosendale, New York, and the area is honeycombed with caves in iron deposits, which make very strong and secure underground storage spaces.

I was not able to discover anything else about Rotron and concluded the investigation—strange, even suggestive, but nothing definite.

My readers are like eyes and ears for me. Among many other things, they have provided me with considerable information about government complicity of interest to the congressional staffers. One wrote that he was retired Air Force and had been involved in counterintelligence. He had assisted in the development of contingency plans designed for Air Force and other military officials to ridicule members of the public who came forward with reports about anything of extraterrestrial origin.

If this is a true statement—and, sadly, I fear that it may be—then our military and intelligence communities are actually engaged in the very sorts of illegal activities that the congressional staffers are concerned about.

After I began cooperating with them, I came under investigation by unknown parties. My New York apartment was staked out by people who were so obvious that they might as well have had "Gumshoe" printed on the backs of their gray suits. I hired a detective who took their license numbers and said they appeared to him to be undercover police. I was about to complain to the city, but he explained that his opinion was that they were federals because the license numbers were all from Ulster County, where, in his experience, he had found that U.S. agencies often register their unmarked cars.

So I complained to the congressional group. A few days later, the cars ceased to jam my street. That became a pattern. Get hassled, complain, they would go away for a time.

In late 1993, I got a piece of e-mail that purported to be the coded file locations of super-secret UFO information in the Defense Department computer system. I sent it to the main congressional investigator.

Spooks started prowling around my neighborhood upstate. A business associate was accosted on an airplane by a group of young men who flashed badges, claimed to be with the National Security Agency, and questioned him about our activities for a couple of hours. They alleged that they were responsible for investigating intrusions into the Defense Department's secure computer systems, but did not ask him directly about the document I had received. My business associate was not aware of the document, in any case.

On May 21, 1994, my upstate cabin was entered by people who were able to suppress the security system, but I determined from the internal records it keeps when they had come and how long they had stayed. They not only examined the contents of my computer, they left a virus on it that took weeks to defeat. They stole a $5,000 endorsed check, but we had it voided before it could be cashed.

The Criminal Investigation Division of the New York State Police investigated this intrusion, but would not proceed because they thought that its structure was highly unusual and I could not produce enough evidence to satisfy them.

On November 10, 1994, there was another entry, at about two in the afternoon. As I had taken steps to increase the security, it was not possible for the entry to be effected without the alarm going off. When sheriff's deputies arrived, however, they found that they could not reach the area of the house because the automatic gate had been rendered inoperative. Later in the day, the gate began working again. The system recorded movement throughout the house over a twenty-minute period. This time nothing was taken.

In September 1994, the flow of mail from the public dropped from an average of 300 letters a month to just a few letters. I sent myself a total of twenty-one letters between September 1994 and January 1995, but none arrived. A postal investigation went nowhere. Ed Conroy told me that, while he was writing his book about me, he had been officially informed that his mail was being opened in the course of an investigation. The only letters that were stickered with forms stating that they had been opened related to UFOs and to me.

I kept the congressional staffers informed of all this, carefully documenting each incident. I note that it is not illegal to be interested in UFOs, and the government does not have the right to pursue investigation of people not under suspicion of criminal activity.

The electronic mail document that I received, it turned out, is readily available in many places online. It can be downloaded, for example, from the New Age Forum library on Compuserve. It's listed in the library section "UFO: Theories" under the title "Hackers Find UFO Information." It is in the public domain, and I have excerpted relevant parts in appendix 1.

20

what is wrong?

Publicly, the United States government knows nothing. Privately, it—or somebody concealing themselves within it—is extremely nervous. As it now seems apparent that the visitors are real, they have reason to be. By simply making a slow pass over New York City at midday, remaining visible long enough to force the television networks to react, the visitors could completely discredit the whole cover-up.

I have been privileged to have communication with a certain number of people in government, stretching across two administrations, who are telling me that there is no public policy that would account either for the harassment that I have endured or that governs any federal knowledge about extraterrestrials whatsoever.

But if there is no policy, then why am I experiencing what certainly appears to be serious investigative and even intimidatory pressure? Since 1985, the only conceivable reason anybody would have an official interest in me has to do with the visitors, and this pressure reached a peak after I transmitted the codes found in "hacker.txt" to congressional investigators.

I am certain that there is no congressional awareness, not even secret, of what would appear to very substantial black budget expenditures in this area. Because of this basic lack of knowledge of the matter on the congressional level, all activities that have been undertaken at any level must flow from a circumvention of the law. The scale is massive, ranging from the small illegality involved in the intimidation of a Linda Jordan or Whitley Strieber or Paul Bennewitz to the large-scale felonies that may have been perpetrated if officials have propagandized the American public. For example, in spreading its Project Mogul explanation for the Roswell incident to Congress and to the people, the Air Force may have been involved in extraordinary crimes. This may have been true earlier, as well, if its Project Blue Book was also propaganda.

In April 1988, I went before an audience at the University of Colorado to speak about the visitors. I was introduced by Dr. Walter Orr Roberts, the President Emeritus of the National Oceanic and Atmospheric Administration. Dr. Roberts was an open-minded and very fair man. Years before, he had been asked to chair Project Blue Book and had turned the job down. When I asked him why, he responded that he had done it because he was told at the outset that the project was intended to draw the conclusion that there is nothing in the UFO controversy, and he did not feel comfortable with the fact that public claims were being made that the study was impartial.

If the Air Force hid information from the Blue Book committee, caused it to be suppressed, or somehow induced the drawing of conclusions it knew to be untrue, there was violation of the law.

Although the government possesses, to an extent, the right to lie to protect duly constituted official secrets, there is no secret so great that it can legally be kept from the appropriate congressional committees.

The nature of our system of secrecy, with its strictly compartmentalized classification, tempts the intelligence community to conceal its mistakes behind a fallacious cloak of national security. If the wall of illegal secrets is ever breached, what we are likely to find on the other side is, in addition to a small amount of amazing information, a sea of misconceived projects on which vast sums have been spent and a staggering array of other abuses, including illegal surveillance of members of the public not involved in criminal activities. It is not against the law to be interested in the visitors or UFOs, but it is against the law to invade the privacy of innocent citizens.

I believe that the reason that this has all happened is that the supervisory links between the intelligence community and the elective government have probably been seriously undermined. It seems likely that there are people making policy without reference to our national leaders and carrying out that policy behind an entirely illegitimate veil of secrecy.

Normally, one would turn to the press for help in a matter like this. In a healthy situation, investigative reporters could be expected to become very aggressive. But if past experience is any indicator of future behavior, the press will continue to respond inadequately.

The reason for this is twofold. First, from the early years of the controversy back in the forties, the press has operated from the basic assumption that the visitors are not real and cannot possibly be real. Two generations of European and American journalists have supported this idea, and most of the great institutions of the press are completely committed to it. Basing their understanding of the facts on what the press has claimed, the entire thinking community of the Western world has supported it as well. As a result of this it has gained an overwhelming cultural momentum that is entirely unsupported by the facts.

The second part of the reason is exclusively American. In this country, the press has gradually ceased to actually uncover its government-related stories and has become more and more reliant on dissemination of releases. This is why the *Times* published the Air Force's transparent explanation of the Roswell debris as the remains of a balloon without the slightest reference to the other side of the controversy—and why, if it should ever readdress the matter, it will only be to justify its former conclusions.

I feel that the weight of this commitment is so great that it cannot be broken by normal proof, such as that I have offered. It will take overwhelming proof. Barring that, I do not see a situation in which any great news organization will alter its stance even to one of neutrality.

However, it is also true that the emergence of the visitors is an organized, coherent process that is moving according to a schedule. From the first intimations of their existence in the late forties to the reports of deep communion that are now beginning to appear, the journey toward contact has been quite systematic. During this entire time, and despite the remarkable way in which the large-scale structure of the evidence suggests a slow, steady approach with every indication of intelligent management, there has been a consistent reluctance on the part of established elements of our culture to investigate rationally.

It is hard to believe that this would have continued as long as it has without substantial pressure being applied on many different levels. By intimidating witnesses, it could be that the holders of the secrets are attempting to interrupt the visitors' schedule. I would doubt that they have much chance of achieving this, given the extraordinary persistence, precision, and insight that the visitors display. It is likely that the secrecy has, to a great extent, played into the visitors' hands, and will collapse exactly when they want it to collapse, and not a moment sooner or later.

Until we begin to see them in an accurate manner, they obviously cannot come into meaningful relationship with us, for the filter of expectation is clearly a powerful one. Because we have never encountered a living mind from outside our world, we do not know the degree to which our expectations, in this case, actually affect the appearance of reality. Given this problem, the visitors could well find themselves unable to reach us without interruption from our own fears, superstitions, and confusion. If this is the case, an ethical approach would have compelled them to minimize contact until our vision became more clear. They would, under this theory, be quite helpless to do much more than they are doing, and secrecy would be needed if the damaging effects of our misconceptions were to be kept to a minimum.

But all this is changing. The fact that they have offered proof of their reality—however gingerly it has been presented—suggests that we are making progress. What concerns me now is that the important elements of the society that are so deeply committed to denial will be unable to adjust when it becomes untenable.

At some point, awareness of them is going to become so general that science, government, and the press are going to take a severe blow. Their viability as institutions will be called into question just when they could be at their most useful.

This problem may be quite apparent to people on the inside. There certainly seems to be an element almost of

desperation at the deeper levels of the cover-up. Barry
Goldwater has reported that General Curtis LeMay
became furious at him when he asked to see remains
that he had heard were stored at Wright-Patterson Air
Force Base. If General LeMay knew that the elective
government had been systematically removed from policy making and supervision in this area, his anger at an
inquisitive senator would be understandable.

That UFOs were a subject of interest at Wright for a
long time is beyond question. On July 6, 1994, a document was declassified stating that, as of October 1947,
the Air Materiel Command at Wright was conducting
wind-tunnel tests of the flying saucer shape based on
models derived from witness accounts.

Shortly after entering office, the Clinton administration was approached—as every administration since
Carter's has been—by UFO organizations asking that
they locate and release information believed to be hidden. In response, the office of the President's Science
Advisor asked for a briefing about UFOs from the CIA.

The CIA replied that it had no information, but it
invited well-known UFO investigator Dr. Bruce
Macabee to conduct a briefing. Macabee apparently convinced administration officials that the CIA had not told
the whole story, because further questions were asked.
A classified briefing was then given. Macabee was not a
participant in this briefing, and I do not know if he was
aware of it.

This briefing may well have revealed the fact that
various intelligence organizations, most notably the Air
Force Office of Special Investigations, have at times
spread stories about UFOs in the public press as a cover
for the visible activities of secret aircraft.

Sometime soon, the Air Force is planning to disclose a
new type of aircraft—the inheritor of technology developed under the project name Aurora—with a revolution-

ary propulsion system that has been the source of much public speculation. This aircraft flies at least seven times the speed of sound and uses something sometimes described in the press as a "pulse-detonation wave" engine, sometimes as a "coronal discharge" device. They will reveal that this device has been tested at Area 51. If the same strategy that has been used in the Project Mogul matter is applied, they will say that testing of this technology explains flying saucers—which are, of course, the actual point of origin of the technology. However, I wish to make clear that I am not suggesting that there has been a direct technology transfer of any kind. I do not think that there has been extensive acquisition of alien technology. I don't think that the intelligence community has much really functional contact with the visitors at all. If they did, the structure of their response would be far more cogent and appropriate that it is.

It is more likely that Aurora has been based not on a knowledge of visitor technology, but on observation of its capabilities. It may be far from that technology. For example, if a two-dimensional creature with absolutely no concept at all of solids observed a ball moving through his flat world, what he would see would be a point that became a line that moved toward him, then receded, became a point again, and disappeared. He could make a line of his own that did that, but he would never have the faintest idea that the ball even existed.

Observably, the visitors have often acted in ways that suggest such large-scale awareness that it may well originate in a perceptual system that is, in effect, more than three-dimensional. Technology designed by such people might be inaccessible to us for perceptual, not intellectual reasons, and until that level of our own brains comes into use we may be able to do no more than emulate, to some extent, those of its capabilities we can comprehend.

I was quite interested in the degree to which Aurora
might emulate the capabilities of UFOs, and tried to
learn all I could about it. I found that it was an ordinary
line-item in the Air Force's budget for many years,
sometimes very richly funded. It was said to be a fighter
aircraft, but certain things that I discovered suggest that
the propulsion system might have some unique elements.

In the early eighties, Project Aurora had a facility in
the southeast that was making substantial electrical
demands on the Tennessee Valley Authority's system.
Residents of the area near this installation often
observed bright lights floating about in the fields and
overhead at night, lights that seemed to some to be flying saucers, to others to appear to be balls of static electricity of some sort. These are not unlike the phenomena
sometimes reported around Area 51 and could represent
Aurora at various stages of development.

I note that one of the few relevant CIA documents
that has been released under the Freedom of
Information Act mentions an assumed magnetic propulsion system for UFOs. The very name of Project Aurora,
referring as it does to the visible manifestation of earth's
magnetic field, suggests a connection.

Could all the secrecy cover a vastly expensive,
decades-long effort to build a flying saucer based only
on backwards-engineering from their observed maneu-
vers and a little crash debris?

I cannot help but mention that there might have been
a similar response to observations of ultra-advanced
technology during World War II. When the natives of
New Guinea saw airplanes for the first time, and
observed them landing and disgorging an incredible
wealth of food, they built "airfields" complete with
bamboo replicas of the planes, in the hope that beer and
cigarettes would come out. If Aurora has indeed been

backwards-engineered, it is possible that the gulf between its technology and that of the visitors is as great as was that between the natives' planes and those of the Air Force. However, Aurora has been somewhat more costly to us than the bamboo replicas were to the natives.

My readers, who were a marvelously sensitive choir of informants, have had reports to deliver. An aircraft was described by a technician who observed it at an air base abroad in 1989 as a large triangular craft, silvery, but translucent. A red light under it was visible through its body. It was floating a few feet off the floor of the hangar in which he saw it. Was this a project Aurora vehicle? Many UFOs have been described as having a triangular shape, most notably enormous craft that seemed to be made of girders and appeared over the Hudson Valley in the seventies and early eighties. Was Aurora operating in the Hudson Valley at that time—an experimental aircraft being flown at night over popu- lated areas? Some of the craft were measured to be a thousand feet long. At the time they were debunked as a flight of ultralight aircraft capable of operating at night with silenced engines.

However, there is another incident that might have involved Aurora. It could be that the extensive series of UFO sightings in Belgium that took place in 1989 were, at least in some cases, Aurora craft being operated to later provide an illustration of how the testing program resulted in UFO claims.

Of course, the whole approach would be fallacious because there are extraordinary sightings reported from long before the United States had anything remotely resembling Aurora. A reader has written me, "Back after World War II, I was engaged in transarctic ferrying mis- sions, moving aircraft to and from occupied Japan. We took many films of flying saucers as they came in above the Arctic circle. Some of this was very clear film." He goes on to say that the film was always moved up the chain of command and he never knew what happened to it. Another recalled that his naval flotilla had encountered a massive cylindrical object floating at low altitude in the Pacific in 1957. This extraordinary device was determined to be 350 feet in diameter and over 4,000 feet long. Photographs were taken. "The film was airlifted to headquarters to be developed, and I would dearly love to know where those photographs are today."

In addition, there were many unexplained sightings in the fifties that could not have been accounted for by secret aircraft. On August 28, 1953, a Ground Observer Corps observer in California contributed a report of fourteen cigar-shaped objects without wings. In 1954 the Maxwell AFB tower observed an object that was given reconnaissance by a helicopter and determined to be an authentic unknown. In June 1955 RB-47 aircraft over Canada observed silver metallic objects on two occasions and tracked them on radar. These are only a few of hundreds of such reports that give the lie to any claims denying the authenticity of the mystery by suggesting that it is explained by our own secret aircraft.

Why must it be this way? What is all this secrecy about? Undoubtedly, in the early fifties, it must have looked like an invasion so horrible and incomprehensible that secrecy and prayer were the only alternatives. Had the president announced that there were aliens here who were absolutely terrifying and completely uncontrollable, the panic would have been intense.

But the invasion did not happen. Fifty years have passed, and the invading army is still lurking around in the shadows. So, obviously, the original conclusion was not correct. It may be that the government legitimately believed that it was protecting us from the visitors when they first came, but now that they have proved not to be an invading force, it would seem that whoever still clings to the old secrets is using the system of classification for the considerably less noble purpose of concealing some serious mistakes.

However, I must also note that individuals formerly at Wright have alluded to a top-secret scientific paper that alleges that the ability of the visitors to enter our reality is mediated by the degree to which we acknowledge their existence and that the "invasion" can be literally held at bay by orchestrated denial and general disbelief.

If science fiction like this is at the heart of the cover-up, then I must conclude that the physicists who had the opportunity to consider the situation were not capable of thinking about it clearly, no matter their credentials.

We have never encountered anything real before that had this same plastic, unfocused quality—at least not in the large-scale universe, which is supposed to function along predictable mechanical lines. Contact, in its present embryonic state, is a sort of clay, and so far we have allowed our emotions to mold it in obedience to our fears. But we are capable of much more. We can reconstruct it in a more realistic mode, and, in the end, we can determine the true nature of what lies on the other side of our present confusion, and learn to relate to it usefully.

The part of the secret government responsible for the situation does not want us to know that it spent billions backwards-engineering a flying saucer while publicly scoffing at their mere existence. It does not want us to know that it does not understand the visitors and that it is trapped in perceptions of them governed by its own fears, just like the rest of us. It lives in terror that the giant is going to climb down the beanstalk of public acceptance, and so spends its energy continually chopping at it.

But human consciousness desires to live and needs to grow, and keeps thrusting upward and breaking through the various levels of denial and derision and cover-up, functioning like the eager, striving weed that it is.

There is no situation in government that illustrates more clearly than this one the fact that the bureaucracy has become, in effect, a dictatorship. In any revamping and downsizing of the overall federal system, there needs to be included a complete restructuring of the intelligence community. For example, the Freedom of Information Act should be greatly strengthened and attempts to evade it, such as that made by NASA, should be criminalized. We should rethink the whole vast system of classification that has come to compromise freedom in our republic. Official secrets should be confined to foreign-policy necessities. The United States government should return to being the open institution of tradition. Organizations such as the CIA, the National Security Agency, and the National Reconnaissance Office, with its clandestine and luxury-loving leadership in their palatial new quarters, cosseted in marble and rare woods, should be consolidated into a single and fundamentally public enterprise. The role of the FBI's intelligence gathering operations should be defined in the context of giving this organization a new charter concentrating federal investigative authority, both domestic and international, under one umbrella. Military intelligence operations such as the Office of Naval Intelligence and the Air Force Office of Special Investigations should be strictly confined to the gathering of hardware-related military intelligence, and the Air Force should be put out of the business of presenting public "studies" such as the Blue Book and Project Mogul rubbish. All federal intelligence activities should be overseen in detail by a civilian review board with absolute powers to declassify, and fully answerable both to Congress and the executive. The clearly stated objective of this board should be to minimize classification, and it should be required to provide public listings of all classified documents and at least a general idea of the areas they cover. Declassification should be automatic and mandatory after twenty-five years.

But the sheer inertia of the situation mitigates against reforms like these. Although the electoral changes of 1994 make it clear that the people are tired of the punishing weight of this generally incompetent and fantastically expensive bureaucracy of ours, it remains to be seen if Congress will ever find a way to open the safe to the owners of the files without compromising our nation's very needed ability to gather and hold genuine secret intelligence.

Despite the overall bleakness of the cover-up picture, there are some signs of restlessness within the elective government. An uneasy General Accounting Office has begun to investigate the possibility of a UFO cover-up, although individuals close to the situation now suggest that its investigation may be just another attempt to strengthen the cover-up initiated by congressmen who are privately briefed and illegally supporting it, because they have been convinced that the public acceptance that will result from official acknowledgment of the visitors will enable the feared invasion. Because it is so extensive, no organization with the investigative power of the GAO could examine this area without discovering at least some clear evidence that the cover-up exists. Whether the GAO will be honest remains to be seen.

Other high-level congressional staff in a position to

know for certain what the intelligence community has disclosed to the appropriate committees and what it has not are more than uneasy, they are angry and concerned that a massive breach of the law is taking place.

One of them expressed his very troubled thoughts in an interview given to me on December 2, 1994.

21

congress smells a rat

I know this man well; as I have stated, I have been working with him and his colleagues since 1992. Whether or not their work will continue in the new Congress, I do not know.

I asked him, "Why have you taken an interest in the question of intelligence community involvement in a possible cover-up of knowledge that UFOs may be unexplained?"

"If the phenomenon is real, it clearly poses a series of national security questions of the first order. Obviously, if there is advanced technology in possession of a hostile force, there is a national security issue of paramount importance. These are issues that the Congress has a legal right to know about."

He had originally entered my life as a result of having read *Majestic*. I wanted to know what about the book had made him do this.

"I wasn't certain that it was fictional. It led me to think that somebody might have opened up to you."

"Of course, that had happened. I told you about the people involved."

"The way it was described in the book was pretty much along the lines that one would expect. It was close to the way that such programs are actually carried out. So I felt that there was a very strong possibility that (a) you had been approached by someone and (b) that the timeline was reasonable. There was a generation of men who would be dying who would maybe be having second thoughts about the reasonableness of keeping secrets that they had kept earlier, and might be breaking the rules they'd lived by."

"Yes."

"This was a likely way for someone like that to go about revealing it. It seemed to me plausible from that perspective."

He had not met with any of the Roswell figures directly, but he knew of conversations that other cleared staffers had had with them. "I believe that you are aware of discussions with General Arthur Exon and Sheridan Ware Cavett by cleared congressional staffers."

"Yes. Cavett totally denies everything. Consistently. Even to people who've interviewed him on behalf of GAO. But he did say something that was interesting. He said, 'Of course, if you did stumble on something, you wouldn't reveal it, would you?' While it could just be the statement of a very dedicated and conservative intelligence officer, it led me to wonder whether or not this man was so dedicated that even now he was still upholding security, or what he perceived to be his oath. When he took his oath, Congress would have been out of the loop."

"You're saying that his oath, as he perceives it, flows from something that is not superseded by the system in place today?"

"It flows from the system that was in place then. The security system that was in place in the late forties really didn't include any kind of regular involvement of Congress. It was only after the excesses of the sixties that congressional oversight became law. The rules that he played under in the forties said that Congress was not supposed to be involved."

"And since the GAO is a congressional body—"

"Exactly. Probably doesn't include Congress in the loop."

"I think that General Exon had that view."

"General Exon is afraid. He was afraid he was being monitored at that point. He was probably afraid his whole house was bugged."

When I originally spoke with General Exon after being introduced to him by my uncle, he was quite straightforward about the fact that he felt that the Roswell debris was extraterrestrial and that the issues it raised had been debated in the White House. In interviews for public attribution that he agreed to later, he was much more guarded.

"My impression is," I said, "that a number of people have made quite specific claims about an extraterrestrial presence on earth while they were on active duty." I was referring to apparent disinformation, such as the story that has been repeated on television and is attributed to former Air Force personnel, about the alien that was captured and interviewed after his throat had been repaired. I wanted to know if he felt that such statements, if they were false and had been made under orders, would be legal.

He pointed out that the bizarre stories could be told for many reasons—even as a prank. However, he continued, "If it is deliberate disinformation, then I think it's probably a violation of the law, because propagandizing the American public is forbidden by statute." He continued, "My sense of this is that some of what has gone out is probably disinformation, and it's very troubling to me. If there is an official kind of locomotion to this, that officials are orchestrating this, then we are in a very serious situation. They are in violation of the law, and whoever is responsible for it is guilty of a conspiracy to defraud the American people. It's a problem area that troubles me. These people may just be jokers who have been in the military. But if there is a concerted official effort to confuse the public about what's going on, there are serious violations of the law involved."

It must not be forgotten at this point, that the combination of this, plus the fact that Congress has apparently been denied its legally mandated oversight in this area, means that every individual presently engaged in any cover-up activity, the spreading of stories and rumors, or investigation of witnesses or maintaining of secrets relating to possible alien presence—should such secrets actually exist—is involved in a felony. No investigation of any witness for UFO-related activity is a legal investigation, and federal and state law enforcement agencies assisting in such investigations at the behest of higher authorities are furthering an illegal conspiracy, as are judges granting orders in their support.

I asked him his current opinion of the Roswell incident, given the fact that the Air Force has now claimed that the debris was the remains of a secret balloon.

He responded, "Well, that's not different from saying it's a weather balloon. To say that it was some kind of a secret balloon doesn't impress me too much. My sense of the Roswell thing is, based on what I've read about it and the investigating I've done, that the evidence is almost overwhelming that this debris was not a balloon and it was a sophisticated device of great importance to the national security establishment. There has never been any kind of a briefing or explanation to Congress that it was anything other than a weather balloon or another known object. The balloon story is false. I'm driven, given my investigation, to conclude that this was not American, it was not under our control, and it was of great interest to us. Whether it was terrestrially based or not I do not know. The fact is, that something happened of great importance and it was covered up. It was covered up in a way that indicates a very concerted, organized effort at the highest levels to do so. Given the statements of witnesses and all the other evidence, one is led to believe that a national security event of the first order occurred. That is my conclusion."

As so the matter stood, in December 1994.

22

Aeon

I felt, after finishing the last chapter, that I might be done with *Breakthrough*. It was a strange feeling because the book is more than a chronicle of eight years with the visitors. In a sense, it is the outcome of my life. I have given all that I can to it, and with all its faults, it is the best effort I can make on behalf of a richer future for us.

Central to my life has always been my great love of children and thus also of mankind, and this more than anything I have ever written is my homage to the wonder and beauty I find in my fellow human beings.

Last night, a man told me that the visitors had predicted that Japan would fall into the sea in 1996. I explained to him that the catastrophe he was seeing was probably inside us, not outside. We are changing; the old mind is what is falling into the sea. He said that the "Gray Empire" is about to attack from its base in Zeta Reticuli and that we'd better get ready to fight them off by allying ourselves with the "Nordic"—the angels to the "gray" demons.

It was the same tired old cold war scenario, this time cast in terms of armageddon and the millennium and remolded to fit fundamentalist Christian beliefs.

I thought to myself, there are so many forces arrayed against the visitors, how can they ever get through to us? And then I thought, "they already have." Of course they have. They've already defeated the fearmongers. Now all that remains is for each of us to come to terms with them in our own way.

I have seen incredible glimpses of what it will be like to possess the new level of mind that they seek to awaken in us. Even though all of my cherished beliefs were challenged, I have come away with my relationship to God immeasurably enhanced. My old childhood prayers have reentered my life, reforged into spiritual arguments of unexpected potency. At the same time, I have found immediate contact with the divine in the commonplace of my life. I have been deeply angered by much unjust treatment because of my work, but have also found that forgiveness can be more than an act of the moment, it can be a way of life. I have surrendered my anger.

My questions, some answered and some not, have come to rest inside me. I not only feel that real communion with the visitors is possible, I have the expectation that it is going to open us to a new scale of being, to enable us to taste at last of the sacred light that floods the universe. Their example offers us the potential to attach ourselves, also, to this mighty dimension of soul.

In light of its value as the one thing that can certainly assure our evolution into the universe, it is understandable to me that they have been willing to put us under such tremendous individual pressure on behalf of our gaining it. I now understand what they meant when they told me, "We have a right."

As a fledgling is pushed from the nest or a baby muscled down the channel of birth, we are being pushed and prodded toward this new life. All of the remarkable effects that we experience in the visitors' company are a promise that we can participate in higher being as fully and completely as they can. Many are already living this, in a small way, as a daily reality. The dead walk again; from the depths of the earth to our highest place in heaven, all our hands are joining.

In early January 1995, there was a repeat of the incident during which I hurled the table across the room. This time, I was sitting in the dark and meditating. Somebody came into the room. I felt a sort of ecstasy of the body, as if all my cells were dancing. This time, I was not afraid, but rather full of pleasure at seeing once again somebody who has become a close friend.

I got up and lay down upon the bed with my eyes closed. For some time, I heard that perfect breathing at my bedside, in and out, in and out, never varying. When the movement came, as I knew it would, I felt a warmth come inside me, and then it seemed as if somebody else was mixed in some way with me, mind and body.

I was in a sharing for which we have made no words. It was not possession. I was never under attack. On the contrary, I tasted of emotions and memories and ideas of such vitality and scope that it could easily take more than a lifetime of words to describe them—if words could even do it. I suppose that the whole of time was shimmering there, time and worlds upon worlds. Then there was a withdrawal—gentle, immensely poignant—that spoke of other days and times yet to come. I saw that the sharing is not actually with a single person, but rather with a whole species or cycle of many species in all their richness, glory, and startling simplicity. I suspect that through the medium of each other, we touched the mystery of all.

From this short period of deep sharing, I have seen that the transformation I have been writing about is not only a change of mind, but a thoroughgoing revision of being. If this evolutionary movement plays itself out as it seems it must, many things are liable to change.

I saw that we have fundamentally misunderstood the true nature of things such as out-of-body experiences. Many—like the Whitley of ten years ago—assume that this is a form of hallucination. Others perceive it as something much more real, as I have since I met the visitors. But the message of this experience, it seems, is not that we have a separate soul or an ability to leave the body, but rather that there we are integrated beings with marvelous capabilities that we have not yet tapped.

The message is clear: we are our own greatest resource, and there is someone here willing to take us by the hand—or nudge us or push us or kick us if need be—to help us find that out.

The reason that the visitors are addressing us on a person-by-person basis is that this is probably the most efficient way to convince us that the larger world is real. The pressure—all the tough treatment, all the fearful stories and corrosive questions—has to do with forcing us to act on our own behalf, because there is nothing else we can do.

I lived this, I faced unendurable terrors in the night for years until I just got sick of my own fear. How did I survive? I'm perfectly healthy, and I've wobbled a few feet on my own in the higher world, which felt very much like my first steps.

Others have gone farther than me, some maybe a lot farther. But many more can go, a critical mass can be reached, we can transform ourselves.

The analogy of the baby at birth is an exact representation of our present state as a species. The earthly womb is reaching her limits. To continue to live and grow, we must evolve. It may be that we will be able to survive as we are for another fifty or hundred years. But what does that little blink of time matter? Human consciousness is the product of billions of years of earthly struggle, and we must cease to look at our future in terms only of a few decades. We must, in each generation, do our part toward the greater goal of advancing the precious creation that is us into eternity.

Many things have fallen away, many fears. For the visitors there remains only love, both for the part of them that appeals to me and the part that I find ugly, and all the equivocal, maddeningly ambiguous material that falls into neither of those categories. In the same way that I have found real love for my fellow man and my own flawed self, I have found it for them. If we discovered a species at our own shuddering edge and had the capacity to literally pour ourselves into its life, we would make many mistakes, especially if we saw that the most important thing we had to offer them was our own fierceness. The visitors are not a monolithic presence. They are at least as complicated as we are, and probably a lot more. In their overall approach to us, with its combination of determination, ugliness, secrecy, and dizzying excitement, we probably see revealed the first true artifact of their culture that we have been able to detect. Beyond that, the vast array of difference between individual encounters must reflect a whole host of different individuals with differing beliefs, modes of approach, ideas and ideals, some kind and wise, others harsh and impatient, some altruistic, others exploitative, and many displaying in their stiff movements, their use of soporifics and their extraordinary wariness, a fear of us that must be at least as great as ours is of them.

We have entered a period of great acceleration, and will obtain explosive new knowledge about ourselves and the nature of the real even as the pressure our numbers place on our planet compromises its ability to nurture us.

The crisis of our species will come when our growing population interrupts biospheric renewal in ways that seriously diminish the planet's ability to support us. In the context of the changes that will follow, there will be severe economic dislocation and political confusion. But mankind's eyes will be opened at the same time by the extraordinary new vision of being that has been placed before us.

Our science will make huge leaps at that point. In our struggle to save ourselves, we will discover the way in which consciousness actually directs the structure of the material world, and become able to design artificial intellects greater than our own, which will propel us higher still. An understanding of gravity will come when we discover the true place of mind in the skein of forces that links the universe together.

We will also see the miracles hidden in the stars. But there is within us as well a strain that leads downward, and because of it all these changes will be accompanied by suffering. It sings many lying songs—mainly versions of the most deceptive tune of all, that all will remain essentially as it is now. It will not remain the same.

Where do the visitors fit into our future? Wherever we want them to. They stand ready to respond in any way they can. I see no reason why scientists, gaining contact with them, cannot expect to obtain a great acceleration of all their disciplines. I think that many ordinary people are going to discover that they possess the potential to lead extraordinary lives.

My method of getting to the visitors has always been to indicate my availability by challenging my fears and maintaining a meditative and contemplative state of mind. As more and more of us turn our faces toward them, I anticipate that they will become less secretive. As we embrace our potential by demonstrating that we can make use of it, the pressure will reduce and we will finally begin to see who is really behind those fearsome masks.

If my own experience is any example, the visitors are prepared to give us the exact minimum amount of knowledge that we need to do things on our own. They are not here to carry us, but to tempt us into walking, which is why they will always stay just out of reach.

I suppose that science will remain institutionally in denial for some time, but I also know that there are already a few physicists who are struggling with their own contact experiences, and I expect that their secret discovery that the visitors are real will soon begin to spread through the scientific and academic undergrounds.

The most difficult thing that our intellectual community will have to face is not that very real visitors of many different kinds may be here, but that physical being has this enormous unguessed dimension that the past identified as the soul, and the Age of Reason rejected as a source of superstition and religious enslavement.

But it exists—not as something separate, but, just like the body, as a property of being. Through it, we penetrate into a vast and very real world mediated by a much more dynamic physics than pertains in this one. Not only that, living human beings can so radically shift their physical perspective that they can actually reach the world of the soul and gain its powers while they are alive.

This may be the hidden message, for example, behind the emergence of the dead into the contact experience.

Science will have to face the fact that classical physics

is not really a physics of actual events, but a way of stabilizing a far more indeterminate reality and that largeness does not solve the indeterminacy that is at the core of the world. It will be discovered that quantum physics is itself only a shadow of a vastly more powerful—and even more predictive and ambiguous—physics that is the actual governing law of reality. It is mastery of this physics that will bring us the key ability to understand and use gravity as an energy of escape into the cosmos, that will enable us to traverse time and thus to an extent reconceive ourselves, and that will provide the means for the instrumentalities of the living to penetrate into the material of the soul's world. It is this that will, in the end, offer to us the potential to readdress our physical surroundings in conscious control of their form.

At that point, we will be able to taste communion not only with our visitors, but also with all life, and most especially to rediscover ourselves as we really are, a continuity of being that stretches back into the beginning of life on earth and forward into the completion of the universe, and that in its rich, selfless truth, exists outside of time as well, another living strand in the veil of consciousness that lies across the face of God.

We will discover then that ecstasy is an energy like heat, without an upper limit. Mankind, completely invested in reality, beyond time and death, fully conscious and completely physical in every way, will no longer fear death or need to hide from eternity. Far from appearing as the horrible chasm filled with demons that we see now, the eternal world will be rediscovered as our natural home, as indeed it has ever been.

Appendices

Appendix 1

HACKER.TXT

The first few pages of Hacker.Txt discuss various UFO conspiracy theories. As there is little in it that is really new, I have omitted it from this appendix. However, the list of allegedly classified datapoints is interesting. A datapoint is a location in a computer that contains files, and there may be many thousands at each datapoint. DDN Locations are Defense Department Network Locations—the computers where the datapoints are actually housed. In general these computers are in various Air Force bases, as noted, but some are listed at naval data centers and some in the Pentagon, at NASA sites, and other locations.

It would be too technical to go into the details of how datapoints are designed. An untrained individual cannot access the DDN, which is elaborately secured. If these data addresses are real, it took considerable computer expertise to find them. Otherwise, they are a clever hoax. Very clever.

I might add that if Congress indeed knows nothing about any of this, these so-called classified datapoints are not legally classified at all but are simply being illegally withheld. There would have been no crime committed by anybody who obtained them whether they had signed a secrecy oath or not.

GENERAL DATAPOINTS CLASSIFIED UFO DATA

HOLLOMAN AIR FORCE BASE

```
Location: New Mexico.
DDN Locations:
NET : 132.5.0.0 : HOLLOMAN :
GATEWAY : 26.9.0.74, 132.5.0.1 : HOLLOMAN-
   GW.AF.MIL : CISCO-MGS : EGP,IP/GW :
GATEWAY : 26.9.0.74, 132.5.0.1 : HOLLOMAN-
   GW.AF.MIL : CISCO-MGS : EGP,IP/GW :
HOST : 26.10.0.74 : HOLLOMAN-TG.AF.MIL : VAX-
   8650 : VMS : TCP/FTP,TCP/TELNET,TCP,SMTP :
HOST : 26.6.0.74 : HOLLOMAN-AM1.AF.MIL :
   WANG-VS100 : VSOS :
   TCP/TELNET,TCP/FTP,TCP/SMTP :
HOST: DDNVAX2.6585TG.AF.MIL 156.6.1.2
```

KIRTLAND AIR FORCE BASE

Office Of Special Investigations. Sandia Labs are here. Also part of NSA Intercept Equipment Division.

DDN Locations:
NET : 131.23.0.0 : KIRTLAND-NET :
NET : 132.62.0.0 : KIRTLAND2 :
GATEWAY : 26.17.0.48, 131.23.0.1 :
KIRTLAND2-GW.AF.MIL,KIRTLAND-GW.AF.MIL :
   CISCO-MGS : UNIX : IP/GW,EGP :
GATEWAY : 26.18.0.87, 132.62.0.1
: KIRTLAND1-GW.AF.MIL,KIRTLAND1606ABW-
   GW.AF.MIL : CISCO-MGS : EGP,IP/GW :
HOST : 26.0.0.48 : KIRTLAND.MT.DDN.MIL : C/30
   : TAC : TCP,ICMP :
HOST : 26.0.0.87 : KIRTLAND2.MT.DDN.MIL : C/30
   : TAC : TCP,ICMP :
HOST : 26.6.0.87 : KIRTLAND-AM1.AF.MIL : WANG-
   VS300 : VS :

NASA

DDN Locations:
Fort Irwin, Barstow, CA:
NET : 134.66.0.0 : IRWIN :
NET : 144.146.0.0 : FTIRWIN1 :
NET : 144.147.0.0 : FTIRWIN2 :
GATEWAY : 26.24.0.85, 26.7.0.230, 144.146.0.1,
   144.147.0.0:
FTIRWIN-GW1.ARMY.MIL : CISCO-GATEWAY : CISCO :
   IP/GW,EGP :
HOST : 26.14.0.39 : IRWIN-ASBN.ARMY.MIL : NCR-
   COMTEN-3650 : COS2 :
HOST : 26.13.0.85 : FTIRWIN-AMEDD.ARMY.MIL :
   ATT-3B2-600G : UNIX:
TCP/FTP,TCP/SMTP,TCP/TELNET :
HOST : 26.14.0.85 : FTIRWIN-IGNET.ARMY.MIL :
   DATAPOINT-8605 : RMS :

```
HOST : 26.15.0.85 : IRWIN-EMH1.ARMY.MIL,FTIR-
  WIN-EMH1.ARMY.MIL :
SPERRY-5000
: UNIX : TCP/FTP,TCP/SMTP,TCP/TELNET :
```

MOFFET FIELD NAVAL BASE
(AMES RESEARCH CENTER)

```
GATEWAY : 26.20.0.16, 192.52.195.1 :
MOFFETT-FLD-MB.DDN.MIL,AMES-MB.DDN.MIL : C/70
  : CHRYSALIS : IP/GW,EGP :
HOST : 26.0.0.16 : MOFFETT.MT.DDN.MIL : C/30 :
  TAC : TCP,ICMP :
```

PENTAGON
(NATIONAL MILITARY COMMAND CENTER)

```
Possible DDN sites:
GATEWAY : 26.9.0.26, 134.205.123.140 : PEN-
  TAGON-GW.HQ.AF.MIL : CISCO-AGS: EGP,IP/GW :
GATEWAY : 26.25.0.26, 131.8.0.1 : PENTAGON-
  GW.AF.MIL,HQUSAFNET-GW.AF.MIL: CISCO-MGS :
  IP/GW,EGP :
GATEWAY : 26.10.0.76, 192.31.75.235 : PEN-
  TAGON-BCN-GW.ARMY.MIL : SUN-360: UNIX :
  IP/GW,EGP :
GATEWAY : 26.26.0.247, 192.31.75.1 : PENTAGON-
  GW.ARMY.MIL : SUN-3/160
: UNIX : EGP,IP/GW :
GATEWAY : 26.31.0.247, 26.16.0.26, 141.116.0.1
  : PENTAGON-GW1.ARMY.MIL : CISCO :
CISCO : IP/GW,EGP :
HOST : 26.0.0.26 : PENTAGON.MT.DDN.MIL : C/30
  : TAC : TCP,ICMP :
```

```
HOST : 26.24.0.26 : OPSNET-PENTAGON.AF.MIL :
   VAX-8500 : VMS : TCP/TELNET,TCP/FTP,TCP/SMTP :
HOST : 26.10.0.76, 192.31.75.235 : PENTAGON-
   BCN.ARMY.MIL : SUN-360 :
UNIX: TCP/FTP,TCP/SMTP,TCP/TELNET :
HOST : 26.0.0.247 : PENTAGON2.MT.DDN.MIL :
   C/30 : TAC : TCP,ICMP :
HOST : 26.7.0.247 : PENTAGON-AMSNET.ARMY.MIL :
   AMDAHL : MVS : TCP/TELNET,TCP/FTP :
HOST : 26.14.0.247 : NSSC-PENTAGON.NAVY.MIL :
   ALTOS-3068A : UNIX :
   TCP/FTP,TCP/TELNET,TCP/SMTP :
HOST : 26.18.0.247 : PENTAGON-EMH4.ARMY.MIL :
   SPERRY-5000/80 : UNIX
   :/TELNET,TCP/FTP,TCP/SMTP :
HOST : 26.26.0.247, 192.31.75.1 : PENTAGON-
   AI.ARMY.MIL : SUN-3/160 :
UNIX: TCP/TELNET,TCP/FTP,TCP/SMTP,TCP/FINGER :


                   UTAH LOCATIONS:

GATEWAY : 26.18.0.20, 131.27.0.1 : HILL-
   GW.AF.MIL,HILLAFBNET-GW.AF.MIL
   : CISCO-MGS :: IP/GW,EGP :
GATEWAY : 26.18.0.20, 131.27.0.1 : HILL-
   GW.AF.MIL,HILLAFBNET-GW.AF.MIL
   : CISCO-MGS :: IP/GW,EGP :
HOST : 26.5.0.20 : HILL.MT.DDN.MIL : C/30 :
   TAC : TCP,ICMP :
HOST : 26.0.0.99 : HILL2.MT.DDN.MIL : C/30 :
   TAC : TCP,ICMP :
HOST : 26.12.0.99 : HILL-AM1.AF.MIL : WANG-
   VS100 : VS
   : TCP/TELNET,TCP/FTP,TCP/SMTP :
```

WRIGHT PATTERSON AFB

Catalogued UFO parts list. Autopsies on
record.
Bodies located in underground facility of
Foreign Technology Building.
DDN Locations:
HOST : 26.0.0.47 : WRIGHTPAT.MT.DDN.MIL : C/30
  : TAC : TCP,ICMP :
HOST : 26.8.0.123 : WRIGHTPAT2.MT.DDN.MIL :
  C/30 : TAC : TCP,ICMP :
HOST : 26.0.0.124 : WRIGHTPAT3.MT.DDN.MIL :
  C/30 : TAC : TCP,ICMP :
HOST : 26.3.0.170 : WAINWRIGHT-IGNET.ARMY.MIL
  : CONVERGENT-TECH-CN-100: CTOS :
HOST : 26.0.0.176 : WRIGHTPAT4.MT.DDN.MIL :
  C/30 : TAC : TCP,ICMP :

NEVADA

NET : 131.216.0.0 : NEVADA :
Random Suspected Nets:
WIN: Top Secret Network. All coordinators have
  last name Win.
NET : 141.8.0.0 : DFN-WIN8 : NET : 141.9.0.0 :
  DFN-WIN9
NET : 141.10.0.0 : DFN-WIN10 : NET :
  141.15.0.0 : DFN-WIN15 :
NET : 141.25.0.0 : DFN-WIN25 : NET :
  141.26.0.0 : DFN-WIN26 :
NET : 141.28.0.0 : DFN-WIN28 : NET :
  141.57.0.0 : DFN-WIN57 :
NET : 141.58.0.0 : DFN-WIN58 : NET :
  141.59.0.0 : DFN-WIN59 :
NET : 141.60.0.0 : DFN-WIN60 : NET :

```
  141.61.0.0 : DFN-WIN61 :
NET : 141.62.0.0 : DFN-WIN62 : NET :
  141.63.0.0 : DFN-WIN63 :
NET : 141.64.0.0 : DFN-WIN64 : NET :
  141.65.0.0 : DFN-WIN65 :
NET : 141.66.0.0 : DFN-WIN66 : NET :
  141.67.0.0 : DFN-WIN67 :
NET : 141.68.0.0 : DFN-WIN68 : NET :
  141.69.0.0 : DFN-WIN69 :
NET : 141.70.0.0 : DFN-WIN70 : NET :
  141.71.0.0 : DFN-WIN71 :
NET : 141.72.0.0 : DFN-WIN72 : NET :
  141.73.0.0 : DFN-WIN73 :
NET : 141.74.0.0 : DFN-WIN74 : NET :
  141.75.0.0 : DFN-WIN75 :
NET : 141.76.0.0 : DFN-WIN76 : NET :
  141.77.0.0 : DFN-WIN77 :
NET : 141.78.0.0 : DFN-WIN78 : NET :
  141.79.0.0 : DFN-WIN79 :
NET : 141.80.0.0 : DFN-WIN80 : NET :
  141.81.0.0 : DFN-WIN81 :
NET : 141.82.0.0 : DFN-WIN82 : NET :
  141.83.0.0 : DFN-WIN83 :
NET : 141.84.0.0 : DFN-WIN84 : NET :
  141.85.0.0 : DFN-WIN85 :
NET : 141.86.0.0 : DFN-WIN86 : NET :
  141.87.0.0 : DFN-WIN87 :
NET : 141.88.0.0 : DFN-WIN88 : NET :
  141.89.0.0 : DFN-WIN89 :
NET : 141.90.0.0 : DFN-WIN90 : NET :
  141.91.0.0 : DFN-WIN91 :
NET : 141.92.0.0 : DFN-WIN92 : NET :
  141.93.0.0 : DFN-WIN93 :
NET : 141.94.0.0 : DFN-WIN94 : NET :
  141.95.0.0 : DFN-WIN95 :
NET : 141.96.0.0 : DFN-WIN96 : NET :
```

   141.97.0.0 : DFN-WIN97 :
NET : 141.98.0.0 : DFN-WIN98 : NET :
   141.99.0.0 : DFN-WIN99 :
NET : 188.1.0.0 : WIN-IP : NET : 192.80.90.0 :
   WINDATA:

SCINET:

Sensitive Compartmented Information Network

NET : 192.12.188.0 : BU-SCINET :

DISNET:

   Defense Integrated Secure Network. Composed
of SCINET, WINCS
   ([World Wide Military and Command Control
System] Intercomputer
   Network Communication Subsystem), and
Secretnet(WIN).